George Eliot

Collection of british authors: Felix Holt

George Eliot

Collection of british authors: Felix Holt

ISBN/EAN: 9783742822376

Manufactured in Europe, USA, Canada, Australia, Japa

Cover: Foto ©Andreas Hilbeck / pixelio.de

Manufactured and distributed by brebook publishing software (www.brebook.com)

George Eliot

Collection of british authors: Felix Holt

EACH VOLUME SOLD SEPARATELY.

COLLECTION
OF
BRITISH AUTHORS

TAUCHNITZ EDITION.

VOL. 898.

FELIX HOLT BY GEORGE ELIOT

IN TWO VOLUMES.

VOL. 2.

LEIPZIG: BERNHARD TAUCHNITZ.
PARIS: C. REINWALD, 15, RUE DES SAINTS PÈRES.

TAUCHNITZ EDITION.

By the same Author,

SCENES OF CLERICAL LIFE . . . . . . 2 vols.
ADAM BEDE . . . . 2 vols.
THE MILL ON THE FLOSS . . . . . . 2 vols.
SILAS MARNER . . . . 1 vol.
ROMOLA . . . . 2 vols.

FELIX HOLT

THE RADICAL

BY

GEORGE ELIOT

AUTHOR OF "ADAM BEDE," "ROMOLA," ETC.

IN TWO VOLUMES.

VOL. II.

LEIPZIG

BERNHARD TAUCHNITZ

1867.

FELIX HOLT,
THE RADICAL.

CHAPTER I.

*Your fellow-man? — Divide the epithet:
Say rather, you're the fellow, he the man.*

WHEN Christian quitted the Free School with the discovery that the young lady whose appearance had first startled him with an indefinable impression in the market-place was the daughter of the old Dissenting preacher who had shown so much agitated curiosity about his name, he felt very much like an uninitiated chess-player who sees that the pieces are in a peculiar position on the board, and might open the way for him to give checkmate, if he only knew how. Ever since his interview with Jermyn, his mind had been occupied with the charade it offered to his ingenuity. What was the real meaning of the lawyer's interest in him, and in his relations with Maurice Christian Bycliffe? Here was a secret; and secrets were often a source of profit, of that agreeable kind which involved little labour. Jermyn had hinted at profit which might possibly come through him; but Christian said inwardly, with well-satisfied self-esteem, that he was not so pitiable a nincompoop as to trust Jermyn. On the

contrary, the only problem before him was to find out
by what combination of independent knowledge he
could outwit Jermyn, elude any purchase the attorney
had on him through his past history, and get a hand
some bonus, by which a somewhat shattered man of
pleasure might live well without a master. Christian,
having early exhausted the more impulsive delights of
life, had become a sober calculator; and he had made
up his mind that, for a man who had long ago run
through his own money, servitude in a great family
was the best kind of retirement after that of a pen-
sioner; but if a better chance offered, a person of talent
must not let it slip through his fingers. He held
various ends of threads, but there was danger in pulling
at them too impatiently. He had not forgotten the surprise which had made him drop the punch-ladle, when
Mr. Crowder, talking in the steward's room, had said
that a scamp named Henry Scaddon had been concerned in a lawsuit about the Transome estate. Again,
Jermyn was the family lawyer of the Transomes; he
knew about the exchange of names between Scaddon
and Bycliffe; he clearly wanted to know as much as
he could about Bycliffe's history. The conclusion was
not remote that Bycliffe had had some claim on the
Transome property, and that a difficulty had arisen
from his being confounded with Henry Scaddon. But
hitherto the other incident which had been apparently
connected with the interchange of names — Mr.
Lyon's demand that he should write down the name
Maurice Christian, accompanied with the question
whether that were his whole name — had had no
visible link with the inferences arrived at through
Crowder and Jermyn.

The discovery made this morning at the Free School that Esther was the daughter of the Dissenting preacher at last suggested a possible link. Until then, Christian had not known why Esther's face had impressed him so peculiarly; but the minister's chief association for him was with Bycliffe, and that association served as a flash to show him that Esther's features and expression, and still more her bearing, now she stood and walked, revived Bycliffe's image. Daughter? There were various ways of being a daughter. Suppose this were a case of adoption: suppose Bycliffe were known to be dead, or thought to be dead. "Begad, if the old parson had fancied the original father was come to life again, it was enough to frighten him a little. Slow and steady," Christian said to himself; "I'll get some talk with the old man again. He's safe enough: one can handle him without cutting one's self. I'll tell him I knew Bycliffe, and was his fellow-prisoner. I'll worm out the truth about this daughter. Could pretty Annette have married again, and married this little scarecrow? There's no knowing what a woman will not do."

Christian could see no distinct result for himself from his industry; but if there were to be any such result, it must be reached by following out every clue; and to the non-legal mind there are dim possibilities in law and heirship which prevent any issue from seeming too miraculous.

The consequence of these meditations was, that Christian hung about Treby more than usual in his leisure time, and that on the first opportunity he accosted Mr. Lyon in the street with suitable civility, stating that since the occasion which had brought them

together some weeks before he had often wished to
renew their conversation, and, with Mr. Lyon's per-
mission, would now ask to do so. After being assured,
as he had been by Jermyn, that this courier, who had
happened by some accident to possess the memorable
locket and pocket-book, was certainly not Annette's
husband, and was ignorant whether Maurice Christian
Bycliffe were living or dead, the minister's mind had
become easy again; his habitual lack of interest in
personal details rendering him gradually oblivious of
Jermyn's precautionary statement that he was pursuing
inquiries, and that if anything of interest turned up,
Mr. Lyon should be made acquainted with it. Hence,
when Christian addressed him, the minister, taken by
surprise and shaken by the recollections of former anx-
ieties, said, helplessly,

"If it is business, sir, you would perhaps do better
to address yourself to Mr. Jermyn."

He could not have said anything that was a more
valuable hint to Christian. He inferred that the minister had made a confidant of Jermyn, and it was needful to be wary.

"On the contrary, sir," he answered, "it may be of
the utmost importance to you that what passes between
us should not be known to Mr. Jermyn."

Mr. Lyon was perplexed, and felt at once that he
was no more in clear daylight concerning Jermyn than
concerning Christian. He dared not neglect the possible duty of hearing what this man had to say, and he
invited him to proceed to Malthouse Yard, where they
could converse in private.

Once in Mr. Lyon's study, Christian opened the
dialogue by saying that since he was in this room be-

fore it had occurred to him that the anxiety he had
observed in Mr. Lyon might be owing to some acquaintance with Maurice Christian Bycliffe — a fellow-
prisoner in France whom he, Christian, had assisted in
getting freed from his imprisonment, and who, in fact,
had been the owner of the trifles which Mr. Lyon had
recently had in his possession and had restored. Christian hastened to say that he knew nothing of Bycliffe's
history since they had parted in France, but that he
knew of his marriage with Annette Ledru, and had
been acquainted with Annette herself. He would be
very glad to know what became of Bycliffe, if he
could, for he liked him uncommonly.

Here Christian paused; but Mr. Lyon only sat
changing colour and trembling. This man's bearing
and tone of mind were made repulsive to him by being
brought in contact with keenly-felt memories, and he
could not readily summon the courage to give answers
or ask questions.

"May I ask if you knew my friend Bycliffe?" said
Christian, trying a more direct method.

"No, sir; I never saw him."

"Ah! well — you have seen a very striking likeness
of him. It's wonderful — unaccountable; but when I
saw Miss Lyon at the Free School the other day, I
could have sworn she was Bycliffe's daughter."

"Sir!" said Mr. Lyon, in his deepest tone, half rising, and holding by the arms of his chair, "these subjects touch me with too sharp a point for you to be
justified in thrusting them on me out of mere levity.
Is there any good you seek or any injury you fear in
relation to them?"

"Precisely, sir. We shall come now to an understanding. Suppose I believed that the young lady who goes by the name of Miss Lyon was the daughter of Bycliffe?"

Mr. Lyon moved his lips silently.

"And suppose I had reason to suspect that there would be some great advantage for her if the law knew who was her father?"

"Sir!" said Mr. Lyon, shaken out of all reticence, "I would not conceal it. She believes herself to be my daughter. But I will bear all things rather than deprive her of a right. Nevertheless I appeal to the pity of any fellow-man, not to thrust himself between her and me, but to let me disclose the truth to her myself."

"All in good time," said Christian. "We must do nothing rash. Then Miss Lyon is Annette's child?"

The minister shivered as if the edge of a knife had been drawn across his hand. But the tone of this question, by the very fact that it intensified his antipathy to Christian, enabled him to collect himself for what must be simply the endurance of a painful operation. After a moment or two he said more coolly, "It is true, sir. Her mother became my wife. Proceed with any statement which may concern my duty."

"I have no more to say than this: If there's a prize that the law might hand over to Bycliffe's daughter, I am much mistaken if there isn't a lawyer who'll take precious good care to keep the law hoodwinked. And that lawyer is Mat Jermyn. Why, my good sir, if you've been taking Jermyn into your confidence, you've been setting the fox to keep off the weasel. It strikes me that when you were made a little anxious about those articles of poor Bycliffe's, you put Jermyn on making inquiries of me. Eh? I think I am right?"

"I do not deny it."

"Ah! — it was very well you did, for by that means I've found out that he's got hold of some secrets about Bycliffe which he means to stifle. Now, sir, if you desire any justice for your daughter, stepdaughter, I should say — don't so much as wink to yourself before Jermyn; and if you've got any papers or things of that sort that may come in evidence, as these confounded rascals the lawyers call it, clutch them tight, for if they get into Jermyn's hands they may soon fly up the chimney. Have I said enough?"

"I had not purposed any further communication with Mr. Jermyn, sir; indeed, I have nothing further to communicate. Except that one fact concerning my daughter's birth, which I have erred in concealing from her, I neither seek disclosures nor do I tremble before them."

"Then I have your word that you will be silent about this conversation between us? It is for your daughter's interest, mind."

"Sir, I shall be silent," said Mr. Lyon, with cold gravity. "Unless," he added, with an acumen as to possibilities rather disturbing to Christian's confident contempt for the old man — "unless I were called upon by some tribunal to declare the whole truth in this relation; in which case I should submit myself to that authority of investigation which is a requisite of social order."

Christian departed, feeling satisfied that he had got the utmost to be obtained at present out of the Dis-

senting preacher, whom he had not dared to question
more closely. He must look out for chance lights, and
perhaps, too, he might catch a stray hint by stirring
the sediment of Mr. Crowder's memory. But he must
not venture on inquiries that might be noticed. He
was in awe of Jermyn.

When Mr. Lyon was alone he paced up and down
among his books, and thought aloud, in order to relieve
himself after the constraint of this interview. "I will
not wait for the urgency of necessity," he said, more
than once. "I will tell the child, without compulsion.
And then I shall fear nothing. And an unwonted
spirit of tenderness has filled her of late. She will forgive me."

CHAPTER II.

*Consideration like an angel came
And whipped the offending Adam out of her;
Leaving her body as a paradise
To envelop and contain celestial spirits.*
                      SHAKSPEARE: *Henry V.*

THE next morning, after much prayer for the needful strength and wisdom, Mr. Lyon came down-stairs with the resolution that another day should not pass without the fulfilment of the task he had laid on himself; but what hour he should choose for his solemn disclosure to Esther, must depend on their mutual occupations. Perhaps he must defer it till they sat up alone together, after Lyddy was gone to bed. But at breakfast Esther said,

"To-day is a holiday, father. My pupils are all going to Duffield to see the wild beasts. What have you got to do to-day? Come, you are eating no breakfast. O, Lyddy, Lyddy, the eggs are hard again. I wish you would not read Alleyne's 'Alarm' before breakfast; it makes you cry and forget the eggs."

"They *are* hard, and that's the truth; but there's hearts as are harder, Miss Esther," said Lyddy.

"I think not," said Esther. "This is leathery enough for the heart of the most obdurate Jew. Pray give it little Zachary for a football."

"Dear, dear, don't you be so light, miss. We may all be dead before night."

"You speak out of season, my good Lyddy," said Mr. Lyon, wearily; "depart into the kitchen."

"What have you got to do to-day, father?" persisted Esther. "I have a holiday."

Mr. Lyon felt as if this were a fresh summons not to delay. "I have something of great moment to do, my dear; and since you are not otherwise demanded, I will ask you to come and sit with me up-stairs."

Esther wondered what there could be on her father's mind more pressing than his morning studies.

She soon knew. Motionless, but mentally stirred as she had never been before, Esther listened to her mother's story, and to the outpouring of her step-father's long-pent-up experience. The rays of the morning sun which fell athwart the books, the sense of the beginning day, had deepened the solemnity more than night would have done. All knowledge which alters our lives penetrates us more when it comes in the early morning: the day that has to be travelled with something new and perhaps for ever sad in its light, is an image of the life that spreads beyond. But at night the time of rest is near.

Mr. Lyon regarded his narrative as a confession — as a revelation to this beloved child of his own miserable weakness and error. But to her it seemed a revelation of another sort: her mind seemed suddenly enlarged by a vision of passion and struggle, of delight and renunciation, in the lot of beings who had hitherto been a dull enigma to her. And in the act of unfolding to her that he was not her real father, but had only striven to cherish her as a father, had only longed to be loved as a father, the odd, way-worn, unworldly man became the object of a new sympathy in which Esther felt herself exalted. Perhaps this knowledge would have been less powerful within her, but for the mental preparation that had come during the last two months from her acquaintance with Felix Holt, which had taught her to doubt the infallibility of her own standard, and raised a presentiment of moral depths that were hidden from her.

Esther had taken her place opposite to her father, and had not moved even her clasped hands while he was speaking. But after the long outpouring in which he seemed to lose the sense of everything but the memories he was giving utterance to, he paused a little while and then said timidly,

"This is a late retrieval of a long error, Esther. I make not excuses for myself, for we ought to strive that our affections be rooted in the truth. Nevertheless you ——."

Esther had risen, and had glided on to the wooden stool on a level with her father's chair, where he was accustomed to lay books. She wanted to speak, but the floodgates could not be opened for words alone. She threw her arms round the old man's neck and sobbed out with a passionate cry, "Father, father! forgive me if I have not loved you enough. I will — I will!"

The old man's little delicate frame was shaken by a surprise and joy that were almost painful in their intensity. He had been going to ask forgiveness of her who asked it for herself. In that moment of supreme complex emotion one ray of the minister's joy was the thought, "Surely the work of grace is begun in her — surely here is a heart that the Lord hath touched."

They sat so, enclasped in silence, while Esther relieved her full heart. When she raised her head, she sat quite still for a minute or two looking fixedly before her, and keeping one little hand in the minister's. Presently she looked at him and said,

"Then you lived like a working man, father; you were very, very poor. Yet my mother had been used to luxury. She was well born — she was a lady."

"It is true, my dear; it was a poor life that I could give her."

Mr. Lyon answered in utter dimness as to the course Esther's mind was taking. He had anticipated before his disclosure, from his long-standing discernment of tendencies in her which were often the cause of silent grief to him, that the discovery likely to have the keenest interest for her would be that her parents had a higher rank than that of the poor Dissenting preacher; but she had shown that other and better sensibilities were predominant. He rebuked himself now for a hasty and shallow judgment concerning the child's inner life, and waited for new clearness.

"But that must be the best life, father," said Esther, suddenly rising, with a flush across her paleness, and standing with her head thrown a little backward, as if some illumination had given her a new decision. "That must be the best life."

"What life, my dear child?"

"Why, that where one bears and does everything because of some great and strong feeling — so that this and that in one's circumstances don't signify."

"Yea, verily; but the feeling that should be thus supreme is devotedness to the Divine Will."

Esther did not speak; her father's words did not fit on to the impressions wrought in her by what he had told her. She sat down again, and said, more quietly,

"Mamma did not speak much of my — first father?"

"Not much, dear. She said he was beautiful to the eye, and good and generous; and that his family was of those who have been long privileged among their fellows. But now I will deliver to you the letters, which, together with a ring and locket, are the only visible memorials she retained of him."

Mr. Lyon reached and delivered to Esther the box containing the relics. "Take them, and examine them in privacy, my dear. And that I may no more err by concealment, I will tell you some late occurrences that bear on these memorials, though to my present apprehension doubtfully and confusedly."

He then narrated to Esther all that had passed between himself and Christian. The possibility — to which Mr. Lyon's alarms had pointed — that her real father might still be living, was a new shock. She could not speak about it to her present father, but it was registered in silence as a painful addition to the uncertainties which she suddenly saw hanging over her life.

"I have little confidence in this man's allegations," Mr. Lyon ended. "I confess his presence and speech are to me as the jarring of metal. He bears the stamp of one who has never conceived aught of more sanctity than the lust of the eye and the pride of life. He hints at some possible inheritance for you, and denounces mysteriously the devices of Mr. Jermyn. All this may or may not have a true foundation. But it is not my part to move in this matter save on a clearer showing."

"Certainly not, father," said Esther, eagerly. A little while ago, these problematic prospects might have set her dreaming pleasantly; but now, for some reasons that she could not have put distinctly into words, they affected her with dread.

CHAPTER III.

To bear with eyes is part of love's rare wit.
SHAKSPEARE: *Sonnets.*

*Custom calls me to't:—
What custom wills, in all things should we do't?
The dust on antique time would lie unswept,
And mountainous error be too highly heaped
For truth to over-peer.* — *Coriolanus.*

IN the afternoon Mr. Lyon went out to see the sick amongst his flock, and Esther, who had been passing the morning in dwelling on the memories and the few remaining relics of her parents, was left alone in the parlour amidst the lingering odours of the early dinner, not easily got rid of in that small house. Rich people, who know nothing of these vulgar details, can hardly imagine their significance in the history of multitudes of human lives in which the sensibilities are never adjusted to the external conditions. Esther always felt so much discomfort from those odours that she usually seized any possibility of escaping from them, and to-day they oppressed her the more because she was weary with long-continued agitation. Why did she not put on her bonnet as usual and get out into the open air? It was one of those pleasant November afternoons — pleasant in the wide country — when the sunshine is on the clinging brown leaves of the young oaks, and the last yellow leaves of the elms flutter down in the fresh but not eager breeze. But Esther sat still on the sofa — pale and with reddened eyelids, her curls all pushed back carelessly, and her elbow resting on the ridgy black horsehair, which usually almost set her teeth on edge if she pressed it even through her sleeve — while her eyes rested blankly on the dull street. Lyddy had said, "Miss, you look sadly; if you can't take a walk, go and lie down." She had never seen the curls in such disorder, and she reflected that there had been a death from typhus recently. But the obstinate Miss only shook her head.

Esther was waiting for the sake of — not a probability, but — a mere possibility, which made the brothy odours endurable. Apparently, in less than half an hour, the possibility came to pass, for she changed her attitude, almost started from her seat, sat down again, and listened eagerly. If Lyddy should send him away, could she herself rush out and call him back? Why not? Such things were permissible where it was understood, from the necessity of the case, that there was only friendship. But Lyddy opened the door and said, "Here's Mr. Holt, miss, wants to know if you'll give him leave to come in. I told him you was sadly."

"O yes, Lyddy, beg him to come in."

"I should not have persevered," said Felix, as they shook hands, "only I know Lyddy's dismal way. But you do look ill," he went on, as he seated himself at the other end of the sofa. "Or rather — for that's a false way of putting it — you look as if you had been very much distressed. Do you mind about my taking notice of it?"

He spoke very kindly, and looked at her more persistently than he had ever done before, when her hair was perfect.

"You are quite right. I am not at all ill. But I have been very much agitated this morning. My father has been telling me things I never heard before about my mother, and giving me things that belonged to her. She died when I was a very little creature."

"Then it is no new pain or trouble for you and Mr. Lyon? I could not help being anxious to know that."

Esther passed her hand over her brow before she answered. "I hardly know whether it is pain, or something better than pleasure. It has made me see things I was blind to before — depths in my father's nature."

As she said this, she looked at Felix, and their eyes met very gravely.

"It is such a beautiful day," he said, "it would do you good to go into the air. Let me take you along the river towards Little Treby, will you?"

"I will put my bonnet on," said Esther unhesitatingly, though they had never walked out together before.

It is true that to get into the fields they had to pass through the street; and when Esther saw some acquaintances, she reflected that her walking alone with Felix might be a subject of remark — all the more because of his cap, patched boots, no cravat, and thick stick. Esther was a little amazed herself at what she had come to. So our lives glide on: the river ends we don't know where, and the sea begins, and then there is no more jumping ashore.

When they were in the streets Esther hardly spoke. Felix talked with his usual readiness, as easily as if he were not doing it solely to divert her thoughts, first about Job Tudge's delicate chest, and the probability that the little white-faced monkey would not live long; and then about a miserable beginning of a night-school, which was all he could get together at Sproxton; and the dismalness of that hamlet, which was a sort of lip to the coalpit on one side and the "public" on the other — and yet a paradise compared with the wynds of Glasgow, where there was little more than a chink of daylight to show the hatred in women's faces.

But soon they got into the fields, where there was a right of way towards Little Treby, now following the course of the river, now crossing towards a lane, and now turning into a cart-track through a plantation.

"Here we are!" said Felix, when they had crossed the wooden bridge, and were treading on the slanting shadows made by the elm trunks. "I think this is delicious. I never feel less unhappy than in these late autumn afternoons when they are sunny."

"Less unhappy! There now!" said Esther, smiling at him with some of her habitual sauciness, "I have caught you in self-contradiction. I have heard you quite furious against puling, melancholy people. If I had said what you have just said, you would have given me a long lecture, and told me to go home and interest myself in the reason of the rule of three."

"Very likely," said Felix, beating the weeds, according to the foible of our common humanity when it has a stick in its hand. "But I don't think myself a fine fellow because I'm melancholy. I don't measure my force by the negations in me, and think my soul must be a mighty one because it is more given to idle

suffering than to beneficent activity. That's what your
favourite gentlemen do, of the Byronic-bilious style."
"I don't admit that those are my favourite gentlemen."
"I've heard you defend them — gentlemen like
your Rénés, who have no particular talent for the
finite, but a general sense that the infinite is the right
thing for them. They might as well boast of nausea
as a proof of a strong inside."
"Stop, stop! You run on in that way to get out
of my reach. I convicted you of confessing that you
are melancholy."
"Yes!" said Felix, thrusting his left hand into his
pocket, with a shrug; "as I could confess to a great
many other things I'm not proud of. The fact is,
there are not many easy lots to be drawn in the world
at present; and such as they are I am not envious of
them. I don't say life is not worth having: it is
worth having to a man who has some sparks of sense
and feeling and bravery in him. And the finest fellow of all would be the one who could be glad to
have lived because the world was chiefly miserable,
and his life had come to help some one who needed it.
He would be the man who had the most powers and
the fewest selfish wants. But I'm not up to the level
of what I see to be best. I'm often a hungry discontented fellow."
"Why have you made your life so hard then?"
said Esther, rather frightened as she asked the question. "It seems to me you have tried to find just the
most difficult task."
"Not at all," said Felix, with curt decision. "My
course was a very simple one. It was pointed out to

me by conditions that I saw as clearly as I see the bars of this stile. It's a difficult stile too," added Felix, striding over. "Shall I help you, or will you be left to yourself?"

"I can do without help, thank you."

"It was all simple enough," continued Felix, as they walked on. "If I meant to put a stop to the sale of those drugs, I must keep my mother, and of course at her age she would not leave the place she had been used to. And I had made up my mind against what they call genteel businesses."

"But suppose every one did as you do? Please to forgive me for saying so; but I cannot see why you could not have lived as honourably with some employment that presupposes education and refinement."

"Because you can't see my history or my nature," said Felix, bluntly. "I have to determine for myself, and not for other men. I don't blame them, or think I am better than they; their circumstances are different. I would never choose to withdraw myself from the labour and common burthen of the world; but I do choose to withdraw myself from the push and the scramble for money and position. Any man is at liberty to call me a fool, and say that mankind are benefited by the push and the scramble in the long-run. But I care for the people who live now and will not be living when the long-run comes. As it is, I prefer going shares with the unlucky."

Esther did not speak, and there was silence between them for a minute or two, till they passed through a gate into a plantation where there was no large timber, but only thin-stemmed trees and underwood, so that the sunlight fell on the mossy spaces which lay open here and there.

"See how beautiful those stooping birch-stems are with the light on them!" said Felix. "Here is an old felled trunk they have not thought worth carrying away. Shall we sit down a little while?"

"Yes, the mossy ground with the dry leaves sprinkled over it is delightful to one's feet." Esther sat down and took off her bonnet, that the light breeze might fall on her head. Felix, too, threw down his cap and stick, lying on the ground with his back against the felled trunk.

"I wish I felt more as you do," she said, looking at the point of her foot, which was playing with a tuft of moss. "I can't help caring very much what happens to me. And you seem to care so little about yourself."

"You are thoroughly mistaken," said Felix. "It is just because I'm a very ambitious fellow, with very hungry passions, wanting a great deal to satisfy me, that I have chosen to give up what people call worldly good. At least that has been one determining reason. It all depends on what a man gets into his consciousness — what life thrusts into his mind, so that it becomes present to him as remorse is present to the guilty, or a mechanical problem to an inventive genius. There are two things I've got present in that way: one of them is the picture of what I should hate to be. I'm determined never to go about making my face simpering or solemn, and telling professional lies for profit; or to get tangled in affairs where I must wink at dishonesty and pocket the proceeds, and justify that knavery as part of a system that I can't alter. If I once went into that sort of struggle for success, I should want to win — I should defend the wrong that I had once identified myself with. I should become everything that I see now beforehand to be detestable. And what's more, I should do this, as men are doing it every day, for a ridiculously small prize — perhaps for none at all — perhaps for the sake of two parlours, a rank eligible for the churchwardenship, a discontented wife and several unhopeful children."

Esther felt a terrible pressure on her heart — the certainty of her remoteness from Felix — the sense that she was utterly trivial to him.

"The other thing that's got into my mind like a splinter," said Felix, after a pause, "is the life of the miserable — the spawning life of vice and hunger. I'll never be one of the sleek dogs. The old Catholics are right, with their higher rule and their lower. Some are called to subject themselves to a harder discipline, and renounce things voluntarily which are lawful for others. It is the old word — 'necessity is laid upon me.'"

"It seems to me you are stricter than my father is."

"No! I quarrel with no delight that is not base or cruel, but one must sometimes accommodate one's self to a small share. That is the lot of the majority. I would wish the minority joy, only they don't want my wishes."

Again there was silence. Esther's cheeks were hot in spite of the breeze that sent her hair floating backward. She felt an inward strain, a demand on her to see things in a light that was not easy or soothing. When Felix had asked her to walk, he had seemed so kind, so alive to what might be her feelings, that she had thought herself nearer to him than she had ever been before; but since they had come out, he had appeared to forget all that. And yet she was conscious that this impatience of hers was very petty. Battling in this way with her own little impulses, and looking at the birch-stems opposite till her gaze was too wide for her to see anything distinctly, she was unaware how long they had remained without speaking. She did not know that Felix had changed his attitude a little, and was resting his elbow on the tree-trunk, while he supported his head, which was turned towards her. Suddenly he said, in a lower tone than was habitual to him,

"You are very beautiful."

She started and looked round at him, to see whether his face would give some help to the interpretation of this novel speech. He was looking up at her quite calmly, very much as a reverential Protestant might look at a picture of the Virgin, with a devoutness suggested by the type rather than by the image. Esther's vanity was not in the least gratified: she felt that, somehow or other, Felix was going to reproach her.

"I wonder," he went on, still looking at her, "whether the subtle measuring of forces will ever come to measuring the force there would be in one beautiful woman whose mind was as noble as her face was beautiful — who made a man's passion for her rush in one current with all the great aims of his life."

Esther's eyes got hot and smarting. It was no use trying to be dignified. She had turned away her head, and now said, rather bitterly, "It is difficult for a woman ever to try to be anything good when she is not believed in — when it is always supposed that she must be contemptible."

"No, dear Esther" — it was the first time Felix had been prompted to call her by her Christian name, and as he did so he laid his large hand on her two little hands, which were clasped on her knees. "You don't believe that I think you contemptible. When I first saw you —"

"I know, I know," said Esther, interrupting him impetuously, but still looking away. "You mean you did think me contemptible then. But it was very narrow of you to judge me in that way, when my life had been so different from yours. I have great faults. I know I am selfish, and think too much of my own small tastes and too little of what affects others. But I am not stupid. I am not unfeeling. I can see what is better."

"But I have not done you injustice since I knew more of you," said Felix, gently.

"Yes, you have," said Esther, turning and smiling at him through her tears. "You talk to me like an angry pedagogue. Were *you* always wise? Remember the time when you were foolish or naughty."

"That is not far off," said Felix, curtly, taking away his hand and clasping it with the other at the back of his head. The talk, which seemed to be introducing a mutual understanding, such as had not existed before, seemed to have undergone some check.

"Shall we get up and walk back now?" said Esther, after a few moments.

"No," said Felix, entreatingly. "Don't move yet. I daresay we shall never walk together or sit here again."

"Why not?"

"Because I am a man who am warned by visions. Those old stories of visions and dreams guiding men have their truth: we are saved by making the future present to ourselves."

"I wish I could get visions, then," said Esther, smiling at him, with an effort at playfulness, in resistance to something vaguely mournful within her.

"That is what I want," said Felix, looking at her very earnestly. "Don't turn your head. Do look at me, and then I shall know if I may go on speaking. I do believe in you; but I want you to have such a vision of the future that you may never lose your best self. Some charm or other may be flung about you — some of your atta-of-rose fascinations — and nothing but a good strong terrible vision will save you. And if it did save you, you might be that woman I was thinking of a little while ago when I looked at your face: the woman whose beauty makes a great task easier to men instead of turning them away from it. I am not likely to see such fine issues; but they may come where a woman's spirit is finely touched. I should like to be sure they would come to you."

"Why are you not likely to know what becomes of me?" said Esther, turning away her eyes in spite of his command. "Why should you not always be my father's friend and mine?"

"O, I shall go away as soon as I can to some large town," said Felix, in his more usual tone, — "some ugly, wicked, miserable place. I want to be a demagogue of a new sort; an honest one, if possible, who will tell the people they are blind and foolish, and neither flatter them nor fatten on them. I have my heritage — an order I belong to. I have the blood of a line of handicraftsmen in my veins, and I want to stand up for the lot of the handicraftsman as a good lot, in which a man may be better trained to all the best functions of his nature than if he belonged to the grimacing set who have visiting-cards, and are proud to be thought richer than their neighbours."

"Would nothing ever make it seem right to you to change your mind?" said Esther (she had rapidly woven some possibilities out of the new uncertainties in her own lot, though she would not for the world have had Felix know of her weaving). "Suppose, by some means or other, a fortune might come to you honourably — by marriage, or in any other unexpected way — would you see no change in your course?"

"No," said Felix, peremptorily; "I will never be rich. I don't count that as any peculiar virtue. Some men do well to accept riches, but that is not my inward vocation: I have no fellow-feeling with the rich as a class; the habits of their lives are odious to me. Thousands of men have wedded poverty because they expect to go to heaven for it; I don't expect to go to heaven for it, but I wed it because it enables me to do what I most want to do on earth. Whatever the hopes for the world may be — whether great or small — I am a man of this generation; I will try to make life less bitter for a few within my reach. It is held reasonable enough to toil for the fortunes of a family, though it may turn to imbecility in the third generation. I choose a family with more chances in it."

Esther looked before her dreamily till she said, "That seems a hard lot; yet it is a great one." She rose to walk back.

"Then you don't think I'm a fool," said Felix, loudly, starting to his feet, and then stooping to gather up his cap and stick.

"Of course you suspected me of that stupidity."

"Well — women, unless they are Saint Theresas or Elizabeth Frys, generally think this sort of thing madness, unless when they read of it in the Bible."

"A woman can hardly ever choose in that way; she is dependent on what happens to her. She must take meaner things, because only meaner things are within her reach."

"Why, can you imagine yourself choosing hardship as the better lot?" said Felix, looking at her with a sudden question in his eyes.

"Yes, I can," she said, flushing over neck and brow.

Their words were charged with a meaning dependent entirely on the secret consciousness of each. Nothing had been said which was necessarily personal. They walked a few yards along the road by which they had come, without further speech, till Felix said gently, "Take my arm." She took it, and they walked home so, entirely without conversation. Felix was struggling as a firm man struggles with a temptation, seeing beyond it and disbelieving its lying promise. Esther was struggling as a woman struggles with the yearning for some expression of love, and with vexation under that subjection to a yearning which is not likely to be satisfied. Each was conscious of a silence which each was unable to break, till they entered Malthouse Lane, and were within a few yards of the minister's door.

"It is getting dusk," Felix then said; "will Mr. Lyon be anxious about you?"

"No, I think not. Lyddy would tell him that I

went out with you, and that you carried a large stick," said Esther, with her light laugh.

Felix went in with Esther to take tea, but the conversation was entirely between him and Mr. Lyon about the tricks of canvassing, the foolish personality of the placards, and the probabilities of Transome's return, as to which Felix declared himself to have become indifferent. This scepticism made the minister uneasy: he had great belief in the old political watchwords, had preached that universal suffrage and no ballot were agreeable to the will of God, and liked to believe that a visible "instrument" was forthcoming in the Radical Candidate who had pronounced emphatically against Whig finality. Felix, being in a perverse mood, contended that universal suffrage would be equally agreeable to the devil; that he would change his politics a little, have a larger traffic, and see himself more fully represented in Parliament.

"Nay, my friend," said the minister, "you are again sporting with paradox; for you will not deny that you glory in the name of Radical, or Root-and-branch man, as they said in the great times when Nonconformity was in its giant youth."

"A Radical — yes; but I want to go to some roots a good deal lower down than the franchise."

"Truly there is a work within which cannot be dispensed with; but it is our preliminary work to free men from the stifled life of political nullity, and bring them into what Milton calls 'the liberal air,' wherein alone can be wrought the final triumphs of the Spirit."

"With all my heart. But while Caliban is Caliban, though you multiply him by a million, he'll worship every Trinculo that carries a bottle. I forget, though — you don't read Shakspeare, Mr. Lyon."

"I am bound to confess that I have so far looked into a volume of Esther's as to conceive your meaning; but the fantasies therein were so little to be reconciled with a steady contemplation of that divine economy which is hidden from sense and revealed to faith, that I forbore the reading, as likely to perturb my ministrations."

Esther sat by in unusual silence. The conviction that Felix willed her exclusion from his life was making it plain that something more than friendship between them was not so thoroughly out of the question as she had always inwardly asserted. In her pain that his choice lay aloof from her, she was compelled frankly to admit ot herself the longing that it had been otherwise, and that he had entreated her to share his difficult life. He was like no one else to her: he had seemed to bring at once a law, and the love that gave strength to obey the law. Yet the next moment, stung by his independence of her, she denied that she loved him; she had only longed for a moral support under the negations of her life. If she were not to have that support, all effort seemed useless.

Esther had been so long used to hear the formulas of her father's belief without feeling or understanding them, that they had lost all power to touch her. The first religious experience of her life — the first self-questioning, the first voluntary subjection, the first longing to acquire the strength of greater motives and obey the more strenuous rule — had come to her through Felix Holt. No wonder that she felt as if the loss of him were inevitable backsliding.

But was it certain that she should lose him? She did not believe that he was really indifferent to her.

CHAPTER IV.

Titus. But what says Jupiter, I ask thee?
Clown. Alas, sir, I know not Jupiter:
 I never drank with him in all my life.
Titus Andronicus.

THE multiplication of uncomplimentary placards noticed by Mr. Lyon and Felix Holt was one of several signs that the days of nomination and election were approaching. The presence of the Revising Barrister in Treby was not only an opportunity for all persons not otherwise busy to show their zeal for the purification of the voting-lists, but also to reconcile private ease and public duty by standing about the streets and lounging at doors.

It was no light business for Trebians to form an opinion; the mere fact of a public functionary with an unfamiliar title was enough to give them pause, as a premiss that was not to be quickly started from. To Mr. Pink the saddler, for example, until some distinct injury or benefit had accrued to him, the existence of the Revising Barrister was like the existence of the young giraffe which Wombwell had lately brought into those parts — it was to be contemplated, and not criticised. Mr. Pink professed a deep-dyed Toryism; but he regarded all fault-finding as Radical and somewhat impious, as disturbing to trade, and likely to offend the gentry or the servants through whom their harness was ordered: there was a Nemesis in things

which made objection unsafe, and even the Reform
Bill was a sort of electric eel which a thriving tradesman had better leave alone. It was only the "Papists"
who lived far enough off to be spoken of uncivilly.

But Mr. Pink was fond of news, which he collected
and retailed with perfect impartiality, noting facts and
rejecting comments. Hence he was well pleased to have
his shop so constant a place of resort for loungers, that
to many Trebians there was a strong association between the pleasures of gossip and the smell of leather.
He had the satisfaction of chalking and cutting, and of
keeping his journeymen close at work, at the very time
that he learned from his visitors who were those whose
votes had been called in question before His Honour,
how Lawyer Jermyn had been too much for Lawyer
Labron about Todd's cottages, and how, in the opinion
of some townsmen, this looking into the value of people's
property, and swearing it down below a certain sum,
was a nasty, inquisitorial kind of thing; while others
observed that being nice to a few pounds was all nonsense — they should put the figure high enough, and
then never mind if a voter's qualification was there-
abouts. But, said Mr. Sims the auctioneer, everything
was done for the sake of the lawyers. Mr. Pink suggested impartially that lawyers must live; but Mr.
Sims, having a ready auctioneering wit, did not see
that so many of them need live, or that babies were
born lawyers. Mr. Pink felt that this speculation was
complicated by the ordering of side-saddles for lawyers'
daughters, and, returning to the firm ground of fact,
stated that it was getting dusk.

The dusk seemed deepened the next moment by a
tall figure obstructing the doorway, at sight of whom

Mr. Pink rubbed his hands and smiled and bowed more than once, with evident solicitude to show honour where honour was due, while he said,

"Mr. Christian, sir, how do you do, sir?"

Christian answered with the condescending familiarity of a superior. "Very badly, I can tell you, with these confounded braces that you were to make such a fine job of. See, old fellow, they've burst out again."

"Very sorry, sir. Can you leave them with me?"

"O yes, I'll leave them. What's the news, eh?" said Christian, half seating himself on a high stool, and beating his boot with a hand-whip.

"Well, sir, we look to you to tell us that," said Mr. Pink, with a knowing smile. "You're at headquarters — eh, sir? That was what I said to Mr. Scales the other day. He came for some straps, Mr. Scales did, and he asked that question in pretty near the same terms that you've done, sir, and I answered him, as I may say, ditto. Not meaning any disrespect to you, sir, but a way of speaking."

"Come, that's gammon, Pink," said Christian. "You know everything. You can tell me, if you will, who is the fellow employed to paste up Transome's handbills?"

"What do you say, Mr. Sims?" said Pink, looking at the auctioneer.

"Why, you know and I know well enough. It's Tommy Trounsem — an old, crippling, half-mad fellow. Most people know Tommy. I've employed him myself for charity."

"Where shall I find him?" said Christian.

"At the Cross-Keys, in Pollard's End, most likely," said Mr. Sims. "I don't know where he puts himself when he isn't at the public."

"He was a stoutish fellow fifteen year ago, when he carried pots," said Mr. Pink.

"Ay, and has snared many a hare in his time," said Mr. Sims. "But he was always a little cracked. Lord bless you! he used to swear he'd a right to the Transome estate."

"Why, what put that notion into his head?" said Christian, who had learned more than he expected.

"The lawing, sir — nothing but the lawing about the estate. There was a deal of it twenty year ago," said Mr. Pink. "Tommy happened to turn up hereabout at that time; a big, lungeous fellow, who would speak disrespectfully of hanybody."

"O, he meant no harm," said Mr. Sims. "He was fond of a drop to drink, and not quite right in the upper storey, and he could hear no difference between Trounsem and Transome. It's an odd way of speaking they have in that part where he was born — a little north'ard. You'll hear it in his tongue now, if you talk to him."

"At the Cross-Keys I shall find him, eh?" said Christian, getting off his stool. "Good-day, Pink, good-day."

Christian went straight from the saddler's to Quorlen's, the Tory printer's, with whom he had contrived a political spree. Quorlen was a new man in Treby, who had so reduced the trade of Dow, the old hereditary printer, that Dow had lapsed to Whiggery and Radicalism and opinions in general, so far as they were contented to express themselves in a small stock of types. Quorlen had brought his Duffield wit with him, and insisted that religion and joking were the handmaids of politics; on which principle he and Christian undertook the joking, and left the religion to the Rector. The joke at present in question was a practical one. Christian, turning into the shop, merely said, "I've found him out — give me the placards;" and, tucking a thickish flat bundle, wrapped in a black glazed cotton bag, under his arm, walked out into the dusk again.

"Suppose now," he said to himself, as he strode along — "suppose there should be some secret to be got out of this old scamp, or some notion that's as good as a secret to those who know how to use it? That would be virtue rewarded. But I'm afraid the old tosspot is not likely to be good for much. There's truth in wine, and there may be some in gin and muddy beer; but whether it's truth worth my knowing, is another question. I've got plenty of truth in my time out of men who were half-seas-over, but never any that was worth a sixpence to me."

The Cross-Keys was a very old-fashioned "public:" its bar was a big rambling kitchen, with an undulating brick floor; the small-paned windows threw an interesting obscurity over the far-off dresser, garnished with pewter and tin, and with large dishes that seemed to speak of better times; the two settles were half pushed under the wide-mouthed chimney; and the grate, with its brick hobs, massive iron crane, and various pothooks, suggested a generous plenty possibly existent in all moods and tenses except the indicative present. One way of getting an idea of our fellow-countrymen's miseries is to go and look at their pleasures. The Cross-Keys had a fungous-featured landlord and a yellow sickly landlady, with a napkin bound round her head like a resuscitated Lazarus; it had doctored ale, an odour of bad tobacco, and remarkably strong cheese. It was not what Astræa, when come back, might be expected to approve as the scene of ecstatic enjoyment for the beings whose special prerogative it is to lift their sublime faces towards heaven. Still, there was ample space on the hearth — accommodation for narrative bagmen or boxmen — room for a man to stretch his legs; his brain was not pressed upon by a white wall within a yard of him, and the light did not stare in mercilessly on bare ugliness, turning the fire to ashes. Compared with some beerhouses of this more advanced period, the Cross-Keys of that day presented a high standard of pleasure.

But though this venerable "public" had not failed to share in the recent political excitement of drinking, the pleasures it offered were not at this early hour of the evening sought by a numerous company. There were only three or four pipes being smoked by the firelight, but it was enough for Christian when he found that one of these was being smoked by the bill-sticker, whose large flat basket, stuffed with placards, leaned near him against the settle. So splendid an apparition as Christian was not a little startling at the Cross-Keys, and was gazed at in expectant silence; but he was a stranger in Pollard's End, and was taken for the highest style of traveller when he declared that he was deucedly thirsty, ordered sixpennyworth of gin and a large jug of water, and, putting a few drops of the spirit into his own glass, invited Tommy Trounsem, who sat next him, to help himself. Tommy was not slower than a shaking hand obliged him to be in accepting this invitation. He was a tall broad-shouldered old fellow, who had once been good-looking; but his cheeks and

chest were both hollow now, and his limbs were
shrunken.

"You've got some bills there, master, eh?" said
Christian, pointing to the basket. "Is there an auction
coming on?"

"Auction? no," said Tommy, with a gruff hoarse-
ness, which was the remnant of a jovial bass, and with
an accent which differed from the Trebian fitfully, as
an early habit is wont to reassert itself. "I've nought
to do wi' auctions; I'm a pol'tical charicter. It's me
am getting Trounsem into Parl'ment."

"Trounsem, says he," the landlord observed, taking
out his pipe with a low laugh. "It's Transome, sir.
Maybe you don't belong to this part. It's the candidate 'ull do most for the working men, and's proved
it too, in the way o' being openhanded and wishing 'em
to enjoy themselves. If I'd twenty votes, I'd give one
for Transome, and I don't care who hears me."

The landlord peeped out from his fungous cluster
of features with a beery confidence that the high figure
of twenty had somehow raised the hypothetic value of
his vote.

"Spilkins, now," said Tommy, waving his hand to
the landlord, "you let one genelman speak to another,
will you? This genelman wants to know about my
bills. Does he, or docsn't he?"

"What then? I spoke according," said the landlord,
mildly holding his own.

"You're all very well, Spilkins," returned Tommy,
"but y'aren't me. I know what the bills are. It's
public business. I'm none o' your common bill-stickers,
master; I've left off sticking up ten guineas reward for
a sheep-stealer, or low stuff like that. These are Troun-

sem's bills; and I'm the rightful family, and so I give him a lift. A Trounsem I am, and a Trounsem I'll be buried; and if Old Nick tries to lay hold on me for poaching, I'll say, 'You be hanged for a lawyer, Old Nick; every hare and pheasant on the Trounsem's land is mine;' and what rises the family, rises old Tommy; and we're going to get into Parl'ment — that's the long and the short on't, master. And I'm the head o' the family, and I stick the bills. There's Johnsons, and Thomsons, and Jacksons, and Billsons; but I'm a Trounsem, I am. What do you say to that, master?"

This appeal, accompanied by a blow on the table, while the landlord winked at the company, was addressed to Christian, who answered, with severe gravity,

"I say there isn't any work more honourable than bill-sticking."

"No, no," said Tommy, wagging his head from side to side. "I thought you'd come in to that. I thought you'd know better than say contrairy. But I'll shake hands wi' you; I don't want to knock any man's head off. I'm a good chap — a sound crock — an old family kep' out o' my rights. I shall go to heaven, for all Old Nick."

As these celestial prospects might imply that a little extra gin was beginning to tell on the bill-sticker, Christian wanted to lose no time in arresting his attention. He laid his hand on Tommy's arm and spoke emphatically.

"But I'll tell you what you bill-stickers are not up to. You should be on the look-out when Debarry's side have stuck up fresh bills, and go and paste yours over them. I know where there's a lot of Debarry's

bills now. Come along with me, and I'll show you.
We'll paste them over, and then we'll come back and
treat the company."

"Hooray!" said Tommy. "Let's be off then."

He was one of the thoroughly inured, originally
hale drunkards, and did not easily lose his head or
legs or the ordinary amount of method in his talk.
Strangers often supposed that Tommy was tipsy when
ho had only taken what he called "one blessed pint,"
chiefly from that glorious contentment with himself
and his adverse fortunes which is not usually characteristic of the sober Briton. He knocked the ashes
out of his pipe, seized his paste-vessel and his basket,
and prepared to start, with a satisfactory promise that
he could know what he was about.

The landlord and some others had confidently concluded that they understood all about Christian now.
He was a Transome's man, come to see after the bill-
sticking in Transome's interest. The landlord, telling
his yellow wife snappishly to open the door for the
gentleman, hoped soon to see him again.

"This is a Transome's house, sir," he observed, "in
respect of entertaining customers of that colour. I do
my duty as a publican, which, if I know it, is to turn
back no genelman's money. I say, give every genelman a chanch, and the more the merrier, in Parl'ment
and out of it. And if anybody says they want but two
Parl'ment men, I say it 'ud be better for trade if there
was six of 'em, and voters according."

"Ay, ay," said Christian; "you're a sensible man,
landlord. You don't mean to vote for Debarry then,
eh?"

"Not nohow," said the landlord, thinking that

where negatives were good the more you heard of them
the better.

As soon as the door had closed behind Christian
and his new companion, Tommy said,

"Now, master, if you're to be my lantern, don't
you be a Jacky Lantern, which I take to mean one as
leads you the wrong way. For I'll tell you what —
if you've had the luck to fall in wi' Tommy Trounsem,
don't you let him drop."

"No, no — to be sure not," said Christian. "Come
along here. We'll go to the Back Brewery wall first."

"No, no; don't you let me drop. Give me a shilling
any day you like, and I'll tell you more nor
you'll hear from Spilkins in a week. There isna many
men like me. I carried pots for fifteen year off and
on — what do you think o' that now, for a man as
might ha' lived up there at Trounsem Park, and snared
his own game? Which I'd ha' done," said Tommy,
wagging his head at Christian in the dimness undisturbed
by gas. "None o' your shooting for me — it's
two to one you'll miss. Snaring's more fishing-like.
You bait your hook, and if it isna the fishes' goodwill to
come, that's nothing again' the sporting genelman.
And that's what I say by snaring."

"But if you'd a right to the Transome estate, how
was it you were kept out of it, old boy? It was some
foul shame or other, eh?"

"It's the law — that's what it is. You're a good
sort o' chap; I don't mind telling you. There's folks
born to property, and there's folks catch hold on it;
and the law's made for them as catch hold. I'm pretty
deep; I see a good deal further than Spilkins. There
was Ned Patch, the pedlar, used to say to me, 'You

canna read, Tommy,' says he. 'No; thank you,' says I; 'I'm not going to crack my headpiece to make myself as big a fool as you.' I was fond o' Ned. Many's the pot we've had together."

"I see well enough you're deep, Tommy. How came you to know you were born to property?"

"It was the regester — the parish regester," said Tommy, with his knowing wag of the head, "that shows as you was born. I allays felt it inside me as I was somebody, and I could see other chaps thought it on me too; and so one day at Littleshaw, where I kep ferrets and a little bit of a public, there comes a fine man looking after me, and walking me up and down wi' questions. And I made out from the clerk as he'd been at the regester; and I gave the clerk a pot or two, and he got it of our parson as the name o' Trounsem was a great name hereabout. And I waits a bit for my fine man to come again. Thinks I, if there's property wants a right owner, I shall be called for; for I didn't know the law then. And I waited and waited, till I see'd no fun i' waiting. So I parted wi' my public and my ferrets — for she was dead a'ready, my wife was, and I hadn't no cumbrance. And off I started a pretty long walk to this countryside, for I could walk for a wager in them days."

"Ah! well, here we are at the Back Brewery wall. Put down your paste and your basket now, old boy, and I'll help you. You paste, and I'll give you the bills, and then you can go on talking."

Tommy obeyed automatically, for he was now carried away by the rare opportunity of talking to a new listener, and was only eager to go on with his story.

As soon as his back was turned, and he was stooping over his paste-pot, Christian, with quick adroitness, exchanged the placards in his own bag for those in Tommy's basket. Christian's placards had not been printed at Treby, but were a new lot which had been sent from Duffield that very day — "highly spiced," Quorlen had said, "coming from a pen that was up to that sort of thing." Christian had read the first of the sheaf, and supposed they were all alike. He proceeded to hand one to Tommy, and said,

"Here, old boy, paste this over the other. And so, when you got into this country-side, what did you do?"

"Do? Why, I put up at a good public and ordered the best, for I'd a bit o' money in my pocket; and I axed about, and they said to me, if it's Trounsem business you're after, you go to Lawyer Jermyn. And I went; and says I, going along, he's maybe the fine man as walked me up and down. But no such thing. I'll tell you what Lawyer Jermyn was. He stands you there, and holds you away from him wi' a pole three yard long. He stares at you, and says nothing, till you feel like a Tomfool; and then he threats you to set the justice on you; and then he's sorry for you, and hands you money, and preaches you a sarmint, and tells you you're a poor man, and he'll give you a bit of advice — and you'd better not be meddling wi' things belonging to the law, else you'll be catched up in a big wheel and fly to bits. And I went of a cold sweat, and I wished I might never come i' sight o' Lawyer Jermyn again. But he says, if you keep i' this neighbourhood, behave yourself well, and I'll pertect you. I were deep enough, but it's no use

being deep, 'cause you can never know the law. And
there's times when the deepest fellow's worst frightened."

"Yes, yes. There! Now for another placard. And
so that was all?"

"All?" said Tommy, turning round and holding
the paste-brush in suspense. "Don't you be running
too quick. Thinks I, 'I'll meddle no more. I've got
a bit o' money — I'll buy a basket, and be a potman.
It's a pleasant life. I shall live at publics and see the
world, and pick up 'quaintance, and get a chanch
penny' But when I'd turned into the Red Lion, and
got myself warm again wi' a drop o' hot, something
jumps into my head. Thinks I, Tommy, you've done
finely for yourself: you're a rat as has broke up your
house to take a journey, and show yourself to a ferret.
And then it jumps into my head: I'd once two ferrets
as turned on one another, and the little un killed the
big un. Says I to the landlady, "Missis, could you tell
me of a lawyer,' says I, 'not very big or fine, but a
second size — a pig-potato, like?' 'That I can,' says
she; 'there's one now in the bar parlour.' 'Be so kind
as bring us together,' says I. And she cries out —
I think I hear her now — 'Mr. Johnson!' And what
do you think?"

At this crisis in Tommy's story the grey clouds,
which had been gradually thinning, opened sufficiently
to let down the sudden moonlight, and show his poor
battered old figure and face in the attitude and with
the expression of a narrator sure of the coming effect
on his auditor; his body and neck stretched a little on
one side, and his paste-brush held out with an alarming intention of tapping Christian's coat-sleeve at the

right moment. Christian started to a safe distance, and said,

"It's wonderful. I can't tell what to think."

"Then never do you deny Old Nick," said Tommy, with solemnity. "I've believed in him more ever since. Who was Johnson? Why, Johnson was the fine man as had walked me up and down with questions. And I out with it to him then and there. And he speaks me civil, and says, 'Come away wi' me, my good fellow.' And he told me a deal o' law. And he says, whether you're a Tommy Trounsem or no, it's no good to you, but only to them as have got hold o' the property. If you was a Tommy Trounsem twenty times over, it 'ud be no good, for the law's bought you out; and your life's no good, only to them as have catched hold o' the property. The more you live, the more they'll stick in. Not as they want you now, says he — you're no good to anybody, and you might howl like a dog for iver, and the law 'ud take no notice on you. Says Johnson, I'm doing a kind thing by you, to tell you. For that's the law. And if you want to know the law, master, you ask Johnson. I heard 'em say after, as he was an understrapper at Jermyn's. I've never forgot it from that day to this. But I saw clear enough, as if the law hadn't been again' me, the Trounsem estate 'ud ha' been mine. But folks are fools hereabouts, and I've left off talking. The more you tell 'em the truth, the more they'll niver believe you. And I went and bought my basket and the pots, and —"

"Come, then, fire away," said Christian. "Here's another placard."

"I'm getting a bit dry, master."

"Well, then, make haste, and you'll have something to drink all the sooner."

Tommy turned to his work again, and Christian, continuing his help, said, "And how long has Mr. Jermyn been employing you?"

"Oh, no particular time — off and on; but a week or two ago he sees me upo' the road, and speaks to me uncommon civil, and tells me to go up to his office, and he'll give me employ. And I was noways unwilling to stick the bills to get the family into Parl'ment. For there's no man can help the law. And the family's the family, whether you carry pots or no. Master, I'm uncommon dry; my head's a turning round; it's talking so long on end."

The unwonted excitement of poor Tommy's memory was producing a reaction.

"Well, Tommy," said Christian, who had just made a discovery among the placards which altered the bent of his thoughts, "you may go back to the Cross-Keys now, if you like; here's a half-crown for you to spend handsomely. I can't go back there myself just yet; but you may give my respects to Spilkins, and mind you paste the rest of the bills early to-morrow morning."

"Ay, ay. But don't you believe too much i' Spilkins," said Tommy, pocketing the half-crown, and showing his gratitude by giving this advice — "he's no harm much — but weak. He thinks he's at the bottom o' things because he scores you up. But I bear him no ill-will. Tommy Trounsem's a good chap; and any day you like to give me half-a-crown, I'll tell you the same story over again. Not now; I'm dry. Come, help me up wi' these things; you're a younger chap than me. Well, I'll tell Spilkins you'll come again another day."

The moonlight, which had lit up poor Tommy's oratorical attitude, had served to light up for Christian the print of the placards. He had expected the copies to be various, and had turned them half over at different depths of the sheaf before drawing out those he offered to the bill-sticker. Suddenly the clearer light had shown him on one of them a name which was just then especially interesting to him, and all the more when occurring in a placard intended to dissuade the electors of North Loamshire from voting for the heir of the Transomes. He hastily turned over the lists that preceded and succeeded, that he might draw out and carry away all of this pattern; for it might turn out to be wiser for him not to contribute to the publicity of handbills which contained allusions to Bycliffe *versus* Transome. There were about a dozen of them; he pressed them together and thrust them into his pocket, returning all the rest to Tommy's basket. To take away this dozen might not be to prevent similar bills from being posted up elsewhere, but he had reason to believe that these were all of the same kind which had been sent to Treby from Duffield.

Christian's interest in his practical joke had died out like a morning rushlight. Apart from this discovery in the placards, old Tommy's story had some indications in it that were worth pondering over. Where was that well-informed Johnson now? Was he still an understrapper of Jermyn's?

With this matter in his thoughts, Christian only turned in hastily at Quorlen's, threw down the black bag which contained the captured Radical handbills, said he had done the job, and hurried back to the Manor that he might study his problem.

CHAPTER V.

I doe believe that, as the gall has severall receptacles in several creatures, soe there's scarce any creature but hath that emunctorye somewhere. — SIR THOMAS BROWNE.

FANCY what a game at chess would be if all the chessmen had passions and intellects, more or less small and cunning: if you were not only uncertain about your adversary's men, but a little uncertain also about your own; if your knight could shuffle himself on to a new square by the sly; if your bishop, in disgust at your castling, could wheedle your pawns out of their places; and if your pawns, hating you because they are pawns, could make away from their appointed posts that you might get checkmate on a sudden. You might be the longest-headed of deductive reasoners, and yet you might be beaten by your own pawns. You would be especially likely to be beaten, if you depended arrogantly on your mathematical imagination, and regarded your passionate pieces with contempt.

Yet this imaginary chess is easy compared with the game a man has to play against his fellow-men with other fellow-men for his instruments. He thinks himself sagacious, perhaps, because he trusts no bond except that of self-interest; but the only self-interest he can safely rely on is what seems to be such to the mind he would use or govern. Can he ever be sure of knowing this?

Matthew Jermyn was under no misgivings as to
the fealty of Johnson. He had "been the making of
Johnson;" and this seems to many men a reason for
expecting devotion, in spite of the fact that they themselves, though very fond of their own persons and lives,
are not at all devoted to the Maker they believe in.
Johnson was a most serviceable subordinate. Being a
man who aimed at respectability, a family man, who
had a good church-pew, subscribed for engravings of
banquet pictures where there were portraits of political
celebrities, and wished his children to be more unques-
tionably genteel than their father, he presented all the
more numerous handles of worldly motive by which a
judicious superior might keep a hold on him. But this
useful regard to respectability had its inconvenience in
relation to such a superior: it was a mark of some
vanity and some pride, which, if they were not touched
just in the right handling-place, were liable to become
raw and sensitive. Jermyn was aware of Johnson's
weaknesses, and thought he had flattered them sufficiently. But on the point of knowing when we are
disagreeable, our human nature is fallible. Our lavender-
water, our smiles, our compliments, and other polite
falsities, are constantly offensive, when in the very nature of them they can only be meant to attract admiration and regard. Jermyn had often been unconsciously
disagreeable to Johnson, over and above the constant
offence of being an ostentatious patron. He would
never let Johnson dine with his wife and daughters;
he would not himself dine at Johnson's house when he
was in town. He often did what was equivalent to
pooh-poohing his conversation by not even appearing
to listen, and by suddenly cutting it short with a query

on a new subject. Jermyn was able and politic enough to have commanded a great deal of success in his life, but he could not help being handsome, arrogant, fond of being heard, indisposed to any kind of comradeship, amorous and bland towards women, cold and self-contained towards men. You will hear very strong denials that an attorney's being handsome could enter into the dislike he excited; but conversation consists a good deal in the denial of what is true. From the British point of view masculine beauty is regarded very much as it is in the drapery business: — as good solely for the fancy department — for young noblemen, artists, poets, and the clergy. Some one who, like Mr. Lingon, was disposed to revile Jermyn (perhaps it was Sir Maximus), had called him "a cursed, sleek, handsome, long-winded, overbearing sycophant;" epithets which expressed, rather confusedly, the mingled character of the dislike he excited. And serviceable John Johnson, himself sleek, and mindful about his broadcloth and his cambric fronts, had what he considered "spirit" enough within him to feel that dislike of Jermyn gradually gathering force through years of obligation and subjection, till it had become an actuating motive disposed to use an opportunity, if not to watch for one.

It was not this motive, however, but rather the ordinary course of business, which accounted for Johnson's playing a double part as an electioneering agent. What men do in elections, is not to be classed either among sins or marks of grace: it would be profane to include business in religion, and conscience refers to failure, not to success. Still, the sense of being galled by Jermyn's harness was an additional reason for cultivating all relations that were independent of him;

and pique at Harold Transome's behaviour to him in Jermyn's office perhaps gave all the more zest to Johnson's use of his pen and ink when he wrote a handbill in the service of Garstin, and Garstin's incomparable agent, Putty, full of innuendoes against Harold Transome, as a descendant of the Durfey-Transomes. It is a natural subject of self-congratulation to a man, when special knowledge, gained long ago without any forecast, turns out to afford a special inspiration in the present; and Johnson felt a new pleasure in the consciousness that he of all people in the world next to Jermyn had the most intimate knowledge of the Transome affairs. Still better — some of these affairs were secrets of Jermyn's. If in an uncomplimentary spirit he might have been called Jermyn's "man of straw," it was a satisfaction to know that the unreality of the man John Johnson was confined to his appearance in annuity deeds, and that elsewhere he was solid, locomotive, and capable of remembering anything for his own pleasure and benefit. To act with doubleness towards a man whose own conduct was double, was so near an approach to virtue that it deserved to be called by no meaner name than Diplomacy.

By such causes it came to pass that Christian held in his hands a bill in which Jermyn was playfully alluded to as Mr. German Cozen, who won games by clever shuffling and odd tricks without any honour, and backed Durfey's crib against Bycliffe, — in which it was adroitly implied that the so-called head of the Transomes was only the tail of the Durfeys, — and that some said the Durfeys would have died out and left their nest empty if it had not been for their German Cozen.

Johnson had not dared to use any recollections except such as might credibly exist in other minds besides his own. In the truth of the case, no one but himself had the prompting to recall these outworn scandals; but it was likely enough that such foul-winged things should be revived by election heats for Johnson to escape all suspicion.

Christian could gather only dim and uncertain inferences from this flat irony and heavy joking; but one chief thing was clear to him. He had been right in his conjecture that Jermyn's interest about Bycliffe had its source in some claim of Bycliffe's on the Transome property. And then, there was that story of the old bill-sticker's, which, closely considered, indicated that the right of the present Transomes depended, or at least had depended, on the continuance of some other lives. Christian in his time had gathered enough legal notions to be aware that possession by one man sometimes depended on the life of another; that a man might sell his own interest in property, and the interest of his descendants, while a claim on that property would still remain to some one else than the purchaser, supposing the descendants became extinct, and the interest they had sold were at an end. But under what conditions the claim might be valid or void in any particular case, was all darkness to him. Suppose Bycliffe had any such claim on the Transome estates: how was Christian to know whether at the present moment it was worth anything more than a bit of rotten parchment? Old Tommy Trounsem had said that Johnson knew all about it. But even if Johnson were still above-ground — and all Johnsons are mortal — he might still be an understrapper of Jermyn's, in which case his knowledge would be on the wrong side of the hedge for the purposes of Henry Scaddon. His immediate care must be to find out all he could about Johnson. He blamed himself for not having questioned Tommy further while he had him at command; but on this head the bill-sticker could hardly know more than the less dilapidated denizens of Treby.

Now it had happened that during the weeks in which Christian had been at work in trying to solve the enigma of Jermyn's interest about Bycliffe, Johnson's mind also had been somewhat occupied with suspicion and conjecture as to new information on the subject of the old Bycliffe claims which Jermyn intended to conceal from him. The letter which, after his interview with Christian, Jermyn had written with a sense of perfect safety to his faithful ally Johnson, was, as we know, written to a Johnson who had found his self-love incompatible with that faithfulness of which it was supposed to be the foundation. Anything that the patron felt it inconvenient for his obliged friend and servant to know, became by that very fact an object of peculiar curiosity. The obliged friend and servant secretly doated on his patron's inconvenience, provided that he himself did not share it; and conjecture naturally became active.

Johnson's legal imagination, being very differently furnished from Christian's, was at no loss to conceive conditions under which there might arise a new claim on the Transome estates. He had before him the whole history of the settlement of those estates made a hundred years ago by John Justus Transome, entailing them, whilst in his possession, on his son Thomas and his heirs-male, with remainder to the Bycliffes in fee.

He knew that Thomas, son of John Justus, proving a
prodigal, had, without the knowledge of his father, the
tenant in possession, sold his own and his descendants'
rights to a lawyer-cousin named Durfey; that, therefore, the title of the Durfey-Transomes, in spite of that
old Durfey's tricks to show the contrary, depended
solely on the purchase of the "base fee" thus created
by Thomas Transome; and that the Bycliffes were the
"remainder-men" who might fairly oust the Durfey-
Transomes if ever the issue of the prodigal Thomas
went clean out of existence, and ceased to represent a
right which he had bargained away from them.

Johnson, as Jermyn's subordinate, had been closely
cognisant of the details concerning the suit instituted
by successive Bycliffes, of whom Maurice Christian
Bycliffe was the last, on the plea that the extinction
of Thomas Transome's line had actually come to pass
— a weary suit, which had eaten into the fortunes of
two families, and had only made the cankerworms fat.
The suit had closed with the death of Maurice Christian Bycliffe in prison; but before his death, Jermyn's
exertions to get evidence that there was still issue of
Thomas Transome's line surviving, as a security of the
Durfey title, had issued in the discovery of a Thomas
Transome at Littleshaw, in Stonyshire, who was the
representative of a pawned inheritance. The death of
Maurice had made this discovery useless — had made
it seem the wiser part to say nothing about it; and the
fact had remained a secret known only to Jermyn and
Johnson. No other Bycliffe was known or believed
to exist, and the Durfey-Transomes might be consi-
dered safe, unless — yes, there was an "unless" which
Johnson could conceive: an heir or heiress of the By-

cliffes — if such a personage turned out to be in existence — might some time raise a new and valid claim when once informed that wretched old Tommy Trounsem the bill-sticker, tottering drunkenly on the edge of the grave, was the last issue remaining above ground from that dissolute Thomas who played his Esau part a century before. While the poor old bill-sticker breathed, the Durfey-Transomes could legally keep their possession in spite of a possible Bycliffe proved real; but not when the parish had buried the bill-sticker.

Still, it is one thing to conceive conditions, and another to see any chance of proving their existence. Johnson at present had no glimpse of such a chance; and even if he ever gained the glimpse, he was not sure that he should ever make any use of it. His inquiries of Medwin, in obedience to Jermyn's letter, had extracted only a negative as to any information possessed by the lawyers of Bycliffe concerning a marriage, or expectation of offspring on his part. But Johnson felt not the less stung by curiosity to know what Jermyn had found out: that he had found something in relation to a possible Bycliffe, Johnson felt pretty sure. And he thought with satisfaction that Jermyn could not hinder him from knowing what he already knew about Thomas Transome's issue. Many things might occur to alter his policy and give a new value to facts. Was it certain that Jermyn would always be fortunate?

When greed and unscrupulousness exhibit themselves on a grand historical scale, and there is question of peace or war or amicable partition, it often occurs that gentlemen of high diplomatic talents have their minds bent on the same object from different points of view. Each, perhaps, is thinking of a certain duchy or province, with a view to arranging the ownership in such a way as shall best serve the purposes of the gentleman with high diplomatic talents in whom each is more especially interested. But these select minds in high office can never miss their aims from ignorance of each other's existence or whereabouts. Their high titles may be learned even by common people from every pocket almanac.

But with meaner diplomatists, who might be mutually useful, such ignorance is often obstructive. Mr. John Johnson and Mr. Christian, otherwise Henry Scaddon, might have had a concentration of purpose and an ingenuity of device fitting them to make a figure in the parcelling of Europe, and yet they might never have met, simply because Johnson knew nothing of Christian, and because Christian did not know where to find Johnson.

CHAPTER VI.

*His nature is too noble for the world:
He would not flatter Neptune for his trident,
Or Jove for his power to thunder. His heart's his mouth:
What his breast forges, that his tongue must vent;
And, being angry, doth forgot that ever
He heard the name of death. — Coriolanus.*

CHRISTIAN and Johnson did meet, however, by means that were quite incalculable. The incident which brought them into communication was due to Felix Holt, who of all men in the world had the least affinity either for the industrious or the idle parasite.

Mr. Lyon had urged Felix to go to Duffield on the 15th of December, to witness the nomination of the candidates for North Loamshire. The minister wished to hear what took place; and the pleasure of gratifying him helped to outweigh some opposing reasons.

"I shall get into a rage at something or other," Felix had said. "I've told you one of my weak points. Where I have any particular business, I must incur the risks my nature brings. But I've no particular business at Duffield. However, I'll make a holiday and go. By dint of seeing folly, I shall get lessons in patience."

The weak point to which Felix referred was his liability to be carried completely out of his own mastery by indignant anger. His strong health, his renunciation of selfish claims, his habitual preoccupation with large thoughts and with purposes independent of everyday casualties, secured him a fine and even tem-

per, free from moodiness or irritability. He was full
of long-suffering towards his unwise mother, who
"pressed him daily with her words and urged him, so
that his soul was vexed;" he had chosen to fill his
days in a way that required the utmost exertion of
patience, that required those little rill-like out-flowings
of goodness which in minds of great energy must be fed
from deep sources of thought and passionate devotedness. In this way his energies served to make him
gentle; and now, in this twenty-sixth year of his life,
they had ceased to make him angry, except in the
presence of something that roused his deep indignation. When once exasperated, the passionateness of his
nature threw off the yoke of a long-trained consciousness in which thought and emotion had been more
and more completely mingled, and concentrated itself
in a rage as ungovernable as that of boyhood. He
was thoroughly aware of the liability, and knew that
in such circumstances he could not answer for himself.
Sensitive people with feeble frames have often the
same sort of fury within them; but they are themselves
shattered, and shatter nothing. Felix had a terrible
arm: he knew that he was dangerous; and he avoided
the conditions that might cause him exasperation, as
he would have avoided intoxicating drinks if he had
been in danger of intemperance.

The nomination-day was a great epoch of successful
trickery, or, to speak in a more parliamentary manner,
of war-stratagem, on the part of skilful agents. And
Mr. Johnson had his share of inward chuckling and
self-approval, as one who might justly expect increasing renown, and be some day in as general request as
the great Putty himself. To have the pleasure and

the praise of electioneering ingenuity, and also to get
paid for it, without too much anxiety whether the ingenuity will achieve its ultimate end, perhaps gives to
some select persons a sort of satisfaction in their
superiority to their more agitated fellow-men that is
worthy to be classed with those generous enjoyments
of having the truth chiefly to yourself, and of seeing
others in danger of drowning while you are high and
dry, which seem to have been regarded as unmixed pri-
vileges by Lucretius and Lord Bacon.

One of Mr. Johnson's great successes was this.
Spratt, the hated manager of the Sproxton Colliery, in
careless confidence that the colliers and other labourers
under him would follow his orders, had provided carts
to carry some loads of voteless enthusiasm to Duffield
on behalf of Garstin; enthusiasm which, being already
paid for by the recognised benefit of Garstin's existence as a capitalist with a share in the Sproxton mines,
was not to cost much in the form of treating. A capitalist was held worthy of pious honour as the cause
why working men existed. But Mr. Spratt did not
sufficiently consider that a cause which has to be proved
by argument or testimony is not an object of passionate
devotion to colliers: a visible cause of beer acts on
them much more strongly. And even if there had
been any love of the far-off Garstin, hatred of the too-
immediate Spratt would have been the stronger motive.
Hence Johnson's calculations, made long ago with
Chubb, the remarkable publican, had been well founded,
and there had been diligent care to supply treating at
Duffield in the name of Transome. After the election
was over, it was not improbable that there would be
much friendly joking between Putty and Johnson as to

the success of this trick against Putty's employer, and Johnson would be conscious of rising in the opinion of his celebrated senior.

For the show of hands and the cheering, the hustling and the pelting, the roaring and the hissing, the hard hits with small missiles, and the soft hits with small jokes, were strong enough on the side of Transome to balance the similar "demonstrations" for Garstin, even with the Debarry interest in his favour. And the inconvenient presence of Spratt was early got rid of by a dexterously managed accident, which sent him bruised and limping from the scene of action. Mr. Chubb had never before felt so thoroughly that the occasion was up to a level with his talents, while the clear daylight in which his virtue would appear when at the election he voted, as his duty to himself bound him, for Garstin only, gave him thorough repose of conscience.

Felix Holt was the only person looking on at the senseless exhibitions of this nomination-day, who knew from the beginning the history of the trick with the Sproxton men. He had been aware all along that the treating at Chubb's had been continued, and that so far Harold Transome's promise had produced no good fruits; and what he was observing to-day, as he watched the uproarious crowd, convinced him that the whole scheme would be carried out just as if he had never spoken about it. He could be fair enough to Transome to allow that he might have wished, and yet have been unable, with his notions of success, to keep his promise; and his bitterness towards the candidate only took the form of contemptuous pity; for Felix was not sparing in his contempt for men who put their

inward honour in pawn by seeking the prizes of the
world. His scorn fell too readily on the fortunate.
But when he saw Johnson passing to and fro, and
speaking to Jermyn on the hustings, he felt himself
getting angry, and jumped off the wheel of the sta-
tionary cart on which he was mounted, that he might
no longer be in sight of this man, whose vitiating cant
had made his blood hot and his fingers tingle on the
first day of encountering him at Sproxton. It was a
little too exasperating to look at this pink-faced rotund
specimen of prosperity, to witness the power for evil
that lay in his vulgar cant, backed by another man's
money, and to know that such stupid iniquity flourished
the flags of Reform, and Liberalism, and justice to the
needy. While the roaring and the scuffling were still
going on, Felix, with his thick stick in his hand, made
his way through the crowd, and walked on through
the Duffield streets till he came out on a grassy suburb,
where the houses surrounded a small common. Here
he walked about in the breezy air, and ate his bread
and apples, telling himself that this angry haste of
his about evils that could only be remedied slowly,
could be nothing else than obstructive, and might
some day — he saw it so clearly that the thought
seemed like a presentiment — be obstructive of his
own work.

"Not to waste energy, to apply force where it
would tell, to do small work close at hand, not waiting
for speculative chances of heroism, but preparing for
them" — these were the rules he had been constantly
urging on himself. But what could be a greater waste
than to beat a scoundrel who had law and opodeldoc
at command? After this meditation, Felix felt cool

and wise enough to return into the town, not, however,
intending to deny himself the satisfaction of a few
pungent words wherever there was place for them.
Blows are sarcasms turned stupid: wit is a form of
force that leaves the limbs at rest.

Anything that could be called a crowd was no
longer to be seen. The show of hands having been
pronounced to be in favour of Debarry and Transome,
and a poll having been demanded for Garstin, the
business of the day might be considered at an end. But
in the street where the hustings were erected, and
where the great hotels stood, there were many groups,
as well as strollers and steady walkers to and fro. Men
in superior greatcoats and well-brushed hats were await-
ing with more or less impatience an important dinner,
either at the Crown, which was Debarry's house, or at
the Three Cranes, which was Garstin's, or at the Fox
and Hounds, which was Transome's. Knots of sober
retailers, who had already dined, were to be seen at
some shop-doors; men in very shabby coats and miscellaneous head-coverings, inhabitants of Duffield and
not county voters, were lounging about in dull silence,
or listening, some to a grimy man in a flannel shirt,
hatless and with turbid red hair, who was insisting on
political points with much more ease than had seemed
to belong to the gentlemen speakers on the hustings,
and others to a Scotch vendor of articles useful to sell,
whose unfamiliar accent seemed to have a guarantee of
truth in it wanting as an association with everyday
English. Some rough-looking pipe-smokers, or distinguished cigar-smokers, chose to walk up and down
in isolation and silence. But the majority of those
who had shown a burning interest in the nomination

had disappeared, and cockades no longer studded a close-pressed crowd, like, and also very unlike, meadow flowers among the grass. The street pavement was strangely painted with fragments of perishable missiles ground flat under heavy feet: but the workers were resting from their toil, and the buzz and tread and the fitfully discernible voices seemed like stillness to Felix after the roar with which the wide space had been filled when he left it.

The group round the speaker in the flannel shirt stood at the corner of a side-street, and the speaker himself was elevated by the head and shoulders above his hearers, not because he was tall, but because he stood on a projecting stone. At the opposite corner of the turning was the great inn of the Fox and Hounds, and this was the ultra-Liberal quarter of the High Street. Felix was at once attracted by this group; he liked the look of the speaker, whose bare arms were powerfully muscular, though he had the pallid complexion of a man who lives chiefly amidst the heat of furnaces. He was leaning against the dark stone building behind him with folded arms, the grimy paleness of his shirt and skin standing out in high relief against the dark stone building behind him. He lifted up one fore-finger, and marked his emphasis with it as he spoke. His voice was high and not strong, but Felix recognised the fluency and the method of a habitual preacher or lecturer.

"It's the fallacy of all monopolists," he was saying. "We know what monopolists are: men who want to keep a trade all to themselves, under the pretence that they'll furnish the public with a better article. We know what that comes to: in some countries a poor man can't afford to buy a spoonful of salt, and yet there's salt enough in the world to pickle every living thing in it. That's the sort of benefit monopolists do to mankind. And these are the men who tell us we're to let politics alone; they'll govern us better without our knowing anything about it. We must mind our business; we are ignorant; we've no time to study great questions. But I tell them this: the greatest question in the world is, how to give every man a man's share in what goes on in life ———"

"Hear, hear!" said Felix, in his sonorous voice, which seemed to give a new impressiveness to what the speaker had said. Every one looked at him: the well-washed face and its educated expression along with a dress more careless than that of most well-to-do workmen on a holiday, made his appearance strangely arresting.

"Not a pig's share," the speaker went on, "not a horse's share, not the share of a machine fed with oil only to make it work and nothing else. It isn't a man's share just to mind your pin-making, or your glass-blowing, and higgle about your own wages, and bring up your family to be ignorant sons of ignorant fathers, and no better prospect; that's a slave's share; we want a freeman's share, and that is to think and speak and act about what concerns us all, and see whether these fine gentlemen who undertake to govern us are doing the best they can for us. They've got the knowledge, say they. Very well, we've got the wants. There's many a one would be idle if hunger didn't pinch him; but the stomach sets us to work. There's a fable told where the nobles are the belly and the people the members. But I make another sort of fable. I say, we are the belly that feels the pinches, and we'll set these aristocrats, these great people who call themselves our brains, to work at some way of satisfying us a bit better. The aristocrats are pretty sure to try and govern for their own benefit; but how are we to be sure they'll try and govern for ours? They must be looked after, I think, like other workmen. We must have what we call inspectors, to see whether the work's well done for us. We want to send our inspectors to Parliament. Well, they say — you've got the Reform Bill; what more can you want? Send your inspectors. But I say, the Reform Bill is a trick — it's nothing but swearing-in special constables to keep the aristocrats safe in their monopoly; it's bribing some of the people with votes to make them hold their tongues about giving votes to the rest. I say, if a man doesn't beg or steal, but works for his bread, the poorer and the more miserable he is, the more he'd need have a vote to send an inspector to Parliament — else the man who is worst off is likely to be forgotten; and I say, he's the man who ought to be first remembered. Else what does their religion mean? Why do they build churches and endow them that their sons may get paid well for preaching a Saviour, and making themselves as little like Him as can be? If I want to believe in Jesus Christ, I must shut my eyes for fear I should see a parson. And what's a bishop? A bishop's a parson dressed up, who sits in the House of Lords to help and throw out Reform Bills. And because it's hard to get anything in the shape of a man to dress himself up like that, and do such work, they give him a palace for it, and plenty of thousands a-year. And then they cry out — 'The Church is in

danger,' — 'the poor man's Church.' And why is it
the poor man's Church? Because he can have a seat
for nothing. I think it *is* for nothing; for it would be
hard to tell what he gets by it. If the poor man had
a vote in the matter, I think he'd choose a different
sort of a Church to what that is. But do you think
the aristocrats will ever alter it, if the belly doesn't
pinch them? Not they. It's part of their monopoly.
They'll supply us with our religion like everything
else, and get a profit on it. They'll give us plenty of
heaven. We may have land *there*. That's the sort of
religion they like — a religion that gives us working
men heaven, and nothing else. But we'll offer to
change with 'em. We'll give them back some of their
heaven, and take it out in something for us and our
children in this world. They don't seem to care so
much about heaven themselves till they feel the gout
very bad; but you won't get them to give up anything
else, if you don't pinch 'em for it. And to pinch them
enough, we must get the suffrage, we must get votes,
that we may send the men to Parliament who will do
our work for us; and we must have Parliament dis-
solved every year, that we may change our man if he
doesn't do what we want him to do; and we must have
the country divided so that the little kings of the
counties can't do as they like, but must be shaken up
in one bag with us. I say, if we working men are
ever to get a man's share, we must have universal
suffrage, and annual Parliaments, and the vote by
ballot, and electoral districts."

"No! — something else before all that," said Felix,
again startling the audience into looking at him. But
the speaker glanced coldly at him and went on.

5*

"That's what Sir Francis Burdett went in for fifteen years ago; and it's the right thing for us, if it was Tomfool who went in for it. You must lay hold of such handles as you can. I don't believe much in Liberal aristocrats; but if there's any fine carved gold-headed stick of an aristocrat will make a broomstick of himself, I'll lose no time but I'll sweep with him. And that's what I think about Transome. And if any of you have acquaintance among county voters, give 'em a hint that you wish 'em to vote for Transome."

At the last word, the speaker stepped down from his slight eminence, and walked away rapidly, like a man whose leisure was exhausted, and who must go about his business. But he had left an appetite in his audience for further oratory, and one of them seemed to express a general sentiment as he turned immediately to Felix, and said, "Come, sir, what do you say?"

Felix did at once what he would very likely have done without being asked — he stepped on to the stone, and took off his cap by an instinctive prompting that always led him to speak uncovered. The effect of his figure in relief against the stone background was unlike that of the previous speaker. He was considerably taller, his head and neck were more massive, and the expression of his mouth and eyes was something very different from the mere acuteness and rather hard-lipped antagonism of the trades-union man. Felix Holt's face had the look of habitual meditative abstraction from objects of mere personal vanity or desire, which is the peculiar stamp of culture, and makes a very roughly-cut face worthy to be called "the human face divine." Even lions and dogs know a distinction between men's glances; and doubtless those Duffield men, in the expectation with which they looked up at Felix, were unconsciously influenced by the grandeur of his full yet firm mouth, and the calm clearness of his grey eyes, which were somehow unlike what they were accustomed to see along with an old brown velveteen coat, and an absence of chin-propping. When he began to speak, the contrast of voice was still stronger than that of appearance. The man in the flannel shirt had not been heard — had probably not cared to be heard — beyond the immediate group of listeners. But Felix at once drew the attention of persons comparatively at a distance.

"In my opinion," he said, almost the moment after he was addressed, "that was a true word spoken by your friend when he said the great question was how to give every man a man's share in life. But I think he expects voting to do more towards it than I do. I want the working men to have power. I'm a working man myself, and I don't want to be anything else. But there are two sorts of power. There's a power to do mischief — to undo what has been done with great expense and labour, to waste and destroy, to be cruel to the weak, to lie and quarrel, and to talk poisonous nonsense. That's the sort of power that ignorant numbers have. It never made a joint stool or planted a potato. Do you think it's likely to do much towards governing a great country, and making wise laws, and giving shelter, food, and clothes to millions of men? Ignorant power comes in the end to the same thing as wicked power; it makes misery. It's another sort of power that I want us working men to have, and I can see plainly enough that our all having votes will do little towards it at present. I hope we, or the children that come after us, will get plenty of political power some time. I tell everybody plainly, I hope there will be great changes, and that some time, whether we live to see it or not, men will have come to be ashamed of things they're proud of now. But I should like to convince you that votes would never give you political power worth having while things are as they are now, and that if you go the right way to work you may get power sooner without votes. Perhaps all you who hear me are sober men, who try to learn as much of the nature of things as you can, and to be as little like fools as possible. A fool or idiot is one who expects things to happen that never can happen; he pours milk into a can without a bottom, and expects the milk to stay there. The more of such vain expectations a man has, the more he is of a fool or idiot. And if any working man expects a vote to do for him what it never can do, he's foolish to that amount, if no more. I think that's clear enough, eh?"

"Hear, hear," said several voices, but they were not those of the original group; they belonged to some strollers who had been attracted by Felix Holt's vibrating voice, and were Tories from the Crown. Among them was Christian, who was smoking a cigar with a pleasure he always felt in being among people who did not know him, and doubtless took him to be something higher than he really was. Hearers from the Fox and Hounds also were slowly adding themselves to the nucleus. Felix, accessible to the pleasure of being listened to, went on with more and more animation:

"The way to get rid of folly is to get rid of vain

expectations, and of thoughts that don't agree with the nature of things. The men who have had true thoughts about water, and what it will do when it is turned into steam and under all sorts of circumstances, have made themselves a great power in the world: they are turning the wheels of engines that will help to change most things. But no engines would have done, if there had been false notions about the way water would act. Now, all the schemes about voting, and districts, and annual Parliaments, and the rest, are engines, and the water or steam — the force that is to work them — must come out of human nature — out of men's passions, feelings, desires. Whether the engines will do good work or bad depends on these feelings; and if we have false expectations about men's characters, we are very much like the idiot who thinks he'll carry milk in a can without a bottom. In my opinion, the notions about what mere voting will do are very much of that sort."

"That's very fine," said a man in dirty fustian, with a scornful laugh. "But how are we to get the power without votes?"

"I'll tell you what's the greatest power under heaven," said Felix, "and that is public opinion — the ruling belief in society about what is right and what is wrong, what is honourable and what is shameful. That's the steam that is to work the engines. How can political freedom make us better, any more than a religion we don't believe in, if people laugh and wink when they see men abuse and defile it? And while public opinion is what it is — while men have no better beliefs about public duty — while corruption is not felt to be a damning disgrace — while men are not ashamed in Parliament and out of it to make public questions which concern the welfare of millions a mere screen for their own petty private ends, — I say, no fresh scheme of voting will much mend our condition. For, take us working men of all sorts. Suppose out of every hundred who had a vote there were thirty who had some soberness, some sense to choose with, some good feeling to make them wish the right thing for all. And suppose there were seventy out of the hundred who were, half of them, not sober, who had no sense to choose one thing in politics more than another, and who had so little good feeling in them that they wasted on their own drinking the money that should have helped to feed and clothe their wives and children; and another half of them who, if they didn't drink, were too ignorant or mean or stupid to see any good for themselves better than pocketing a five-shilling piece when it was offered them. Where would be the political power of the thirty sober men? The power would lie with the seventy drunken and stupid votes; and I'll tell you what sort of men would get the power — what sort of men would end by returning whom they pleased to "Parliament."

Felix had seen every face around him, and had particularly noticed a recent addition to his audience; but now he looked before him without appearing to fix his glance on any one. In spite of his cooling meditations an hour ago, his pulse was getting quickened by indignation, and the desire to crush what he hated was likely to vent itself in articulation. His tone became more biting.

"They would be men who would undertake to do the business for a candidate; and return him: men who have no real opinions, but who pilfer the words of every opinion, and turn them into a cant which will serve their purpose at the moment; men who look out for dirty work to make their fortunes by, because dirty work wants little talent and no conscience; men who know all the ins and outs of bribery, because there is not a cranny in their own souls where a bribe can't enter. Such men as these will be the masters wherever there's a majority of voters who care more for money, more for drink, more for some mean little end which is their own and nobody else's, than for anything that has ever been called Right in the world. For suppose there's a poor voter named Jack, who has seven children, and twelve or fifteen shillings a-week wages, perhaps less. Jack can't read — I don't say whose fault that is — he never had the chance to learn; he knows so little that he perhaps thinks God made the poor-laws, and if anybody said the pattern of the workhouse was laid down in the Testament, he wouldn't be able to contradict them. What is poor Jack likely to do when he sees a smart stranger coming to him, who happens to be just one of those men that I say will be the masters till public opinion gets too hot for them? He's a middle-sized man, we'll say; stout, with coat upon coat of fine broadcloth, open enough to show a fine gold chain: none of your dark, scowling men, but one with an innocent pink-and-white skin and very smooth light hair — a most respectable man, who calls himself by a good, sound, well-known English name — as Green, or Baker, or Wilson, or, let us say, Johnson——"

Felix was interrupted by an explosion of laughter from a majority of the bystanders. Some eyes had been turned on Johnson, who stood on the right hand of Felix, at the very beginning of the description, and these were gradually followed by others, till at last every hearer's attention was fixed on him, and the first burst of laughter from the two or three who knew the attorney's name, let every one sufficiently into the secret to make the amusement common. Johnson, who had kept his ground till his name was mentioned, now turned away, looking unusually white after being unusually red, and feeling by an attorney's instinct for his pocket-book, as if he felt it was a case for taking down the names of witnesses.

All the well-dressed hearers turned away too, thinking they had had the cream of the speech in the joke against Johnson, which, as a thing worth telling, helped to recall them to the scene of dinner.

"Who is this Johnson?" said Christian to a young man who had been standing near him, and had been one of the first to laugh. Christian's curiosity had naturally been awakened by what might prove a golden opportunity.

"O — a London attorney. He acts for Transome. That tremendous fellow at the corner there is some red-hot Radical demagogue, and Johnson has offended him, I suppose; else he wouldn't have turned in that way on a man of their own party."

"I had heard there was a Johnson who was an understrapper of Jermyn's," said Christian.

"Well, so this man may have been for what I know. But he's a London man now — a very busy fellow — on his own legs in Bedford Row. Ha ha! It's capital, though, when these Liberals get a slap in the face from the working men they're so very fond of."

Another turn along the street enabled Christian to come to a resolution. Having seen Jermyn drive away an hour before, he was in no fear: he walked at once to the Fox and Hounds and asked to speak to Mr. Johnson. A brief interview, in which Christian ascertained that he had before him the Johnson mentioned by the bill-sticker, issued in the appointment of a longer one at a later hour; and before they left Duffield they had come not exactly to a mutual understanding, but to an exchange of information mutually welcome.

Christian had been very cautious in the commencement, only intimating that he knew something important which some chance hints had induced him to think might be interesting to Mr. Johnson, but that this entirely depended on how far he had a common interest with Mr. Jermyn. Johnson replied that he had much business in which that gentleman was not concerned, but that to a certain extent they had a common interest. Probably then, Christian observed, the affairs of the Transome estate were part of the business in which Mr. Jermyn and Mr. Johnson might be understood to represent each other — in which case he need not detain Mr. Johnson? At this hint Johnson could not conceal that he was becoming eager. He had no idea what Christian's information was, but there were many grounds on which Johnson desired to know as much as he could about the Transome affairs independently of Jermyn. By little and little an understanding was arrived at. Christian told of his interview with Tommy Trounsem, and stated that if Johnson could show him whether the knowledge could have any legal value, he could bring evidence that a legitimate child of Bycliffe's existed: he felt certain of his fact, and of his proof. Johnson explained, that in this case the death of the old bill-sticker would give the child the first valid claim to the Bycliffe heirship; that for his own part he should be glad to further a true claim, but that caution must be observed. How did Christian know that Jermyn was informed on this subject? Christian, more and more convinced that Johnson would be glad to counteract Jermyn, at length became explicit about Esther, but still withheld his own real name, and the nature of his relations with Bycliffe. He said he would bring the rest of his information when Mr. Johnson took the case up seriously, and placed it in the hands of Bycliffe's old lawyers — of course he would do that? Johnson replied that he would certainly do that; but that there were legal niceties which Mr. Christian was probably not acquainted with; that Esther's claim had not yet accrued; and that hurry was useless.

The two men parted, each in distrust of the other, but each well pleased to have learned something. Johnson was not at all sure how he should act, but thought it likely that events would soon guide him. Christian was beginning to meditate a way of securing his own ends without depending in the least on Johnson's procedure. It was enough for him that he was now assured of Esther's legal claim on the Transome estates.

CHAPTER VII.

> "In the copia of the factious language the word Tory was entertained, ... and being a vocal clever-sounding word, readily pronounced, it kept its hold, and took possession of the foul mouths of the faction. ... The Loyalists began to cheer up and to take heart of grace, and in the working of this crisis, according to the common laws of scolding, they considered which way to make payment for so much of Tory as they had been treated with, to clear scores. ... Immediately the train took, and ran like wild-fire and became general. And so the account of Tory was balanced, and soon began to run up a sharp score on the other side." — NORTH'S *Examen*, p. 321.

AT last the great epoch of the election for North Loamshire had arrived. The roads approaching Treby were early traversed by a larger number of vehicles, horsemen, and also foot-passengers, than were ever seen there at the annual fair. Treby was the polling-place for many voters whose faces were quite strange in the town; and if there were some strangers who did not come to poll, though they had business not unconnected with the election, they were not liable to be regarded with suspicion or especial curiosity. It was understood that no division of a county had ever been more thoroughly canvassed, and that there would be a hard run between Garstin and Transome. Mr. Johnson's headquarters were at Duffield; but it was a maxim which he repeated after the great Putty, that a capable agent makes himself omnipresent; and quite apart from the express between him and Jermyn, Mr. John Johnson's presence in the universe had potent effects on this December day at Treby Magna.

A slight drizzling rain which was observed by some Tories who looked out of their bedroom windows before six o'clock, made them hope that, after all, the day might pass off better than alarmists had expected. The rain was felt to be somehow on the side of quiet and Conservatism; but soon the breaking of the clouds and the mild gleams of a December sun brought back previous apprehensions. As there were already precedents for riot at a Reformed election, and as the Trebian district had had its confidence in the natural course of things somewhat shaken by a landed proprietor with an old name offering himself as a Radical candidate, the election had been looked forward to by many with a vague sense that it would be an occasion something like a fighting match, when bad characters would probably assemble, and there might be struggles and alarms for respectable men, which would make it expedient for them to take a little neat brandy as a precaution beforehand and a restorative afterwards. The tenants on the Transome estate were comparatively fearless: poor Mr. Goffe, of Rabbit's End, considered that "one thing was as mauling as another," and that an election was no worse than the sheep-rot; while Mr. Dibbs, taking the more cheerful view of a prosperous man, reflected that if the Radicals were dangerous, it was safer to be on their side. It was the voters for Debarry and Garstin who considered that they alone had the right to regard themselves as targets for evil-minded men; and Mr. Crowder, if he could have got his ideas countenanced, would have recommended a muster of farm-servants with defensive pitchforks on the side of Church and King. But the bolder men were rather gratified by the prospect of being groaned at, so that they might face about and groan in return.

Mr. Crow, the high constable of Treby, inwardly rehearsed a brief address to a riotous crowd in case it should be wanted, having been warned by the Rector that it was a primary duty on these occasions to keep a watch against provocation as well as violence. The Rector, with a brother magistrate who was on the spot, had thought it desirable to swear in some special constables, but the presence of loyal men not absolutely required for the polling was not looked at in the light of a provocation. The Benefit Clubs from various quarters made a show, some with the orange-coloured ribbons and streamers of the true Tory candidate, some with the mazarine of the Whig. The orange-coloured bands played "Auld Langsyne," and a louder mazarine band came across them with "O whistle and I will come to thee, my lad" — probably as the tune the most symbolical of Liberalism which their repertory would furnish. There was not a single club bearing the Radical blue: the Sproxton Club members wore the mazarine, and Mr. Chubb wore so much of it that he looked (at a sufficient distance) like a very large gentianella. It was generally understood that "these brave fellows," representing the fine institution of Benefit Clubs, and holding aloft the motto, "Let brotherly love continue," were a civil force calculated to encourage voters of sound opinions and keep up their spirits. But a considerable number of unadorned heavy navvies, colliers, and stone-pit men, who used their freedom as British subjects to be present in Treby on this great occasion, looked like a possibly uncivil force whose politics were dubious until it was clearly seen for whom they cheered and for whom they groaned.

Thus the way up to the polling-booths was variously lined, and those who walked it, to whatever side they belonged, had the advantage of hearing from the opposite side what were the most marked defects or excesses in their personal appearance; for the Trebians of that day held, without being aware that they had Cicero's authority for it, that the bodily blemishes of an opponent were a legitimate ground for ridicule; but if the voter frustrated wit by being handsome, he was groaned at and satirised according to a formula, in which the adjective was Tory, Whig, or Radical, as the case might be, and the substantive a blank to be filled up after the taste of the speaker.

Some of the more timid had chosen to go through this ordeal as early as possible in the morning. One of the earliest was Mr. Timothy Rose, the gentleman-farmer from Leek Malton. He had left home with some foreboding, having swathed his more vital parts in layers of flannel, and put on two greatcoats as a soft kind of armour. But reflecting with some trepidation that there were no resources for protecting his head, he once more wavered in his intention to vote; he once more observed to Mrs. Rose that these were hard times when a man of independent property was expected to vote "willy-nilly;" but finally, coerced by the sense that he should be looked ill on "in these times" if he did not stand by the gentlemen round about, he set out in his gig, taking with him a powerful waggoner, whom he ordered to keep him in sight as he went to the polling-booth. It was hardly more than nine o'clock when Mr. Rose, having thus come up to the level of his times, cheered himself with a little cherry-brandy at the Marquis, drove away in a much more courageous spirit, and got down at Mr. Nolan's, just outside the town. The retired Londoner, he considered, was a man of experience, who would estimate properly the judicious course he had taken, and could make it known to others. Mr. Nolan was superintending the removal of some shrubs in his garden.

"Well, Mr. Nolan," said Rose, twinkling a self-complacent look over the red prominence of his cheeks, "have you been to give your vote yet?"

"No; all in good time. I shall go presently."

"Well, I wouldn't lose an hour, I wouldn't. I said to myself, if I've got to do gentlemen a favour, I'll do it at once. You see, I've got no landlord, Nolan — I'm in that position o' life that I can be independent."

"Just so, my dear sir," said the wiry-faced Nolan, pinching his under-lip between his thumb and finger, and giving one of those wonderful universal shrugs, by which he seemed to be recalling all his garments from a tendency to disperse themselves. "Come in and see Mrs. Nolan?"

"No, no, thankye. Mrs. Rose expects me back. But, as I was saying, I'm a independent man, and I consider it's not my part to show favour to one more than another, but to make things as even as I can. If I'd been a tenant to anybody, well, in course I must have voted for my landlord — that stands to sense. But I wish everybody well; and if one's returned to Parliament more than another, nobody can say it's my doing; for when you can vote for two, you can make things even. So I gave one to Debarry and one to Transome; and I wish Garstin no ill, but I can't help the odd number, and he hangs on to Debarry, they say."

"God bless me, sir," said Mr. Nolan, coughing down a laugh, "don't you perceive that you might as well have stayed at home and not voted at all, unless you would rather send a Radical to Parliament than a sober Whig?"

"Well, I'm sorry you should have anything to say against what I've done, Nolan," said Mr. Rose, rather crestfallen, though sustained by inward warmth. "I thought you'd agree with me, as you're a sensible man. But the most a independent man can do is to try and please all; and if he hasn't the luck — here's wishing I may do it another time," added Mr. Rose, apparently confounding a toast with a salutation, for he put out his hand for a passing shake, and then stepped into his gig again.

At the time that Mr. Timothy Rose left the town, the crowd in King Street and in the market-place, where the polling-booths stood, was fluctuating. Voters as yet were scanty, and brave fellows who had come from any distance this morning, or who had sat up late drinking the night before, required some reinforcement of their strength and spirits. Every public-house in Treby, not excepting the venerable and sombre Cross-Keys, was lively with changing and numerous company. Not, of course, that there was any treating: treating necessarily had stopped, from moral scruples, when once "the writs were out;" but there was drinking, which did equally well under any name.

Poor Tommy Trounsem, breakfasting here on Falstaff's proportion of bread, and something which, for gentility's sake, I will call sack, was more than usually

victorious over the ills of life, and felt himself one of
the heroes of the day. He had an immense light-blue
cockade in his hat, and an amount of silver in a dirty
little canvas bag which astonished himself. For some
reason, at first inscrutable to him, he had been paid
for his bill-sticking with great liberality at Mr. Jermyn's
office, in spite of his having been the victim of a trick
by which he had once lost his own bills and pasted up
Debarry's; but he soon saw that this was simply a recognition of his merit as "an old family kept out of
its rights," and also of his peculiar share in an occasion when the family was to get into Parliament.
Under these circumstances, it was due from him that
he should show himself prominently where business
was going forward, and give additional value by his
presence to every vote for Transome. With this view
he got a half-pint bottle filled with his peculiar kind of
"sack," and hastened back to the market-place, feeling
good-natured and patronising towards all political parties, and only so far partial as his family bound him
to be.

But a disposition to concentrate at that extremity
of King Street which issued in the market-place was
not universal among the increasing crowd. Some of
them seemed attracted towards another nucleus at the
other extremity of King Street, near the Seven Stars.
This was Garstin's chief house, where his committee
sat, and it was also a point which must necessarily be
passed by many voters entering the town on the
eastern side. It seemed natural that the mazarine
colours should be visible here, and that Pack, the tall
"shepherd" of the Sproxton men, should be seen moving to and fro where there would be a frequent oppor-

tunity of cheering the voters for a gentleman who had the chief share in the Sproxton mines. But the side lanes and entries out of King Street were numerous enough to relieve any pressure if there was need to make way. The lanes had a distinguished reputation. Two of them had odours of brewing; one had a side entrance to Mr. Tiliot's wine and spirit vaults; up another Mr. Muscat's cheeses were frequently being unloaded; and even some of the entries had those cheerful suggestions of plentiful provision which were among the characteristics of Treby.

Between ten and eleven the voters came in more rapid succession, and the whole scene became spirited. Cheers, sarcasms, and oaths, which seemed to have a flavour of wit for many hearers, were beginning to be reinforced by more practical demonstrations, dubiously jocose. There was a disposition in the crowd to close and hem in the way for voters, either going or coming, until they had paid some kind of toll. It was difficult to see who set the example in the transition from words to deeds. Some thought it was due to Jacob Cuff, a Tory charity-man, who was a well-known ornament of the pothouse, and gave his mind much leisure for amusing devices; but questions of origination in stirring periods are notoriously hard to settle. It is by no means necessary in human things that there should be only one beginner. This, however, is certain — that Mr. Chubb, who wished it to be noticed that he voted for Garstin solely, was one of the first to get rather more notice than he wished, and that he had his hat knocked off and crushed in the interest of Debarry by Tories opposed to coalition. On the other hand, some said it was at the same time that Mr. Pink, the saddler, being stopped on his way and made to declare that he was going to vote for Debarry, got himself well chalked as to his coat, and pushed up an entry, where he remained the prisoner of terror combined with the want of any back outlet, and never gave his vote that day.

The second Tory joke was performed with much gusto. The majority of the Transome tenants came in a body from the Ram Inn, with Mr. Banks the bailiff leading them. Poor Goffe was the last of them, and his worn melancholy look and forward-leaning gait gave the jocose Cuff the notion that the farmer was not what he called "compus." Mr. Goffe was cut off from his companions and hemmed in; asked, by voices with hot breath close to his ear, how many horses he had, how many cows, how many fat pigs; then jostled from one to another, who made trumpets with their hands and deafened him by telling him to vote for Debarry. In this way the melancholy Goffe was hustled on till he was at the polling-booth — filled with confused alarms, the immediate alarm being that of having to go back in still worse fashion than he had come. Arriving in this way after the other tenants had left, he astonished all hearers who knew him for a tenant of the Transomes by saying "Debarry," and was jostled back trembling amid shouts of laughter.

By stages of this kind the fun grew faster, and was in danger of getting rather serious. The Tories began to feel that their jokes were returned by others of a heavier sort, and that the main strength of the crowd was not on the side of sound opinion, but might come to be on the side of sound cudgelling and kicking. The navvies and pitmen in dishabille seemed to be multiplying, and to be clearly not belonging to the party of Order. The shops were freely resorted to for various forms of playful missiles and weapons; and news came to the magistrates, watching from the large window of the Marquis, that a gentleman coming in on horseback at the other end of the street to vote for Garstin had had his horse turned round and frightened into a headlong gallop out of it again.

Mr. Crow and his subordinates, and all the special constables, felt that it was necessary to make some energetic effort, or else every voter would be intimidated and the poll must be adjourned. The Rector determined to get on horseback and go amidst the crowd with the constables; and he sent a message to Mr. Lingon, who was at the Ram, calling on him to do the same. "Sporting Jack" was sure the good fellows meant no harm, but he was courageous enough to face any bodily dangers, and rode out in his brown leggings and coloured bandanna, speaking persuasively.

It was nearly twelve o'clock when this sally was made: the constables and magistrates tried the most pacific measures, and they seemed to succeed. There was a rapid thinning of the crowd: the most boisterous disappeared, or seemed to do so by becoming quiet; missiles ceased to fly, and a sufficient way was cleared for voters along King Street. The magistrates returned to their quarters, and the constables took convenient posts of observation. Mr. Wace, who was one of Debarry's committee, had suggested to the Rector that it might be wise to send for the military from Duffield, with orders that they should station themselves at Hathercote, three miles off: there was so much pro-

perty in the town that it would be better to make it
secure against risks. But the Rector felt that this was
not the part of a moderate and wise magistrate, unless
the signs of riot recurred. He was a brave man, and
fond of thinking that his own authority sufficed for the
maintenance of the general good in Treby.

CHAPTER VIII.

*Go from me. Yet I feel that I shall stand
Henceforward in thy shadow. Never more
Alone upon the threshold of my door
Of individual life, I shall command
The uses of my soul, nor lift my hand
Serenely in the sunshine as before
Without the sense of that which I forbore—
Thy touch upon the palm. The widest land
Doom takes to part us, leaves thy heart in mine
With pulses that beat double. What I do
And what I dream include thee, as the wine
Must taste of its own grapes. And when I sue
God for myself, He hears that name of thine,
And sees within my eyes the tears of two.*
Mrs. Browning.

Felix Holt, seated at his work without his pupils, who had asked for a holiday with a notion that the wooden booths promised some sort of show, noticed about eleven o'clock that the noises which reached him from the main street were getting more and more tumultuous. He had long seen bad auguries for this election, but, like all people who dread the prophetic wisdom that ends in desiring the fulfilment of its own evil forebodings, he had checked himself with remembering that, though many conditions were possible which might bring on violence, there were just as many which might avert it. There would, perhaps, be no other mischief than what he was already certain of. With these thoughts he had sat down quietly to his work, meaning not to vex his soul by going to look on at things he would fain have made different if he

could. But he was of a fibre that vibrated too strongly
to the life around him to shut himself away in quiet,
even from suffering and irremediable wrong. As the
noises grew louder, and wrought more and more
strongly on his imagination, he was obliged to lay
down his delicate wheel-work. His mother came from
her turnip-paring in the kitchen, where little Job was
her companion, to observe that they must be killing
everybody in the High Street, and that the election,
which had never been before at Treby, must have
come for a judgment; that there were mercies where
you didn't look for them, and that she thanked God in
His wisdom for making her live up a back street.

Felix snatched his cap and rushed out. But when
he got to the turning into the market-place the magistrates were already on horseback there, the constables
were moving about, and Felix observed that there was
no strong spirit of resistance to them. He stayed long
enough to see the partial dispersion of the crowd and
the restoration of tolerable quiet, and then went back
to Mrs. Holt to tell her that there was nothing to fear
now: he was going out again, and she must not be in
any anxiety at his absence. She might set by his
dinner for him.

Felix had been thinking of Esther and her probable alarm at the noises that must have reached her
more distinctly than they had reached him, for
Malthouse Yard was removed but a little way from the
main street. Mr. Lyon was away from home, having
been called to preach charity sermons and attend meetings in a distant town; and Esther, with the plaintive
Lyddy for her sole companion, was not cheerfully
circumstanced. Felix had not been to see her yet

since her father's departure, but to-day he gave way to new reasons.

"Miss Esther was in the garret," Lyddy said, trying to see what was going on. But before she was fetched she came running down the stairs, drawn by the knock at the door, which had shaken the small dwelling.

"I am so thankful to see you," she said, eagerly. "Pray come in."

When she had shut the parlour door behind them, Felix said, "I suspected that you might have been made anxious by the noises. I came to tell you that things are quiet now. Though, indeed, you can hear that they are."

"I *was* frightened," said Esther. "The shouting and roaring of rude men is so hideous. It is a relief to me that my father is not at home — that he is out of the reach of any danger he might have fallen into if he had been here. But I gave you credit for being in the midst of the danger," she added, smiling, with a determination not to show much feeling. "Sit down and tell me what has happened."

They sat down at the extremities of the old black sofa, and Felix said,

"To tell you the truth, I had shut myself up, and tried to be as indifferent to the election as if I'd been one of the fishes in the Lapp, till the noises got too strong for me. But I only saw the tail end of the disturbance. The poor noisy simpletons seemed to give way before the magistrates and the constables. I hope nobody has been much hurt. The fear is that they may turn out again by-and-by; their giving way so soon may not be altogether a good sign. There's a great number of heavy fellows in the town. If they go and drink more, the last end may be worse than the first. However——"

Felix broke off, as if this talk were futile, clasped his hands behind his head, and, leaning backward, looked at Esther, who was looking at him.

"May I stay here a little while?" he said, after a moment, which seemed long.

"Pray do," said Esther, colouring. To relieve herself she took some work and bowed her head over her stitching. It was in reality a little heaven to her that Felix was there, but she saw beyond it — saw that by-and-by he would be gone, and that they should be farther on their way, not towards meeting, but parting. His will was impregnable. He was a rock, and she was no more to him than the white clinging mist-cloud.

"I wish I could be sure that you see things just as I do," he said, abruptly, after a minute's silence.

"I am sure you see them much more wisely than I do," said Esther, almost bitterly, without looking up.

"There are some people one must wish to judge one truly. Not to wish it would be mere hardness. I know you think I am a man without feeling — at least, without strong affections. You think I love nothing but my own resolutions."

"Suppose I reply in the same sort of strain?" said Esther, with a little toss of the head.

"How?"

"Why, that you think me a shallow woman, incapable of believing what is best in you, setting down everything that is too high for me as a deficiency."

"Don't parry what I say. Answer me." There

was an expression of painful beseeching in the tone with which Felix said this. Esther let her work fall on her lap and looked at him, but she was unable to speak.

"I want you to tell me — once — that you know it would be easier to me to give myself up to loving and being loved, as other men do, when they can, than to ⸺."

This breaking-off in speech was something quite new in Felix. For the first time he had lost his self-possession, and turned his eyes away. He was at variance with himself. He had begun what he felt that he ought not to finish.

Esther, like a woman as she was — a woman waiting for love, never able to ask for it — had her joy in these signs of her power; but they made her generous, not chary, as they might have done if she had had a pettier disposition. She said, with deep yet timid earnestness,

"What you have chosen to do has only convinced me that your love would be the better worth having."

All the finest part of Esther's nature trembled in those words. To be right in great memorable moments, is perhaps the thing we need most desire for ourselves.

Felix as quick as lightning turned his look upon her again, and, leaning forward, took her sweet hand and held it to his lips some moments before he let it fall again and raised his head.

"We shall always be the better for thinking of each other," he said, leaning his elbow on the back of the sofa, and supporting his head as he looked at her with calm sadness. "This thing can never come to me twice over. It is my knighthood. That was always a business of great cost."

He smiled at her, but she sat biting her inner lip, and pressing her hands together. She desired to be worthy of what she reverenced in Felix, but the inevitable renunciation was too difficult. She saw herself wandering through the future weak and forsaken. The charming sauciness was all gone from her face, but the memory of it made this child-like dependent sorrow all the more touching.

"Tell me what you would ——" Felix burst out, leaning nearer to her; but the next instant he started up, went to the table, took his cap in his hand, and came in front of her.

"Good-bye," he said, very gently, not daring to put out his hand. But Esther put up hers instead of speaking. He just pressed it and then went away.

She heard the doors close behind him, and felt free to be miserable. She cried bitterly. If she might have married Felix Holt, she could have been a good woman. She felt no trust that she could ever be good without him.

Felix reproached himself. He would have done better not to speak in that way. But the prompting to which he had chiefly listened had been the desire to prove to Esther that he set a high value on her feelings. He could not help seeing that he was very important to her; and he was too simple and sincere a man to ape a sort of humility which would not have made him any the better if he had possessed it. Such pretences turn our lives into sorry dramas. And Felix wished Esther to know that her love was dear to him as the beloved dead are dear. He felt that they must

not marry — that they would ruin each other's lives.
But he had longed for her to know fully that his will
to be always apart from her was renunciation, not an
easy preference. In this he was thoroughly generous;
and yet, now some subtle, mysterious conjuncture of
impressions and circumstances had made him speak,
he questioned the wisdom of what he had done. Express confessions give definiteness to memories that
might more easily melt away without them; and Felix
felt for Esther's pain as the strong soldier, who can
march on hungering without fear that he shall faint,
feels for the young brother — the maiden-cheeked
conscript whose load is too heavy for him.

CHAPTER IX.

Mischief, thou art afoot.
      Julius Cæsar.

FELIX could not go home again immediately after quitting Esther. He got out of the town, skirted it a little while, looking across the December stillness of the fields, and then re-entered it by the main road into the market-place, thinking that, after all, it would be better for him to look at the busy doings of men than to listen in solitude to the voices within him; and he wished to know how things were going on.

It was now nearly half-past one, and Felix perceived that the street was filling with more than the previous crowd. By the time he got in front of the booths, he was himself so surrounded by men who were being thrust hither and thither that retreat would have been impossible; and he went where he was obliged to go, although his height and strength were above the average even in a crowd where there were so many heavy-armed workmen used to the pick-axe. Almost all shabby-coated Trebians must have been there, but the entries and back-streets of the town did not supply the mass of the crowd; and besides the rural incomers, both of the more decent and the rougher sort, Felix, as he was pushed along, thought he discerned here and there men of the keener aspect which is only common in manufacturing towns.

But at present there was no evidence of any distinctly mischievous design. There was only evidence that the majority of the crowd were excited with drink, and that their actions could hardly be calculated on more than those of oxen and pigs congregated amidst hootings and pushings. The confused deafening shouts, the incidental fighting, the knocking over, pulling and scuffling, seemed to increase every moment. Such of the constables as were mixed with the crowd were quite helpless; and if an official staff was seen above the heads, it moved about fitfully, showing as little sign of a guiding hand as the summit of a buoy on the waves. Doubtless many hurts and bruises had been received, but no one could know the amount of injuries that were widely scattered.

It was clear that no more voting could be done, and the poll had been adjourned. The probabilities of serious mischief had grown strong enough to prevail over the Rector's objection to getting military aid within reach; and when Felix re-entered the town, a galloping messenger had already been despatched to Duffield. The Rector wished to ride out again, and read the Riot Act from a point where he could be better heard than from the window of the Marquis; but Mr. Crow, the high constable, who had returned from closer observation, insisted that the risk would be too great. New special constables had been sworn in, but Mr. Crow said prophetically that if once mischief began, the mob was past caring for constables.

But the Rector's voice was ringing and penetrating, and when he appeared on the narrow balcony and read the formula, commanding all men to go to their homes or about their lawful business, there was a strong transient effect. Every one within hearing listened, and for a few moments after the final words, "God save the King!" the comparative silence continued. Then the people began to move, the buzz rose again, and grew, and grew, till it turned to shouts and roaring as before. The movement was that of a flood hemmed in; it carried nobody away. Whether the crowd would obey the order to disperse themselves within an hour, was a doubt that approached nearer and nearer to a negative certainty.

Presently Mr. Crow, who held himself a tactician, took a well-intentioned step, which went far to fulfil his own prophecy. He had arrived with the magistrates by a back way at the Seven Stars, and here again the Riot Act was read from a window, with much the same result as before. The Rector had returned by the same way to the Marquis, as the headquarters most suited for administration, but Mr. Crowe remained at the other extremity of King Street, where some awe-striking presence was certainly needed. Seeing that the time was passing, and all effect from the voice of law had disappeared, he showed himself at an upper window, and addressed the crowd, telling them that the soldiers had been sent for, and that if they did not disperse they would have cavalry upon them instead of constables.

Mr. Crow, like some other high constables more celebrated in history, "enjoyed a bad reputation;" that is to say, he enjoyed many things which caused his reputation to be bad, and he was anything but popular in Treby. It is probable that a pleasant message would have lost something from his lips, and what he actually said was so unpleasant, that, instead of persuading the crowd, it appeared to enrage them. Some one, snatching a raw potato from a sack in the green-

grocer's shop behind him, threw it at the constable, and
hit him on the mouth. Straightway raw potatoes and
turnips were flying by twenties at the windows of the
Seven Stars, and the panes were smashed. Felix, who
was half-way up the street, heard the voices turning to
a savage roar, and saw a rush towards the hardware
shop, which furnished more effective weapons and missiles than turnips and potatoes. Then a cry ran along
that the Tories had sent for the soldiers, and if those
among the mob who called themselves Tories as willingly as anything else were disposed to take whatever
called itself the Tory side, they only helped the main
result of reckless disorder.

But there were proofs that the predominant will of
the crowd was against "Debarry's men," and in favour
of Transome. Several shops were invaded, and they
were all of them "Tory shops." The tradesmen who
could do so, now locked their doors and barricaded
their windows within. There was a panic among
the householders of this hitherto peaceful town, and
a general anxiety for the military to arrive. The
Rector was in painful anxiety on this head: he had
sent out two messengers as secretly as he could towards
Hathercote, to order the soldiers to ride straight to the
town; but he feared that these messengers had been
somehow intercepted.

It was three o'clock: more than an hour had
elapsed since the reading of the Riot Act. The Rector
of Treby Magna wrote an indignant message and sent
it to the Ram, to Mr. Lingon, the Rector of Little Treby, saying that there was evidently a Radical animus
in the mob, and that Mr. Transome's party should hold

themselves peculiarly responsible. Where was Mr. Jermyn?

Mr. Lingon replied that he was going himself out towards Duffield to see after the soldiers. As for Jermyn, he was not that attorney's sponsor: he believed that Jermyn was gone away somewhere on business — to fetch voters.

A serious effort was now being made by all the civil force at command. The December day would soon be passing into evening, and all disorder would be aggravated by obscurity. The horrors of fire were as likely to happen as any minor evil. The constables, as many of them as could do so, armed themselves with carbines and sabres: all the respectable inhabitants who had any courage, prepared themselves to struggle for order; and many felt with Mr. Wace and Mr. Tiliot that the nearest duty was to defend the breweries and the spirit and wine vaults, where the property was of a sort at once most likely to be threatened and most dangerous in its effects. The Rector, with fine determination, got on horseback again, as the best mode of leading the constables, who could only act efficiently in a close body. By his direction the column of armed men avoided the main street, and made their way along a back road, that they might occupy the two chief lanes leading to the wine-vaults and the brewery, and bear down on the crowd from these openings, which it was especially desirable to guard.

Meanwhile Felix Holt had been hotly occupied in King Street. After the first window-smashing at the Seven Stars, there was a sufficient reason for damaging that inn to the utmost. The destructive spirit tends towards completeness; and any object once maimed or otherwise injured, is as readily doomed by unreasoning men as by unreasoning boys. Also the Seven Stars sheltered Spratt; and to some Sproxton men in front of that inn it was exasperating that Spratt should be safe and sound on a day when blows were going, and justice might be rendered. And again, there was the general desirableness of being inside a public-house.

Felix had at last been willingly urged on to this spot. Hitherto swayed by the crowd, he had been able to do nothing but defend himself and keep on his legs; but he foresaw that the people would burst into the inn; he heard cries of "Spratt!" "Fetch him out!" "We'll pitch him out!" "Pummel him!" It was not unlikely that lives might be sacrificed; and it was intolerable to Felix to be witnessing the blind outrages of this mad crowd, and yet be doing nothing to counteract them. Even some vain effort would satisfy him better than mere gazing. Within the walls of the inn he might save some one. He went in with a miscellaneous set, who dispersed themselves with different objects — some to the taproom, and to search for the cellar; some up-stairs to search in all rooms for Spratt, or any one else perhaps, as a temporary scapegoat for Spratt. Guided by the screams of women, Felix at last got to a high up-stairs passage, where the landlady and some of her servants were running away in helpless terror from two or three half-tipsy men, who had been emptying a spirit-decanter in the bar. Assuming the tone of a mob-leader, he cried out, "Here, boys, here's better fun this way — come with me!" and drew the men back with him along the passage. They reached the lower staircase in time to see the unhappy Spratt being dragged, coatless and screaming, down the steps. No one at present was striking or kicking him; it seemed as if he were being reserved for punishment on some wider area, where the satisfaction might be more generally shared. Felix followed close, determined, if he could, to rescue both assailers and assaulted from the worst consequences. His mind was busy with possible devices.

Down the stairs, out along the stones through the gateway, Spratt was dragged as a mere heap of linen and cloth rags. When he was got outside the gateway, there was an immense hooting and roaring, though many there had no grudge against him, and only guessed that others had the grudge. But this was the narrower part of the street; it widened as it went onwards, and Spratt was dragged on, his enemies crying, "We'll make a ring — we'll see how frightened he looks!"

"Kick him, and have done with him," Felix heard another say. "Let's go to Tiliot's vaults — there's more gin there!"

Here were two hideous threats. In dragging Spratt onward the people were getting very near to the lane leading up to Tiliot's. Felix kept as close as he could to the threatened victim. He had thrown away his own stick, and carried a bludgeon which had escaped from the hands of an invader at the Seven Stars; his head was bare; he looked, to undiscerning eyes, like a leading spirit of the mob. In this condition he was observed by several persons looking anxiously from their upper windows, and finally observed to push himself, by violent efforts, close behind the dragged man.

Meanwhile the foremost among the constables, who, coming by the back way, had now reached the opening of Tiliot's Lane, discerned that the crowd had a victim amongst them. One spirited fellow, named Tucker, who was a regular constable, feeling that no time was to be lost in meditation, called on his neighbour to follow him, and with the sabre that happened to be his weapon got a way for himself where he was not expected, by dint of quick resolution. At this moment Spratt had been let go — had been dropped, in fact, almost lifeless with terror, on the street stones, and the men round him had retreated for a little space, as if to amuse themselves with looking at him. Felix had taken his opportunity; and seeing the first step towards a plan he was bent on, he sprang forward close to the cowering Spratt. As he did this, Tucker had cut his way to the spot, and imagining Felix to be the destined executioner of Spratt — for any discrimination of Tucker's lay in his muscles rather than his eyes — he rushed up to Felix, meaning to collar him and throw him down. But Felix had rapid senses and quick thoughts; he discerned the situation; he chose between two evils. Quick as lightning he frustrated the constable, fell upon him, and tried to master his weapon. In the struggle, which was watched without interference, the constable fell undermost, and Felix got his weapon. He started up with the bare sabre in his hand. The crowd round him cried "Hurray!" with a sense that he was on their side against the constable. Tucker did not rise immediately; but Felix did not imagine that he was much hurt.

"Don't touch him!" said Felix. "Let him go: Here, bring Spratt, and follow me."

Felix was perfectly conscious that he was in the midst of a tangled business. But he had chiefly before his imagination the horrors that might come if the mass of wild chaotic desires and impulses around him were not diverted from any further attack on places where they would get in the midst of intoxicating and inflammable materials. It was not a moment in which a spirit like his could calculate the effect of misunderstanding as to himself: nature never makes men who are at once energetically sympathetic and minutely calculating. He believed he had the power, and he was resolved to try, to carry the dangerous mass out of mischief till the military came to awe them — which he supposed, from Mr. Crowe's announcement long ago, must be a near event.

He was followed the more willingly, because Tiliot's Lane was seen by the hindmost to be now defended by constables, some of whom had fire-arms; and where there is no strong counter-movement, any proposition to do something unspecified stimulates stupid curiosity. To many of the Sproxton men who were within sight of him, Felix was known personally, and vaguely believed to be a man who meant many queer things, not at all of an everyday kind. Pressing along like a leader, with the sabre in his hand, and inviting them to bring on Spratt, there seemed a better reason for following him than for doing anything else. A man with a definite will and an energetic personality acts as a sort of flag to draw and bind together the foolish units of a mob. It was on this sort of influence over men whose mental state was a mere medley of appetites and confused impressions, that Felix had dared to count. He hurried them along with words of invitation, telling them to hold up Spratt and not drag him; and those behind followed him, with a growing belief that he had some design worth knowing, while those in front were urged along partly by the same notion, partly by the sense that there was a motive in those behind them, not knowing what the motive was. It was that mixture of pushing forward and being pushed forward, which is a brief history of most human things.

What Felix really intended to do, was to get the crowd by the nearest way out of the town, and induce them to skirt it on the north side with him, keeping up in them the idea that he was leading them to execute some stratagem by which they would surprise something worth attacking, and circumvent the constables who were defending the lanes. In the mean time he trusted that the soldiers would have arrived, and with this sort of mob, which was animated by no real political passion or fury against social distinctions, it was in the highest degree unlikely that there would be any resistance to a military force. The presence of fifty soldiers would probably be enough to scatter the rioting hundreds. How numerous the mob was, no one ever knew: many inhabitants afterwards were ready to swear that there must have been at least two thousand rioters. Felix knew he was incurring great risks; but "his blood was up:" we hardly allow enough in common life for the results of that enkindled passionate enthusiasm which, under other conditions, makes world-famous deeds.

He was making for a point where the street branched off on one side towards a speedy opening between hedgerows, on the other towards the shabby wideness

of Pollard's End. At this forking of the street there
was a large space, in the centre of which there was a
small stone platform, mounting by three steps, with an
old green finger-post upon it. Felix went straight to
this platform and stepped upon it, crying "Halt!" in a
loud voice to the men behind and before him, and calling to those who held Spratt to bring him there. All
came to a stand with faces towards the finger-post, and
perhaps for the first time the extremities of the crowd
got a definite idea that a man with a sabre in his hand
was taking the command.

"Now!" said Felix, when Spratt had been brought
on to the stone platform, faint and trembling, "has
anybody got cord? if not, handkerchiefs knotted fast;
give them to me."

He drew out his own handkerchief, and two or
three others were mustered and handed to him. He
ordered them to be knotted together, while curious
eyes were fixed on him. Was he going to have Spratt
hanged? Felix kept fast hold of his weapon, and
ordered others to act.

"Now, put it round his waist, wind his arms in,
draw them a little backward — so! and tie it fast on
the other side of the post."

When that was done, Felix said, imperatively,

"Leave him there — we shall come back to him;
let us make haste; march along, lads! Up Park Street
and down Hobb's Lane."

It was the best chance he could think of for saving
Spratt's life. And he succeeded. The pleasure of
seeing the helpless man tied up sufficed for the moment, if there were any who had ferocity enough to
count much on coming back to him. Nobody's imagi-

nation represented the certainty that some one out of the houses at hand would soon come and untie him when he was left alone.

And the rioters pushed up Park Street, a noisy stream, with Felix still in the midst of them, though he was labouring hard to get his way to the front. He wished to determine the course of the crowd along a by-road called Hobb's Lane, which would have taken them to the other — the Duffield end of the town. He urged several of the men round him, one of whom was no less a person than the big Dredge, our old Sproxton acquaintance, to get forward, and be sure that all the fellows would go down the lane, else they would spoil sport. Hitherto Felix had been successful, and he had gone along with an unbroken impulse. But soon something occurred which brought with a terrible shock the sense that his plan might turn out to be as mad as all bold projects are seen to be when they have failed.

Mingled with the more headlong and half-drunken crowd there were some sharp-visaged men who loved the irrationality of riots for something else than its own sake, and who at present were not so much the richer as they desired to be, for the pains they had taken in coming to the Treby election, induced by certain prognostics gathered at Duffield on the nomination-day that there might be the conditions favourable to that confusion which was always a harvest-time. It was known to some of these sharp men that Park Street led out towards the grand house of Treby Manor, which was as good — nay, better for their purpose than the bank. While Felix was entertaining his ardent purpose, these other sons of Adam were entertain-

ing another ardent purpose of their peculiar sort, and
the moment was come when they were to have their
triumph.

From the front ranks backward towards Felix
there ran a new summons — a new invitation.

"Let us go to Treby Manor!"

From that moment Felix was powerless; a new definite suggestion overrode his vaguer influence. There
was a determined rush past Hobb's Lane, and not
down it. Felix was carried along too. He did not
know whether to wish the contrary. Once on the road,
out of the town, with openings into fields and with the
wide park at hand, it would have been easy for him
to liberate himself from the crowd. At first it seemed
to him the better part to do this, and to get back to
the town as fast as he could, in the hope of finding the
military and getting a detachment to come and save
the Manor. But he reflected that the course of the mob
had been sufficiently seen, and that there were plenty
of people in Park Street to carry the information faster
than he could. It seemed more necessary that he
should secure the presence of some help for the family
at the Manor by going there himself. The Debarrys
were not of the class he was wont to be anxious about;
but Felix Holt's conscience was alive to the accusation
that any danger they might be in now was brought on
by a deed of his. In these moments of bitter vexation
and disappointment, it did occur to him that very unpleasant consequences might be hanging over him of a
kind quite different from inward dissatisfaction; but it
was useless now to think of averting such consequences.
As he was pressed along with the multitude into Treby
Park, his very movement seemed to him only an im-

age of the day's fatalities, in which the multitudinous small wickednesses of small selfish ends, really undirected towards any larger result, had issued in widely-shared mischief that might yet be hideous.

The light was declining: already the candles shone through many windows of the Manor. Already the foremost part of the crowd had burst into the offices, and adroit men were busy in the right places to find plate, after setting others to force the butler into unlocking the cellars; and Felix had only just been able to force his way on to the front terrace, with the hope of getting to the rooms where he would find the ladies of the household and comfort them with the assurance that rescue must soon come, when the sound of horses' feet convinced him that the rescue was nearer than he had expected. Just as he heard the horses, he had approached the large window of a room, where a brilliant light suspended from the ceiling showed him a group of women clinging together in terror. Others of the crowd were pushing their way up the terrace-steps and gravel-slopes at various points. Hearing the horses, he kept his post in front of the window, and, motioning with his sabre, cried out to the on-comers, "Keep back! I hear the soldiers coming." Some scrambled back, some paused automatically.

The louder and louder sound of the hoofs changed its pace and distribution. "Halt! Fire!" Bang! bang! bang! — came deafening the ears of the men on the terrace.

Before they had time or nerve to move, there was a rushing sound closer to them — again. "Fire!" a bullet whizzed, and passed through Felix Holt's shoulder

— the shoulder of the arm that held the naked weapon which shone in the light from the window.

Felix fell. The rioters ran confusedly, like terrified sheep. Some of the soldiers, turning, drove them along with the flat of their swords. The greater difficulty was to clear the invaded offices.

The Rector, who with another magistrate and several other gentlemen on horseback had accompanied the soldiers, now jumped on to the terrace, and hurried to the ladies of the family.

Presently there was a group round Felix, who had fainted, and, reviving, had fainted again. He had had little food during the day, and had been overwrought. Two of the group were civilians, but only one of them knew Felix, the other being a magistrate not resident in Treby. The one who knew Felix was Mr. John Johnson, whose zeal for the public peace had brought him from Duffield when he heard that the soldiers were summoned.

"I know this man very well," said Mr. Johnson. "He is a dangerous character — quite revolutionary."

It was a weary night; and the next day, Felix, whose wound was declared trivial, was lodged in Loamford Jail. He was committed on three counts — for having assaulted a constable, for having committed manslaughter (Tucker was dead from spinal concussion), and for having led a riotous onslaught on a dwelling-house.

Four other men were committed: one of them for possessing himself of a gold cup with the Debarry arms on it; the three others, one of whom was the collier Dredge, for riot and assault.

That morning Treby town was no longer in terror; but it was in much sadness. Other men, more innocent than the hated Spratt, were groaning under severe bodily injuries. And poor Tucker's corpse was not the only one that had been lifted from the pavement. It is true that none grieved much for the other dead man, unless it be grief to say, "Poor old fellow!" He had been trampled upon, doubtless where he fell drunkenly, near the entrance of the Seven Stars. This second corpse was old Tommy Trounsem, the bill-sticker — otherwise Thomas Transome, the last of a very old family-line.

CHAPTER X.

*The fields are hoary with December's frost.
I too am hoary with the chills of age.
But through the fields and through the untrodden woods
Is rest and stillness — only in my heart
The pall of winter shrouds a throbbing life.*

A WEEK after that Treby Riot, Harold Transome was at Transome Court. He had returned from a hasty visit to town, to keep his Christmas at this delightful country home, not in the best Christmas spirits. He had lost the election; but if that had been his only annoyance, he had good humour and good sense enough to have borne it as well as most men, and to have paid the eight or nine thousand, which had been the price of ascertaining that he was not to sit in the next Parliament, without useless grumbling. But the disappointments of life can never, any more than its pleasures, be estimated singly; and the healthiest and most agreeable of men is exposed to that coincidence of various vexations, each heightening the effect of the other, which may produce in him something corresponding to the spontaneous and externally unaccountable moodiness of the morbid and disagreeable.

Harold might not have grieved much at a small riot in Treby, even if it had caused some expenses to fall on the county; but the turn which the riot had actually taken, was a bitter morsel for rumination, on more grounds than one. However the disturbances had arisen and been aggravated — and probably no one knew the whole truth on these points — the conspicuous, gravest incidents had all tended to throw the blame on the Radical party, that is to say, on Transome and on Transome's agents; and so far the candidateship and its results had done Harold dishonour in the county: precisely the opposite effect to that which was a dear object of his ambition. More than this, Harold's conscience was active enough to be very unpleasantly affected by what had befallen Felix Holt. His memory, always good, was particularly vivid in its retention of Felix Holt's complaint to him about the treating of the Sproxton men, and of the subsequent irritating scene in Jermyn's office, when the personage with the inauspicious name of Johnson had expounded to him the impossibility of revising an electioneering scheme once begun, and of turning your vehicle back when it had already begun to roll downhill. Remembering Felix Holt's words of indignant warning about hiring men with drink in them to make a noise, Harold could not resist the urgent impression that the offences for which Felix was committed were fatalities, not brought about by any willing co-operation of his with the rioters, but arising probably from some ill-judged efforts to counteract their violence. And this impression, which insisted on growing into a conviction, became in one of its phases an uneasy sense that he held evidence which would at once tend to exonerate Felix, and to place himself and his agents in anything but a desirable light. It was likely that some one else could give equivalent evidence in favour of Felix — the little talkative Dissenting preacher, for example; but, anyhow, the affair with the Sproxton men would be ripped open and made the worst of by the opposite parties. The man who

has failed in the use of some indirectness, is helped very
little by the fact that his rivals are men to whom that
indirectness is a something human, very far from being
alien. There remains this grand distinction, that he has
failed, and that the jet of light is thrown entirely on
his misdoings.

In this matter Harold felt himself a victim. Could
he hinder the tricks of his agents? In this particular
case he had tried to hinder them, and had tried in vain.
He had not loved the two agents in question, to begin
with; and now at this later stage of events he was more
innocent than ever of bearing them anything but the
most sincere ill-will. He was more utterly exasperated
with them than he would probably have been if his one
great passion had been for public virtue. Jermyn, with
his John Johnson, had added this ugly dirty business
of the Treby election to all the long-accumulating list
of offences, which Harold was resolved to visit on him
to the utmost. He had seen some handbills carrying
the insinuation that there was a discreditable indebtedness to Jermyn on the part of the Transomes. If any
such notions existed apart from electioneering slander,
there was all the more reason for letting the world see
Jermyn severely punished for abusing his power over
the family affairs, and tampering with the family property. And the world certainly should see this with
as little delay as possible. The cool confident assuming fellow should be bled to the last drop in compen-
sation, and all connection with him be finally got rid
of. Now that the election was done with, Harold meant
to devote himself to private affairs, till everything lay
in complete order under his own supervision.

This morning he was seated as usual in his private

room, which had now been handsomely fitted up for
him. It was but the third morning after the first
Christmas he had spent in his English home for fifteen
years, and the home looked like an eminently desirable
one. The white frost lay on the broad lawn, on the
many-formed leaves of the evergreens, and on the
giant trees at a distance. Logs of dry oak blazed on
the hearth; the carpet was like warm moss under his
feet; he had breakfasted just according to his taste,
and he had the interesting occupations of a large proprietor to fill the morning. All through the house
now, steps were noiseless on carpets or on fine matting; there was warmth in hall and corridors; there
were servants enough to do everything, and to do it at
the right time. Skilful Dominic was always at hand
to meet his master's demands, and his bland presence
diffused itself like a smile over the household, in-
fecting the gloomy English mind with the belief that
life was easy, and making his real predominance seem
as soft and light as a down quilt. Old Mr. Transome
had gathered new courage and strength since little
Harry and Dominic had come, and since Harold had insisted on his taking drives. Mrs. Transome herself
was seen on a fresh background with a gown of rich
new stuff. And if, in spite of this, she did not seem
happy, Harold either did not observe it, or kindly
ignored it as the necessary frailty of elderly women
whose lives have had too much of dulness and privation. Our minds get tricks and attitudes as our bodies
do, thought Harold, and age stiffens them into unalter-
ableness. "Poor mother! I confess I should not like to be
an elderly woman myself. One requires a good deal
of the purring cat for that, or else of the loving grandame.

I wish she would take more to little Harry. I suppose she has her suspicions about the lad's mother, and is as rigid in those matters as in her Toryism. However, I do what I can; it would be difficult to say what there is wanting to her in the way of indulgence and luxury to make up for the old niggardly life."

And certainly Transome Court was now such a home as many women would covet. Yet even Harold's own satisfaction in the midst of its elegant comfort needed at present to be sustained by the expectation of gratified resentment. He was obviously less bright and enjoying than usual, and his mother, who watched him closely without daring to ask questions, had gathered hints and drawn inferences enough to make her feel sure that there was some storm gathering between him and Jermyn. She did not dare to ask questions, and yet she had not resisted the temptation to say something bitter about Harold's failure to get returned as a Radical, helping, with feminine self-defeat, to exclude herself more completely from any consultation by him. In this way poor women, whose power lies solely in their influence, make themselves like music out of tune, and only move men to run away.

This morning Harold had ordered his letters to be brought to him at the breakfast-table, which was not his usual practice. His mother could see that there were London business letters about which he was eager, and she had found out that the letter brought by a clerk the day before was to make an appointment with Harold for Jermyn to come to Transome Court at eleven this morning. She observed Harold swallow his coffee and push away his plate with an early abstraction from the business of breakfast which was not at all after his usual manner. She herself ate nothing; her sips of tea seemed to excite her; her cheeks flushed, and her hands were cold. She was still young and ardent in her terrors; the passions of the past were living in her dread.

When Harold left the table she went into the long drawing-room, where she might relieve her restlessness by walking up and down, and catch the sound of Jermyn's entrance into Harold's room, which was close by. Here she moved to and fro amongst the rose-coloured satin of chairs and curtains — the great story of this world reduced for her to the little tale of her own existence — dull obscurity everywhere, except where the keen light fell on the narrow track of her own lot, wide only for a woman's anguish. At last she heard the expected ring and footstep, and the opening and closing door. Unable to walk about any longer, she sank into a large cushioned chair, helpless and prayerless. She was not thinking of God's anger or mercy, but of her son's. She was thinking of what might be brought, not by death, but by life.

CHAPTER XI.

M. Check to your queen!
N.   Nay, your own king is bare,
  And moving so, you give yourself checkmate.

WHEN Jermyn entered the room, Harold, who was seated at his library table examining papers, with his back towards the light and his face towards the door, moved his head coldly. Jermyn said an ungracious "Good-morning" — as little as possible like a salutation to one who might regard himself as a patron. On the attorney's handsome face there was a black cloud of defiant determination, slightly startling to Harold, who had expected to feel that the overpowering weight of temper in the interview was on his own side. Nobody was ever prepared beforehand for this expression of Jermyn's face, which seemed as strongly contrasted with the cold impenetrableness which he preserved under the ordinary annoyances of business as with the bland radiance of his lighter moments.

Harold himself did not look amiable just then, but his anger was of the sort that seeks a vent without waiting to give a fatal blow; it was that of a nature more subtly mixed than Jermyn's — less animally forcible, less unwavering in selfishness, and with more of high-bred pride. He looked at Jermyn with increased disgust and secret wonder.

"Sit down," he said, curtly.

Jermyn seated himself in silence, opened his great-coat, and took some papers from a side-pocket.

"I have written to Makepeace," said Harold, "to tell him to take the entire management of the election expenses. So you will transmit your accounts to him."

"Very well. I am come this morning on other business."

"If it's about the riot and the prisoners, I have only to say that I shall enter into no plans. If I am called on, I shall say what I know about that young fellow Felix Holt. People may prove what they can about Johnson's damnable tricks, or yours either."

"I am not come to speak about the riot. I agree with you in thinking that quite a subordinate subject." (When Jermyn had the black cloud over his face, he never hesitated or drawled, and made no Latin quotations.)

"Be so good, then, as to open your business at once," said Harold, in a tone of imperious indifference.

"That is precisely what I wish to do. I have here information from a London correspondent that you are about to file a bill against me in Chancery." Jermyn, as he spoke, laid his hand on the papers before him, and looked straight at Harold.

"In that case the question for you is, how far your conduct as the family solicitor will bear investigation. But it is a question which you will consider quite apart from me."

"Doubtless. But prior to that there is a question which we must consider together."

The tone in which Jermyn said this gave an unpleasant shock to Harold's sense of mastery. Was it possible that he should have the weapon wrenched out of his hand?

"I shall know what to think of that," he replied, as haughtily as ever, "when you have stated what the question is."

"Simply, whether you will choose to retain the family estates, or lay yourself open to be forthwith legally deprived of them."

"I presume you refer to some underhand scheme of your own, on a par with the annuities you have drained us by in the name of Johnson," said Harold, feeling a new movement of anger. "If so, you had better state your scheme to my lawyers, Dymock and Halliwell."

"No. I think you will approve of my stating in your own ear first of all, that it depends on my will whether you remain an important landed proprietor in North Loamshire, or whether you retire from the county with the remainder of the fortune you have acquired in trade."

Jermyn paused, as if to leave time for this morsel to be tasted.

"What do you mean?" said Harold, sharply.

"Not any scheme of mine; but a state of the facts, resulting from the settlement of the estate made in 1729: a state of the facts which renders your father's title and your own title to the family estates utterly worthless as soon as the true claimant is made aware of his right."

"And you intend to inform him?"

"That depends. I am the only person who has the requisite knowledge. It rests with you to decide whether I shall use that knowledge against you; or

whether I shall use it in your favour — by putting
an end to the evidence that would serve to oust you
in spite of your 'robust title of occupancy.'"

Jermyn paused again. He had been speaking
slowly, but without the least hesitation, and with a
bitter definiteness of enunciation. There was a moment
or two before Harold answered, and then he said
abruptly,

"I don't believe you."

"I thought you were more shrewd," said Jermyn,
with a touch of scorn. "I thought you understood
that I had had too much experience to waste my time
in telling fables to persuade a man who has put himself
into the attitude of my deadly enemy."

"Well, then, say at once what your proofs are,"
said Harold, shaking in spite of himself, and getting
nervous.

"I have no inclination to be lengthy. It is not
more than a few weeks since I ascertained that there
is in existence an heir of the Bycliffe's, the old adver-
saries of your family. More curiously, it is only a few
days ago — in fact, only since the day of the riot —
that the Bycliffe claim has become valid, and that the
right of remainder accrues to the heir in question."

"And how, pray?" said Harold, rising from his
chair, and making a turn in the room, with his hands
thrust in his pockets. Jermyn rose too, and stood near
the hearth facing Harold, as he moved to and fro.

"By the death of an old fellow who got drunk,
and was trampled to death in the riot. He was the
last of that Thomas Transome's line, by the purchase
of whose interest your family got its title to the estate.
Your title died with him. It was supposed that the

line had become extinct before — and on that supposition the old Bycliffes founded their claim. But I hunted up this man just about the time the last suit was closed. His death would have been of no consequence to you if there had not been a Bycliffe in existence; but I happen to know that there is, and that the fact can be legally proved."

For a minute or two Harold did not speak, but continued to pace the room, while Jermyn kept his position, holding his hands behind him. At last Harold said, from the other end of the room, speaking in a scornful tone,

"That sounds alarming. But it is not to be proved simply by your statement."

"Clearly. I have here a document, with a copy, which will back my statement. It is the opinion given on the case more than twenty years ago, and it bears the signature of the Attorney-General and the first conveyancer of the day."

Jermyn took up the papers he had laid on the table, opening them slowly and coolly as he went on speaking, and as Harold advanced towards him.

"You may suppose that we spared no pains to ascertain the state of the title in the last suit against Maurice Christian Bycliffe, which threatened to be a hard run. This document is the result of a consultation; it gives an opinion which must be taken as a final authority. You may cast your eyes over that, if you please; I will wait your time. Or you may read the summing-up here," Jermyn ended, holding out one of the papers to Harold, and pointing to a final passage.

Harold took the paper, with a slight gesture of

impatience. He did not choose to obey Jermyn's indication, and confine himself to the summing-up. He ran through the document. But in truth he was too much excited really to follow the details, and was rather acting than reading, till at length he threw himself into his chair and consented to bend his attention on the passage to which Jermyn had pointed. The attorney watched him as he read and twice re-read: —

"*To sum up . . . . . we are of opinion that the title of the present possessors of the Transome estates can be strictly proved to rest solely upon a base fee created under the original settlement of 1729, and to be good so long only as issue exists of the tenant in tail by whom that base fee was created. We feel satisfied by the evidence that such issue exists in the person of Thomas Transome, otherwise Trounsem, of Littleshaw. But upon his decease without issue we are of opinion that the right in remainder of the Bycliffe family will arise, which right would not be barred by any statute of limitation.*"

When Harold's eyes were on the signatures to this document for the third time, Jermyn said,

"As it turned out, the case being closed by the death of the claimant, we had no occasion for producing Thomas Transome, who was the old fellow I tell you of. The inquiries about him set him agog, and after they were dropped he came into this neighbourhood, thinking there was something fine in store for him. Here, if you like to take it, is a memorandum about him. I repeat, that he died in the riot. The proof is ready. And I repeat, that, to my knowledge, and mine only, there is a Bycliffe in existence; and that I know how the proof can be made out."

Harold rose from his chair again, and again paced the room. He was not prepared with any defiance.

"And where is he — this Bycliffe?" he said at last, stopping in his walk, and facing round towards Jermyn.

"I decline to say more till you promise to suspend proceedings against me."

Harold turned again, and looked out of the window, without speaking for a moment or two. It was impossible that there should not be a conflict within him, and at present it was a very confused one. At last he said,

"This person is in ignorance of his claim?"

"Yes."

"Has been brought up in an inferior station?"

"Yes," said Jermyn, keen enough to guess part of what was going on in Harold's mind. "There is no harm in leaving him in ignorance. The question is a purely legal one. And, as I said before, the complete knowledge of the case, as one of evidence, lies exclusively with me. I can nullify the evidence, or I can make it tell with certainty against you. The choice lies with you."

"I must have time to think of this," said Harold, conscious of a terrible pressure.

"I can give you no time unless you promise me to suspend proceedings."

"And then, when I ask you, you will lay the details before me?"

"Not without a thorough understanding beforehand. If I engage not to use my knowledge against you, you must engage in writing that on being satisfied by the details, you will cancel all hostile proceedings against me, and will not institute fresh ones on the strength of any occurrences now past."

"Well, I must have time," said Harold, more than ever inclined to thrash the attorney, but feeling bound hand and foot with knots that he was not sure he could ever unfasten.

"That is to say," said Jermyn, with his black-browed persistence, "you will write to suspend proceedings."

Again Harold paused. He was more than ever exasperated, but he was threatened, mortified, and confounded by the necessity for an immediate decision between alternatives almost equally hateful to him. It was with difficulty that he could prevail on himself to speak any conclusive words. He walked as far as he could from Jermyn — to the other end of the room — then walked back to his chair and threw himself into it. At last he said, without looking at Jermyn, "I agree — I must have time."

"Very well. It is a bargain."

"No further than this," said Harold, hastily, flashing a look at Jermyn — "no further than this, that I require time, and therefore I give it to you."

"Of course. You require time to consider whether the pleasure of trying to ruin me — me to whom you are really indebted — is worth the loss of the Transome estates. — I shall wish you good-morning."

Harold did not speak to him or look at him again, and Jermyn walked out of the room. As he appeared outside the door and closed it behind him, Mrs. Transome showed her white face at another door which opened on a level with Harold's in such a way that it was just possible for Jermyn not to see her. He availed himself of that possibility, and walked straight across the hall, where there was no servant in attendance to let him out, as if he believed that no one was looking at him who could expect recognition. He did not want to speak to Mrs. Transome at present; he had nothing to ask from her, and one disagreeable interview had been enough for him this morning.

She was convinced that he had avoided her, and she was too proud to arrest him. She was as insignificant now in his eyes as in her son's. "Men have no memories in their hearts," she said to herself, bitterly. Turning into her sitting-room, she heard the voices of Mr. Transome and little Harry at play together. She would have given a great deal at this moment if her feeble husband had not always lived in dread of her temper and her tyranny, so that he might have been fond of her now. She felt herself loveless; if she was important to any one, it was only to her old waiting-woman Denner.

CHAPTER XII.

*Are these things then necessities?
Then let us meet them like necessities.*
SHAKSPEARE: *Henry IV.*

*See now the virtue living in a word!
Hobson will think of swearing it was noon
When he saw Dobson at the May-day fair,
To prove poor Dobson did not rob the mail.
'Tis neighbourly to save a neighbour's neck:
What harm in lying when you mean no harm?
But say 'tis perjury, then Hobson quakes —
He'll none of perjury.*
                        *Thus words embalm
*The conscience of mankind; and Roman laws
Bring still a conscience to poor Hobson's aid.*

FEW men would have felt otherwise than Harold Transome felt, if, having a reversion tantamount to possession of a fine estate, carrying an association with an old name and considerable social importance, they were suddenly informed that there was a person who had a legal right to deprive them of these advantages; that person's right having never been contemplated by any one as more than a chance, and being quite unknown to himself. In ordinary cases a shorter possession than Harold's family had enjoyed was allowed by the law to constitute an indefeasible right; and if in rare and peculiar instances the law left the possessor of a long inheritance exposed to deprivation as a consequence of old obscure transactions, the moral reasons for giving legal validity to the title of long occupancy were not the less strong. Nobody would have said that Harold was bound to hunt out this alleged remainder-man and urge his rights upon him; on the contrary, all the world would have laughed at such conduct, and he would have been thought an interesting patient for a mad-doctor. The unconscious remainder-man was probably much better off left in his original station: Harold would not have been called upon to consider his existence, if it had not been presented to him in the shape of a threat from one who had power to execute the threat.

In fact, what he would have done had the circumstances been different was much clearer than what he should choose to do or feel himself compelled to do in the actual crisis. He would not have been disgraced if, on a valid claim being urged, he had got his lawyers to fight it out for him on the chance of eluding the claim by some adroit technical management. Nobody off the stage could be sentimental about these things, or pretend to shed tears of joy because an estate was handed over from a gentleman to a mendicant sailor with a wooden leg. And this chance remainder-man was perhaps some such specimen of inheritance as the drunken fellow killed in the riot. All the world would think the actual Transomes in the right to contest any adverse claim to the utmost. But then — it was not certain that they would win in the contest; and not winning, they would incur other loss besides that of the estate. There had been a little too much of such loss already.

But why, if it were not wrong to contest the claim, should he feel the most uncomfortable scruples about robbing the claim of its sting by getting rid of its evidence? It was a mortal disappointment — it was a sacrifice of indemnification — to abstain from punishing

Jermyn. But even if he brought his mind to contemplate that as the wiser course, he still shrank from what looked like complicity with Jermyn; he still shrank from the secret nullification of a just legal claim. If he had only known the details, if he had known who this alleged heir was, he might have seen his way to some course that would not have grated on his sense of honour and dignity. But Jermyn had been too acute to let Harold know this: he had even carefully kept to the masculine pronoun. And he believed that there was no one besides himself who would or could make Harold any wiser. He went home persuaded that between this interview and the next which they would have together, Harold would be left to an inward debate, founded entirely on the information he himself had given. And he had not much doubt that the result would be what he desired. Harold was no fool: there were many good things he liked better in life than an irrational vindictiveness.

And it did happen that, after writing to London in fulfilment of his pledge, Harold spent many hours over that inward debate, which was not very different from what Jermyn imagined. He took it everywhere with him, on foot and on horseback, and it was his companion through a great deal of the night. His nature was not of a kind given to internal conflict, and he had never before been long undecided and puzzled. This unaccustomed state of mind was so painfully irksome to him — he rebelled so impatiently against the oppression of circumstances in which his quick temperament and habitual decision could not help him — that it added tenfold to his hatred of Jermyn, who was the cause of it. And thus, as the temptation to avoid all risk of losing the estate grew and grew till scruples looked minute by the side of it, the difficulty of bringing himself to make a compact with Jermyn seemed more and more insurmountable.

But we have seen that the attorney was much too confident in his calculations. And while Harold was being galled by his subjection to Jermyn's knowledge, independent information was on its way to him. The messenger was Christian, who, after as complete a survey of probabilities as he was capable of, had come to the conclusion that the most profitable investment he could make of his peculiar experience and testimony in relation to Bycliffe and Bycliffe's daughter, was to place them at the disposal of Harold Transome. He was afraid of Jermyn; he utterly distrusted Johnson; but he thought he was secure in relying on Harold Transome's care for his own interest; and he preferred above all issues the prospect of forthwith leaving the country with a sum that at least for a good while would put him at his ease.

When, only three mornings after the interview with Jermyn, Dominic opened the door of Harold's sitting-room, and said that "Meester Chreestian," Mr. Philip Debarry's courier and an acquaintance of his own at Naples, requested to be admitted on business of importance, Harold's immediate thought was that the business referred to the so-called political affairs which were just now his chief association with the name of Debarry, though it seemed an oddness requiring explanation that a servant should be personally an intermediary. He assented, expecting something rather disagreeable than otherwise.

Christian wore this morning those perfect manners

of a subordinate who is not servile, which he always adopted towards his unquestionable superiors. Mr. Debarry, who preferred having some one about him with as little resemblance as possible to a regular servant, had a singular liking for the adroit, quiet-mannered Christian, and would have been amazed to see the insolent assumption he was capable of in the presence of people like Mr. Lyon, who were of no account in society. Christian had that sort of cleverness which is said to "know the world" — that is to say, he knew the price-current of most things.

Aware that he was looked at as a messenger while he remained standing near the door with his hat in his hand, he said, with respectful ease,

"You will probably be surprised, sir, at my coming to speak to you on my own account; and, in fact, I could not have thought of doing so if my business did not happen to be something of more importance to you than to any one else."

"You don't come from Mr. Debarry, then?" said Harold, with some surprise.

"No, sir. My business is a secret; and, if you please, must remain so."

"Is it a pledge you are demanding from me?" said Harold, rather suspiciously, having no ground for confidence in a man of Christian's position.

"Yes, sir; I am obliged to ask no less than that you will pledge yourself not to take Mr. Jermyn into confidence concerning what passes between us."

"With all my heart," said Harold, something like a gleam passing over his face. His circulation had become more rapid. "But what have you had to do with Jermyn?"

"He has not mentioned me to you then — has he, sir?"

"No; certainly not — never."

Christian thought, "Aha, Mr. Jermyn! you are keeping the secret well, are you?" He said, aloud,

"Then Mr. Jermyn has never mentioned to you, sir, what I believe he is aware of — that there is danger of a new suit being raised against you on the part of a Bycliffe, to get the estate?"

"Ah!" said Harold, starting up, and placing himself with his back against the mantelpiece. He was electrified by surprise at the quarter from which this information was coming. Any fresh alarm was counteracted by the flashing thought that he might be enabled to act independently of Jermyn; and in the rush of feelings he could utter no more than an interjection. Christian concluded that Harold had had no previous hint.

"It is this fact, sir, that I came to tell you of."

"From some other motive than kindness to me, I presume," said Harold, with a slight approach to a smile.

"Certainly," said Christian, as quietly as if he had been stating yesterday's weather. "I should not have the folly to use any affectation with you, Mr. Transome. I lost considerable property early in life, and am now in the receipt of a salary simply. In the affair I have just mentioned to you I can give evidence which will turn the scale against you. I have no wish to do so, if you will make it worth my while to leave the country."

Harold listened as if he had been a legendary hero, selected for peculiar solicitation by the Evil One. Here was temptation in a more alluring form than before, because it was sweetened by the prospect of eluding Jermyn. But the desire to gain time served all the purposes of caution and resistance, and his indifference to the speaker in this case helped him to preserve perfect self-command.

"You are aware," he said, coolly, "that silence is not a commodity worth purchasing unless it is loaded. There are many persons, I dare say, who would like me to pay their travelling expenses for them. But they might hardly be able to show me that it was worth my while."

"You wish me to state what I know?"

"Well, that is a necessary preliminary to any further conversation."

"I think you will see, Mr. Transome, that, as a matter of justice, the knowledge I can give is worth something, quite apart from my future appearance or non-appearance as a witness. I must take care of my own interest, and if anything should hinder you from choosing to satisfy me for taking an essential witness out of the way, I must at least be paid for bringing you the information."

"Can you tell me who and where this Bycliffe is?"

"I can."

"— And give me a notion of the whole affair?"

"Yes: I have talked to a lawyer — not Jermyn — who is at the bottom of the law in the affair."

"You must not count on any wish of mine to suppress evidence or remove a witness. But name your price for the information."

"In that case I must be paid the higher for my information. Say, two thousand pounds."

"Two thousand devils!" burst out Harold, throwing himself into his chair again, and turning his shoulder towards Christian. New thoughts crowded upon him. "This fellow may want to decamp for some reason or other," he said to himself. "More people besides Jermyn know about his evidence, it seems. The whole thing may look black for me if it comes out. I shall be believed to have bribed him to run away, whether or not." Thus the outside conscience came in aid of the inner.

"I will not give you one sixpence for your information," he said, resolutely, "until time has made it clear that you do not intend to decamp, but will be forthcoming when you are called for. On those terms I have no objection to give you a note, specifying that after the fulfilment of that condition — that is, after the occurrence of a suit, or the understanding that no suit is to occur — I will pay you a certain sum in consideration of the information you now give me!"

Christian felt himself caught in a vice. In the first instance he had counted confidently on Harold's ready seizure of his offer to disappear, and after some words had seemed to cast a doubt on this presupposition, he had inwardly determined to go away, whether Harold wished it or not, if he could get a sufficient sum. He did not reply immediately, and Harold waited in silence, inwardly anxious to know what Christian could tell, but with a vision at present so far cleared that he was determined not to risk incurring the imputation of having anything to do with scoundrelism. We are very much indebted to such a linking of events as makes a doubtful action look wrong.

Christian was reflecting that if he stayed, and faced

some possible inconveniences of being known publicly as Henry Scaddon for the sake of what he might get from Esther, it would at least be wise to be certain of some money from Harold Transome, since he turned out to be of so peculiar a disposition as to insist on a punctilious honesty to his own disadvantage. Did he think of making a bargain with the other side? If so, he might be content to wait for the knowledge till it came in some other way. Christian was beginning to be afraid lest he should get nothing by this clever move of coming to Transome Court. At last he said,

"I think, sir, two thousand would not be an unreasonable sum, on those conditions."

"I will not give two thousand."

"Allow me to say, sir, you must consider that there is no one whose interest it is to tell you as much as I shall, even if they could; since Mr. Jermyn, who knows it, has not thought fit to tell you. There may be use you don't think of in getting the information at once."

"Well?"

"I think a gentleman should act liberally under such circumstances."

"So I will."

"I could not take less than a thousand pounds. It really would not be worth my while. If Mr. Jermyn knew I gave you the information, he would endeavour to injure me."

"I will give you a thousand," said Harold, immediately, for Christian had unconsciously touched a sure spring. "At least, I'll give you a note to the effect I spoke of."

He wrote as he had promised, and gave the paper to Christian

"Now, don't be circuitous," said Harold. "You seem to have a business-like gift of speech. Who and where is this Bycliffe?"

"You will be surprised to hear, sir, that she is supposed to be the daughter of the old preacher, Lyon, in Malthouse Yard."

"Good God! How can that be?" said Harold. At once, the first occasion on which he had seen Esther rose in his memory — the little dark parlour — the graceful girl in blue, with the surprisingly distinguished manners and appearance.

"In this way. Old Lyon, by some strange means or other, married Bycliffe's widow when this girl was a baby. And the preacher didn't want the girl to know that he was not her real father: he told me that himself. But she is the image of Bycliffe, whom I knew well — an uncommonly fine woman — steps like a queen."

"I have seen her," said Harold, more than ever glad to have purchased this knowledge. "But now, go on."

Christian proceeded to tell all he knew, including his conversation with Jermyn, except so far as it had an unpleasant relation to himself.

"Then," said Harold, as the details seemed to have come to a close, "you believe that Miss Lyon and her supposed father are at present unaware of the claims that might be urged for her on the strength of her birth?"

"I believe so. But I need not tell you that where the lawyers are on the scent you can never be sure of anything long together. I must remind you, sir, that you have promised to protect me from Mr. Jermyn by keeping my confidence."

"Never fear. Depend upon it, I shall betray nothing to Mr. Jermyn."

Christian was dismissed with a "good-morning;" and while he cultivated some friendly reminiscences with Dominic, Harold sat chewing the cud of his new knowledge, and finding it not altogether so bitter as he had expected.

From the first, after his interview with Jermyn, the recoil of Harold's mind from the idea of strangling a legal right threw him on the alternative of attempting a compromise. Some middle course might be possible, which would be a less evil than a costly lawsuit, or than the total renunciation of the estates. And now he had learned that the new claimant was a woman — a young woman, brought up under circumstances that would make the fourth of the Transome property seem to her an immense fortune. Both the sex and the social condition were of the sort that lies open to many softening influences. And having seen Esther, it was inevitable that, amongst the various issues, agreeable and disagreeable, depicted by Harold's imagination, there should present itself a possibility that would unite the two claims — his own, which he felt to be the rational, and Esther's, which apparently was the legal claim.

Harold, as he had constantly said to his mother, was "not a marrying man;" he did not contemplate bringing a wife to Transome Court for many years to come, if at all. Having little Harry as an heir, he preferred freedom. Western women were not to his taste: they showed a transition from the feebly animal to the thinking being, which was simply troublesome. Harold preferred a slow-witted large-eyed woman, silent and affectionate, with a load of black hair weighing much more heavily than her brains. He had seen no such woman in England, except one whom he had brought with him from the East.

Therefore Harold did not care to be married until or unless some surprising chance presented itself; and now that such a chance had occurred to suggest marriage to him, he would not admit to himself that he contemplated marrying Esther as a plan; he was only obliged to see that such an issue was not inconceivable. He was not going to take any step expressly directed towards that end: what he had made up his mind to, as the course most satisfactory to his nature under present urgencies, was to behave to Esther with a frank gentlemanliness, which must win her good-will, and incline her to save his family interest as much as possible. He was helped to this determination by the pleasure of frustrating Jermyn's contrivance to shield himself from punishment; and his most distinct and cheering prospect was, that within a very short space of time he should not only have effected a satisfactory compromise with Esther, but should have made Jermyn aware, by a very disagreeable form of announcement, that Harold Transome was no longer afraid of him. Jermyn should bite the dust.

At the end of these meditations he felt satisfied with himself and light-hearted. He had rejected two dishonest propositions, and he was going to do something that seemed eminently graceful. But he needed his mother's assistance, and it was necessary that he should both confide in her and persuade her.

Within two hours after Christian left him, Harold begged his mother to come into his private room, and there he told her the strange and startling story, omitting, however, any particulars which would involve the identification of Christian as his informant. Harold felt that his engagement demanded this reticence; and he told his mother that he was bound to conceal the source of that knowledge which he had got independently of Jermyn.

Mrs. Transome said little in the course of the story: she made no exclamations, but she listened with close attention, and asked a few questions so much to the point as to surprise Harold. When he showed her the copy of the legal opinion which Jermyn had left with him, she said she knew it very well; she had a copy herself. The particulars of that last lawsuit were too well engraven on her mind: it happened at a time when there was no one to supersede her, and she was the virtual head of the family affairs. She was prepared to understand how the estate might be in danger; but nothing had prepared her for the strange details — for the way in which the new claimant had been reared and brought within the range of converging motives that had led to this revelation, least of all for the part Jermyn had come to play in the revelation. Mrs. Transome saw these things through the medium of certain dominant emotions that made them seem like a long-ripening retribution. Harold perceived that she was painfully agitated, that she trembled, and that her white lips would not readily lend themselves to speech. And this was hardly more than he expected. He had not liked the revelation himself when it had first come to him.

But he did not guess what it was in his narrative which had most pierced his mother. It was something that made the threat about the estate only a secondary alarm. Now, for the first time, she heard of the intended proceedings against Jermyn. Harold had not chosen to speak of them before; but having at last called his mother into consultation, there was nothing in his mind to hinder him from speaking without reserve of his determination to visit on the attorney his shameful maladministration of the family affairs.

Harold went through the whole narrative — of what he called Jermyn's scheme to catch him in a vice, and his power of triumphantly frustrating that scheme — in his usual rapid way, speaking with a final decisiveness of tone: and his mother felt that if she urged any counter-consideration at all, she could only do so when he had no more to say.

"Now, what I want you to do, mother, if you can see this matter as I see it," Harold said in conclusion, "is to go with me to call on this girl in Malthouse Yard. I will open the affair to her; it appears she is not likely to have been informed yet; and you will invite her to visit you here at once, that all scandal, all hatching of law-mischief, may be avoided, and the thing may be brought to an amicable conclusion."

"It seems almost incredible — extraordinary — a girl in her position," said Mrs. Transome, with difficulty. It would have seemed the bitterest humiliating penance if another sort of suffering had left any room in her heart.

"I assure you she is a lady; I saw her when I was canvassing, and was amazed at the time. You will be quite struck with her. It is no indignity for you to invite her."

"Oh," said Mrs. Transome, with low-toned bitterness, "I must put up with all things as they are determined for me. When shall we go?"

"Well," said Harold, looking at his watch, "it is hardly two yet. We could really go to-day, when you have lunched. It is better to lose no time. I'll order the carriage."

"Stay," said Mrs. Transome, making a desperate effort. "There is plenty of time. I shall not lunch. I have a word to say."

Harold withdrew his hand from the bell, and leaned against the mantelpiece to listen.

"You see I comply with your wish at once, Harold?".

"Yes, mother, I'm much obliged to you for making no difficulties."

"You ought to listen to me in return."

"Pray go on," said Harold, expecting to be annoyed.

"What is the good of having these Chancery proceedings against Jermyn?"

"Good? This good: that fellow has burdened the estate with annuities and mortgages to the extent of three thousand a-year; and the bulk of them, I am certain, he holds himself under the name of another man. And the advances this yearly interest represents, have not been much more than twenty thousand. Of course he has hoodwinked you, and my father never gave attention to these things. He has been up to all sorts of devil's work with the deeds; he didn't count on my coming back from Smyrna to fill poor Durfey's place. He shall feel the difference. And the good will be, that I shall save almost all the annuities for the rest of my father's life, which may be ten years or more, and I shall get back some of the money, and I shall punish a scoundrel. That is the good."

"He will be ruined."

"That's what I intend," said Harold, sharply.

"He exerted himself a great deal for us in the old suits: every one said he had wonderful zeal and ability," said Mrs. Transome, getting courage and warmth as she went on. Her temper was rising.

"What he did, he did for his own sake, you may depend on that," said Harold, with a scornful laugh.

"There were very painful things in that last suit. You seem anxious, about this young woman, to avoid all further scandal and contests in the family. Why don't you wish to do it in this case? Jermyn might be willing to arrange things amicably — to make restitution as far as he can — if he has done anything wrong."

"I will arrange nothing amicably with him," said Harold, decisively. "If he has ever done anything scandalous as our agent, let him bear the infamy. And the right way to throw the infamy on him is to show the world that he has robbed us, and that I mean to punish him. Why do you wish to shield such a fellow, mother? It has been chiefly through him that you have had to lead such a thrifty miserable life — you who used to make as brilliant a figure as a woman need wish."

Mrs. Transome's rising temper was turned into a horrible sensation, as painful as a sudden concussion from something hard and immovable when we have struck out with our fist, intending to hit something warm, soft, and breathing, like ourselves. Poor Mrs.

Transome's strokes were sent jarring back on her by a hard unalterable past. She did not speak in answer to Harold, but rose from the chair as if she gave up the debate.

"Women are frightened at everything, I know," said Harold, kindly, feeling that he had been a little harsh after his mother's compliance. "And you have been used for so many years to think Jermyn a law of nature. Come, mother," he went on, looking at her gently, and resting his hands on her shoulders, "look cheerful. We shall get through all these difficulties. And this girl — I daresay she will be quite an interesting visitor for you. You have not had any young girl about you for a long while. Who knows? she may fall deeply in love with me, and I may be obliged to marry her."

He spoke laughingly, only thinking how he could make his mother smile. But she looked at him seriously and said, "Do you mean that, Harold?"

"Am I not capable of making a conquest? Not too fat yet — a handsome, well-rounded youth of thirty-four?"

She was forced to look straight at the beaming face, with its rich dark colour, just bent a little over her. Why could she not be happy in this son whose future she had once dreamed of, and who had been as fortunate as she had ever hoped? The tears came, not plenteously, but making her dark eyes as large and bright as youth had once made them without tears.

"There, there!" said Harold, coaxingly. "Don't be afraid. You shall not have a daughter-in-law unless she is a pearl. Now we will get ready to go."

In half an hour from that time Mrs. Transome came down, looking majestic in sables and velvet, ready to call on "the girl in Malthouse Yard." She had composed herself to go through this task. She saw there was nothing better to be done. After the resolutions Harold had taken, some sort of compromise with this oddly-placed heiress was the result most to be hoped for; if the compromise turned out to be a marriage — well, she had no reason to care much: she was already powerless. It remained to be seen what this girl was.

The carriage was to be driven round the back way, to avoid too much observation. But the late election affairs might account for Mr. Lyon's receiving a visit from the unsuccessful Radical candidate.

CHAPTER XIII.

I also could speak as ye do; if your soul were in my soul's stead, I could heap up words against you, and shake mine head at you. — Book of Job.

In the interval since Esther parted with Felix Holt on the day of the riot, she had gone through so much emotion, and had already had so strong a shock of surprise, that she was prepared to receive any new incident of an unwonted kind with comparative equanimity.

When Mr. Lyon had got home again from his preaching excursion, Felix was already on his way to Loamford Jail. The little minister was terribly shaken by the news. He saw no clear explanation of Felix Holt's conduct; for the statements Esther had heard were so conflicting that she had not been able to gather distinctly what had come out in the examination by the magistrates. But Mr. Lyon felt confident that Felix was innocent of any wish to abet a riot or the infliction of injuries; what he chiefly feared was that in the fatal encounter with Tucker he had been moved by a rash temper, not sufficiently guarded against by a prayerful and humble spirit.

"My poor young friend is being taught with mysterious severity the evil of a too confident self-reliance," he said to Esther, as they sat opposite to each other, listening and speaking sadly.

"You will go and see him, father?"

"Verily will I. But I must straightway go and see that poor afflicted woman, whose soul is doubtless whirled about in this trouble like a shapeless and unstable thing driven by divided winds." Mr. Lyon rose and took his hat hastily, ready to walk out, with his greatcoat flying open and exposing his small person to the keen air.

"Stay, father, pray, till you have had some food," said Esther, putting her hand on his arm. "You look quite weary and shattered."

"Child, I cannot stay. I can neither eat bread nor drink water till I have learned more about this young man's deeds, what can be proved and what cannot be proved against him. I fear he has none to stand by him in this town, for even by the friends of our church I have been ofttimes rebuked because he seemed dear to me. But, Esther, my beloved child —"

Here Mr. Lyon grasped her arm, and seemed in the need of speech to forget his previous haste. "I bear in mind this: the Lord knoweth them that are His; but we — we are left to judge by uncertain signs, that so we may learn to exercise hope and faith towards one another; and in this uncertainty I cling with awful hope to those whom the world loves not because their conscience, albeit mistakenly, is at war with the habits of the world. Our great faith, my Esther, is the faith of martyrs: I will not lightly turn away from any man who endures harshness because he will not lie; nay, though I would not wantonly grasp at ease of mind through an arbitrary choice of doctrine, I cannot but believe that the merits of the Divine Sacrifice are wider than our utmost charity. I once believed otherwise—but not now, not now."

The minister paused, and seemed to be abstractedly

gazing at some memory: he was always liable to be
snatched away by thoughts from the pursuit of a purpose which had seemed pressing. Esther seised the opportunity and prevailed on him to fortify himself with
some of Lyddy's porridge before he went out on his
tiring task of seeking definite trustworthy knowledge
from the lips of various witnesses, beginning with that
feminine darkener of counsel, poor Mrs. Holt.

She, regarding all her trouble about Felix in the
light of a fulfilment of her own prophecies, treated the
sad history with a preference for edification above accuracy, and for mystery above relevance, worthy of a
commentator on the Apocalypse. She insisted chiefly,
not on the important facts that Felix had sat at his
work till after eleven, like a deaf man, had rushed out
in surprise and alarm, had come back to report with
satisfaction that things were quiet, and had asked her
to set by his dinner for him — facts which would tell
as evidence that Felix was disconnected with any project of disturbances, and was averse to them. These
things came out incidentally in her long plaint to the
minister; but what Mrs. Holt felt it essential to state
was, that long before Michaelmas was turned, sitting in
her chair, she had said to Felix that there would be a
judgment on him for being so certain sure about the
Pills and the Elixir.

"And now, Mr. Lyon," said the poor woman, who
had dressed herself in a gown previously cast off, a
front all out of curl, and a cap with no starch in it,
while she held little coughing Job on her knee, —
"and now you see — my words have come true sooner
than I thought they would. Felix may contradict me
if he will; but there he is in prison, and here am I

with nothing in the world to bless myself with but half-a-crown a-week as I've saved by my own scraping, and this house I've got to pay rent for. It's not me has done wrong, Mr. Lyon; there's nobody can say it of me—not the orphin child on my knee is more innicent o' riot and murder and anything else as is bad. But when you've got a son so masterful and stopping medicines as Providence has sent, and his betters have been taking up and down the country since before he was a baby, it's o' no use being good here below. But he *was* a baby, Mr. Lyon, and I gave him the breast," —here poor Mrs. Holt's motherly love overcame her expository eagerness, and she fell more and more to crying as she spoke—" And to think there's folks saying now as he'll be transported, and his hair shaved off, and the treadmill, and everything. O dear!"

As Mrs. Holt broke off into sobbing, little Job also, who had got a confused yet profound sense of sorrow, and of Felix being hurt and gone away, set up a little wail of wondering misery.

"Nay, Mistress Holt," said the minister soothingly, "enlarge not your grief by more than warrantable grounds. I have good hope that my young friend your son will be delivered from any severe consequences beyond the death of the man Tucker, which I fear will ever be a sore burthen on his memory. I feel confident that a jury of his countrymen will discern between misfortune, or it may be misjudgment, and an evil will, and that he will be acquitted of any grave offence."

"He never stole anything in his life, Mr. Lyon," said Mrs. Holt, reviving. "Nobody can throw it in my face as my son ran away with money like the young man at the Bank—though he looked most re-

spectable, and far different on a Sunday to what Felix
ever did. And I know it's very hard fighting with
constables; but they say Tucker's wife'll be a deal
better off than she was before, for the great folks'll
pension her, and she'll be put on all the charities, and
her children at the Free School, and everything. Your
trouble's easy borne when everybody gives it a lift for
you; and if judge and jury wants to do right by Felix,
they'll think of his poor mother, with the bread took
out of her mouth, all but half-a-crown a-week and
furniture—which, to be sure, is most excellent, and of
my own buying—and got to keep this orphin child as
Felix himself brought on me. And I might send him
back to his old grandfather on parish pay, but I'm not
that woman, Mr. Lyon: I've a tender heart. And here's
his little feet and toes, like marbil; do but look"—
here Mrs. Holt drew off Job's sock and shoe, and
showed a well-washed little foot—" and you'll perhaps
say I might take a lodger; but it's easy talking; it
isn't everybody at a loose-end wants a parlour and a
bedroom; and if anything bad happens to Felix, I may
as well go and sit in the parish Pound, and nobody to
buy me out; for it's beyond everything how the church
members find fault with my son. But I think they
might leave his mother to find fault; for queer and
masterful he might be, and flying in the face of the
very Scripture about the physic, but he was most clever
beyond anything—that I *will* say—and was his own
father's lawful child, and me his mother, that was Mary
Wall thirty years before ever I married his father."
Here Mrs. Holt's feelings again became too much for
her, but she struggled on to say, sobbingly, "And if
they're to transport him, I should like to go to the

prison and take the orphin child; for he was most fond of having him on his lap, and said he'd never marry; and there was One above overheard him, for he's been took at his word."

Mr. Lyon listened with low groans, and then tried to comfort her by saying that he would himself go to Loamford as soon as possible, and would give his soul no rest till he had done all he could do for Felix.

On one point Mrs. Holt's plaint tallied with his own forebodings, and he found them verified: the state of feeling in Treby among the Liberal Dissenting flock was unfavourable to Felix. None who had observed his conduct from the windows saw anything tending to excuse him, and his own account of his motives, given on his examination, was spoken of with head-shaking; if it had not been for his habit of always thinking himself wiser than other people, he would never have entertained such a wild scheme. He had set himself up for something extraordinary, and had spoken ill of respectable tradespeople. He had put a stop to the making of saleable drugs, contrary to the nature of buying and selling, and to a due reliance on what Providence might effect in the human inside through the instrumentality of remedies unsuitable to the stomach, looked at in a merely secular light; and the result was what might have been expected. He had brought his mother to poverty, and himself into trouble. And what for? He had done no good to "the cause;" if he had fought about Church-rates, or had been worsted in some struggle in which he was distinctly the champion of Dissent and Liberalism, his case would have been one for gold, silver, and copper subscriptions, in order to procure the best defence; sermons might have been preached on him, and his name might have floated on flags from Newcastle to Dorchester. But there seemed to be no edification in what had befallen Felix. The riot at Treby, "turn it which way you would," as Mr. Muscat observed, was no great credit to Liberalism; and what Mr. Lyon had to testify as to Felix Holt's conduct in the matter of the Sproxton men, only made it clear that the defence of Felix was the accusation of his party. The whole affair, Mr. Nutwood said, was dark and inscrutable, and seemed not to be one in which the interference of God's servants would tend to give the glory where the glory was due. That a candidate for whom the richer church members had all voted should have his name associated with the encouragement of drunkenness, riot, and plunder, was an occasion for the enemy to blaspheme; and it was not clear how the enemy's mouth would be stopped by exertions in favour of a rash young man, whose interference had made things worse instead of better. Mr. Lyon was warned lest his human partialities should blind him to the interests of truth; it was God's cause that was endangered in this matter.

The little minister's soul was bruised; he himself was keenly alive to the complication of public and private regards in this affair, and suffered a good deal at the thought of Tory triumph in the demonstration that, excepting the attack on the Seven Stars, which called itself a Whig house, all damage to property had been borne by Tories. He cared intensely for his opinions, and would have liked events to speak for them in a sort of picture-writing that everybody could understand. The enthusiasms of the world are not to be stimulated by a commentary in small and subtle characters which alone can tell the whole truth; and the picture-writing in Felix Holt's troubles was of an entirely puzzling kind: if he were a martyr, neither side wanted to claim him. Yet the minister, as we have seen, found in his Christian faith a reason for clinging the more to one who had not a large party to back him. That little man's heart was heroic: he was not one of those Liberals who make their anxiety for "the cause" of Liberalism a plea for cowardly desertion.

Besides himself, he believed there was no one who could bear testimony to the remonstrances of Felix concerning the treating of the Sproxton men, except Jermyn, Johnson, and Harold Transome. Though he had the vaguest idea of what could be done in the case, he fixed his mind on the probability that Mr. Transome would be moved to the utmost exertion, if only as an atonement; but he dared not take any step until he had consulted Felix, who he foresaw was likely to have a very strong determination as to the help he would accept or not accept.

This last expectation was fulfilled. Mr. Lyon returned to Esther, after his day's journey to Loamford and back, with less of trouble and perplexity in his mind: he had at least got a definite course marked out, to which he must resign himself. Felix had declared that he would receive no aid from Harold Transome, except the aid he might give as an honest witness. There was nothing to be done for him but what was perfectly simple and direct. Even if the pleading of counsel had been permitted (and at that time it was not) on behalf of a prisoner on trial for felony, Felix would have declined it: he would in any case have spoken in his own defence. He had a perfectly simple account to give, and needed not to avail himself of any legal adroitness. He consented to accept the services of a respectable solicitor in Loamford, who offered to conduct his case without any fees. The work was plain and easy, Felix said. The only witnesses who had to be hunted up at all were some who could testify that he had tried to take the crowd down Hobb's Lane, and that they had gone to the Manor in spite of him.

"Then he is not so much cast down as you feared, father?" said Esther.

"No, child; albeit he is pale and much shaken for one so stalwart. He hath no grief, he says, save for the poor man Tucker, and for his mother; otherwise his heart is without a burthen. We discoursed greatly on the sad effect of all this for his mother, and on the perplexed condition of human things, whereby even right action seems to bring evil consequences, if we have respect only to our own brief lives, and not to that larger rule whereby we are stewards of the eternal dealings, and not contrivers of our own success."

"Did he say nothing about me, father?" said Esther, trembling a little, but unable to repress her egoism.

"Yea; he asked if you were well, and sent his affectionate regards. Nay, he bade me say something which appears to refer to your discourse together when I was not present. 'Tell her,' he said, 'whatever they sentence me to, she knows they can't rob me of my vocation. With poverty for my bride, and preaching and pedagoguy for my business, I am sure of a handsome establishment.' He laughed — doubtless bearing in mind some playfulness of thine."

Mr. Lyon seemed to be looking at Esther as he

smiled, but she was not near enough for him to discern the expression of her face. Just then it seemed made for melancholy rather than for playfulness. Hers was not a childish beauty; and when the sparkle of mischief, wit, and vanity was out of her eyes, and the large look of abstracted sorrow was there, you would have been surprised by a certain grandeur which the smiles had hidden. That changing face was the perfect symbol of her mixed susceptible nature, in which battle was inevitable, and the side of victory uncertain.

She began to look on all that had passed between herself and Felix as something not buried, but embalmed and kept as a relic in a private sanctuary. The very entireness of her preoccupation about him, the perpetual repetition in her memory of all that had passed between them, tended to produce this effect. She lived with him in the past; in the future she seemed shut out from him. He was an influence above her life, rather than a part of it; some time or other, perhaps, he would be to her as if he belonged to the solemn admonishing skies, checking her self-satisfied pettiness with the suggestion of a wider life.

But not yet — not while her trouble was so fresh. For it was still *her* trouble, and not Felix Holt's. Perhaps it was a subtraction from his power over her, that she could never think of him with pity, because he always seemed to her too great and strong to be pitied: he wanted nothing. He evaded calamity by choosing privation. The best part of a woman's love is worship; but it is hard to her to be sent away with her precious spikenard rejected, and her long tresses too, that were let fall ready to soothe the wearied feet.

While Esther was carrying these things in her

heart, the January days were beginning to pass by with their wonted wintry monotony, except that there was rather more of good cheer than usual remaining from the feast of Twelfth Night among the triumphant Tories, and rather more scandal than usual excited among the mortified Dissenters by the wilfulness of their minister. He had actually mentioned Felix Holt by name in his evening sermon, and offered up a petition for him in the evening prayer, also by name — not as "a young Ishmaelite, whom we would fain see brought back from the lawless life of the desert, and seated in the same fold even with the sons of Judah and of Benjamin," a suitable periphrasis which Brother Kemp threw off without any effort, and with all the felicity of a suggestive critic. Poor Mrs. Holt, indeed, even in the midst of her grief, experienced a proud satisfaction, that though not a church member she was now an object of congregational remark and ministerial allusion. Feeling herself a spotless character standing out in relief on a dark background of affliction, and a practical contradiction to that extreme doctrine of human depravity which she had never "given in to," she was naturally gratified and soothed by a notice which must be a recognition. But more influential hearers were of opinion, that in a man who had so many long sentences at command as Mr. Lyon, so many parentheses and modifying clauses, this naked use of a non-scriptural Treby name in an address to the Almighty was all the more offensive. In a low unlettered local preacher of the Wesleyan persuasion such things might pass; but a certain style in prayer was demanded from Independents, the most educated body in the ranks of orthodox Dissent. To Mr. Lyon such notions seemed painfully perverse, and the next morning he was declaring to Esther his resolution stoutly to withstand them, and to count nothing common or unclean on which a blessing could be asked, when the tenor of his thoughts was completely changed by a great shock of surprise which made both himself and Esther sit looking at each other in speechless amazement.

The cause was a letter brought by a special messenger from Duffield; a heavy letter addressed to Esther in a business-like manner, quite unexampled in her correspondence. And the contents of the letter were more startling than its exterior. It began:

Madam, — Herewith we send you a brief abstract of evidence which has come within our knowledge, that the right of remainder whereby the lineal issue of Edward Bycliffe can claim possession of the estates of which the entail was settled by John Justus Transome in 1729, now first accrues to you as the sole and lawful issue of Maurice Christian Bycliffe. We are confident of success in the prosecution of this claim, which will result to you in the possession of estates to the value, at the lowest, of from five to six thousand per annum ——

It was at this point that Esther, who was reading aloud, let her hand fall with the letter on her lap, and with a palpitating heart looked at her father, who looked again, in silence that lasted for two or three minutes. A certain terror was upon them both, though the thoughts that laid that weight on the tongue of each were different.

It was Mr. Lyon who spoke first.

"This, then, is what the man named Christian

referred to. I distrusted him, yet it seems he spoke truly."

"But," said Esther, whose imagination ran necessarily to those conditions of wealth which she could best appreciate, "do they mean that the Transomes would be turned out of Transome Court, and that I should go and live there? It seems quite an impossible thing."

"Nay, child, I know not. I am ignorant in these things, and the thought of worldly grandeur for you hath more of terror than of gladness for me. Nevertheless we must duly weigh all things, not considering aught that befalls us as a bare event, but rather as an occasion for faithful stewardship. Let us go to my study and consider this writing further."

How this announcement, which to Esther seemed as unprepared as if it had fallen from the skies, came to be made to her by solicitors other than Batt & Cowley, the old lawyers of the Bycliffes, was by a sequence as natural, that is to say, as legally-natural, as any in the world. The secret worker of the apparent wonder was Mr. Johnson, who, on the very day when he wrote to give his patron, Mr. Jermyn, the serious warning that a bill was likely to be filed in Chancery against him, had carried forward with added zeal the business already commenced, of arranging with another firm his share in the profits likely to result from the prosecution of Esther Bycliffe's claim.

Jermyn's star was certainly going down, and Johnson did not feel an unmitigated grief. Beyond some troublesome declarations as to his actual share in transactions in which his name had been used, Johnson saw nothing formidable in prospect for himself. He was not going to be ruined, though Jermyn probably was: he was not a highflyer, but a mere climbing-bird, who could hold on and get his livelihood just as well if his wings were clipped a little. And, in the mean time, here was something to be gained in this Bycliffe business, which, it was not unpleasant to think, was a nut that Jermyn had intended to keep for his own particular cracking, and which would be rather a severe astonishment to Mr. Harold Transome, whose manners towards respectable agents were such as leave a smart in a man of spirit.

Under the stimulus of small many-mixed motives like these, a great deal of business has been done in the world by well-clad and, in 1833, clean-shaven men, whose names are on charity-lists, and who do not know that they are base. Mr. Johnson's character was not much more exceptional than his double chin.

No system, religious or political, I believe, has laid it down as a principle that all men are alike virtuous, or even that all the people rated for £80 houses are an honour to their species.

CHAPTER XIV.

*The down we rest on in our aëry dreams
Has not been plucked from birds that live and smart;
'Tis but warm snow, that melts not.*

THE story and the prospect revealed to Esther by the lawyers' letter, which she and her father studied together, had made an impression on her very different from what she had been used to figure to herself in her many day-dreams as to the effect of a sudden elevation in rank and fortune. In her day-dreams she had not traced out the means by which such a change could be brought about; in fact, the change had seemed impossible to her, except in her little private Utopia, which, like other Utopias, was filled with delightful results, independent of processes. But her mind had fixed itself habitually on the signs and luxuries of ladyhood, for which she had the keenest perception. She had seen the very mat in her carriage, had scented the dried rose-leaves in her corridors, had felt the soft carpets under her pretty feet, and seen herself, as she rose from her sofa cushions, in the crystal panel that reflected a long drawing-room, where the conservatory flowers and the pictures of fair women left her still with the supremacy of charm. She had trodden the marble-firm gravel of her garden-walks and the soft deep turf of her lawn; she had had her servants about her filled with adoring respect, because of her kindness as well as her grace and beauty; and she had had several accomplished cavaliers all at once suing for her hand — one of whom, uniting very high birth with long dark eyelashes and the most distinguished talents, she secretly preferred, though his pride and hers hindered an avowal, and supplied the inestimable interest of retardation. The glimpses she had had in her brief life as a family governess, supplied her ready faculty with details enough of delightful still life to furnish her day-dreams; and no one who has not, like Esther, a strong natural prompting and susceptibility towards such things, and has at the same time suffered from the presence of opposite conditions, can understand how powerfully those minor accidents of rank which please the fastidious sense can preoccupy the imagination.

It seemed that almost everything in her day-dreams — cavaliers apart — must be found at Transome Court. But now that fancy was becoming real, and the impossible appeared possible, Esther found the balance of her attention reversed: now that her ladyhood was not simply in Utopia, she found herself arrested and painfully grasped by the means through which the ladyhood was to be obtained. To her inexperience this strange story of an alienated inheritance, of such a last representative of pure-blooded lineage as old Thomas Transome the bill-sticker, above all of the dispossession hanging over those who actually held, and had expected always to hold, the wealth and position which were suddenly announced to be rightfully hers — all these things made a picture, not for her own tastes and fancies to float in with Elysian indulgence, but in which she was compelled to gaze on the degrading hard experience of other human beings, and on a humiliating loss which was the obverse of her own proud gain. Even in her times of most untroubled egoism Esther shrank from anything ungenerous; and the fact that she had a very lively image of Harold Transome and his gipsy-eyed boy in her mind, gave additional distinctness to the thought that if she entered they must depart. Of the elder Transomes she had a dimmer vision, and they were necessarily in the background to her sympathy.

She and her father sat with their hands locked, as they might have done if they had been listening to a solemn oracle in the days of old revealing unknown kinship and rightful heirdom. It was not that Esther had any thought of renouncing her fortune; she was incapable, in these moments, of condensing her vague ideas and feelings into any distinct plan of action, nor indeed did it seem that she was called upon to act with any promptitude. It was only that she was conscious of being strangely awed by something that was called good fortune; and the awe shut out any scheme of rejection as much as any triumphant joy in acceptance. Her first father, she learned, had died disappointed and in wrongful imprisonment, and an undefined sense of Nemesis seemed half to sanctify her inheritance, and counteract its apparent arbitrariness.

Felix Holt was present in her mind throughout: what he would say was an imaginary commentary that she was constantly framing, and the words that she most frequently gave him — for she dramatised under the inspiration of a sadness slightly bitter — were of this kind: "That is clearly your destiny — to be aristocratic, to be rich. I always saw that our lots lay widely apart. You are not fit for poverty, or any work of difficulty. But remember what I once said to you about a vision of consequences; take care where your fortune leads you."

Her father had not spoken since they had ended
their study and discussion of the story and the evidence
as it was presented to them. Into this he had entered
with his usual penetrating activity; but he was so
accustomed to the impersonal study of narrative, that
even in these exceptional moments the habit of half a
century asserted itself, and he seemed sometimes not to
distinguish the case of Esther's inheritance from a story
in ancient history, until some detail recalled him to the
profound feeling that a great, great change might be
coming over the life of this child who was so close to
him. At last he relapsed into total silence, and for
some time Esther was not moved to interrupt it. He
had sunk back in his chair, with his hand locked in
hers, and was pursuing a sort of prayerful meditation:
he lifted up no formal petition, but it was as if his soul
travelled again over the facts he had been considering
in the company of a guide ready to inspire and correct
him. He was striving to purify his feeling in this
matter from selfish or worldly dross — a striving which
is that prayer without ceasing, sure to wrest an answer
by its sublime importunity.

There is no knowing how long they might have sat
in this way, if it had not been for the inevitable Lyddy
reminding them dismally of dinner.

"Yes, Lyddy, we come," said Esther; and then,
before moving,

"Is there any advice you have in your mind for
me, father?" The sense of awe was growing in Esther.
Her intensest life was no longer in her dreams, where
she made things to her own mind: she was moving in
a world charged with forces.

"Not yet, my dear — save this: that you will seek

special illumination in this juncture, and, above all, be watchful that your soul be not lifted up within you by what, rightly considered, is rather an increase of charge, and a call upon you to walk along a path which is indeed easy to the flesh, but dangerous to the spirit."

"You would always live with me, father?" Esther spoke under a strong impulse — partly affection, partly the need to grasp at some moral help. But she had no sooner uttered the words than they raised a vision, showing, as by a flash of lightning, the incongruity of that past which had created the sanctities and affections of her life with that future which was coming to her.... The little rusty old minister, with the one luxury of his Sunday evening pipe, smoked up the kitchen chimney, coming to live in the midst of grandeur ... but no! her father, with the grandeur of his past sorrow and his long struggling labours, forsaking his vocation, and vulgarly accepting an existence unsuited to him.... Esther's face flushed with the excitement of this vision and its reversed interpretation, which five months ago she would have been incapable of seeing. Her question to her father seemed like a mockery; she was ashamed. He answered slowly,

"Touch not that chord yet, child. I must learn to think of thy lot according to the demands of Providence. We will rest a while from the subject; and I will seek calmness in my ordinary duties."

The next morning nothing more was said. Mr. Lyon was absorbed in his sermon-making, for it was near the end of the week, and Esther was obliged to attend to her pupils. Mrs. Holt came by invitation with little Job to share their dinner of roast-meat; and, after much of what the minister called unprofitable discourse, she was quitting the house when she hastened back with an astonished face, to tell Mr. Lyon and Esther, who were already in wonder at crashing, thundering sounds on the pavement, that there was a carriage stopping and stamping at the entry into Malthouse Yard, with "all sorts of fine liveries," and a lady and gentleman inside. Mr. Lyon and Esther looked at each other, both having the same name in their minds.

"If it's Mr. Transome or somebody else as is great, Mr. Lyon," urged Mrs. Holt, "you'll remember my son, and say he's got a mother with a character they may inquire into as much as they like. And never mind what Felix says, for he's so masterful he'd stay in prison and be transported whether or no, only to have his own way. For it's not to be thought but what the great people could get him off if they would; and it's very hard with a King in the country and all the texts in Proverbs about the King's countenance, and Solomon and the live baby ——"

Mr. Lyon lifted up his hand deprecatingly, and Mrs. Holt retreated from the parlour-door to a corner of the kitchen, the outer doorway being occupied by Dominic, who was inquiring if Mr. and Miss Lyon were at home, and could receive Mrs. Transome and Mr. Harold Transome. While Dominic went back to the carriage Mrs. Holt escaped with her tiny companion to Zachary's, the pew-opener, observing to Lyddy that she knew herself, and was not that woman to stay where she might not be wanted; whereupon Lyddy, differing fundamentally, admonished her parting ear that it was well if she knew herself to be dust and ashes — silently extending the application of this remark to Mrs. Transome as she saw the tall lady sweep in arrayed in her rich black and fur, with that fine gentleman behind her whose thick topknot of wavy hair, sparkling ring, dark complexion, and general air of worldly exaltation unconnected with chapel, were painfully suggestive to Lyddy of Herod, Pontius Pilate, or the much-quoted Gallio.

Harold Transome, greeting Esther gracefully, presented his mother, whose eagle-like glance, fixed on her from the first moment of entering, seemed to Esther to pierce her through. Mrs. Transome hardly noticed Mr. Lyon, not from studied haughtiness, but from sheer mental inability to consider him — as a person ignorant of natural history is unable to consider a fresh-water polype otherwise than as a sort of animated weed, certainly not fit for table. But Harold saw that his mother was agreeably struck by Esther, who indeed showed to much advantage. She was not at all taken by surprise, and maintained a dignified quietude; but her previous knowledge and reflection about the possible dispossession of these Transomes gave her a softened feeling towards them which tinged her manners very agreeably.

Harold was carefully polite to the minister, throwing out a word to make him understand that he had an important part in the important business which had brought this unannounced visit; and the four made a group seated not far off each other near the window, Mrs. Transome and Esther being on the sofa.

"You must be astonished at a visit from me, Miss Lyon," Mrs. Transome began; "I seldom come to Treby Magna. Now I see you, the visit is an unexpected pleasure; but the cause of my coming is business of a serious nature, which my son will communicate to you."

"I ought to begin by saying that what I have to announce to you is the reverse of disagreeable, Miss Lyon," said Harold, with lively ease. "I don't suppose the world would consider it very good news for me; but a rejected candidate, Mr. Lyon," Harold went on, turning graciously to the minister, "begins to be inured to loss and misfortune."

"Truly, sir," said Mr. Lyon, with a rather sad solemnity, "your allusion hath a grievous hearing for me, but I will not retard your present purpose by further remark."

"You will never guess what I have to disclose," said Harold, again looking at Esther, "unless, indeed, you have had some previous intimation of it."

"Does it refer to law and inheritance?" said Esther, with a smile. She was already brightened by Harold's manner. The news seemed to be losing its chillness, and to be something really belonging to warm, comfortable, interesting life.

"Then you have already heard of it?" said Harold, inwardly vexed, but sufficiently prepared not to seem so.

"Only yesterday," said Esther, quite simply. "I received a letter from some lawyers with a statement of many surprising things, showing that I was an heiress" — here she turned very prettily to address Mrs. Transome — "which, as you may imagine, is one of the last things I could have supposed myself to be."

"My dear," said Mrs. Transome with elderly grace, just laying her hand for an instant on Esther's, "it is a lot that would become you admirably."

Esther blushed, and said playfully,

"O, I know what to buy with fifty pounds a-year, but I know the price of nothing beyond that."

Her father sat looking at her through his spectacles, stroking his chin. It was amazing to herself that she was taking so lightly now what had caused her such deep emotion yesterday.

"I daresay, then," said Harold, "you are more fully possessed of particulars than I am. So that my mother and I need only tell you what no one else can tell you — that is, what are her and my feelings and wishes under these new and unexpected circumstances."

"I am most anxious," said Esther, with a grave beautiful look of respect to Mrs. Transome — "most anxious on that point. Indeed, being of course in uncertainty about it, I have not yet known whether I could rejoice." Mrs. Transome's glance had softened. She liked Esther to look at her.

"Our chief anxiety," she said, knowing what Harold wished her to say, "is, that there may be no contest, no useless expenditure of money. Of course we will surrender what can be rightfully claimed."

"My mother expresses our feeling precisely, Miss Lyon," said Harold. "And I'm sure, Mr. Lyon, you will understand our desire."

"Assuredly, sir. My daughter would in any case have had my advice to seek a conclusion which would involve no strife. We endeavour, sir, in our body, to hold to the apostolic rule that one Christian brother should not go to law with another; and I, for my part, would extend this rule to all my fellow-men, apprehending that the practice of our courts is little consistent with the simplicity that is in Christ."

"If it is to depend on my will," said Esther, "there

is nothing that would be more repugnant to me than any struggle on such a subject. But can't the lawyers go on doing what they will in spite of me? It seems that this is what they mean."

"Not exactly," said Harold, smiling. "Of course they live by such struggles as you dislike. But we can thwart them by determining not to quarrel. It is desirable that we should consider the affair together, and put it into the hands of honourable solicitors. I assure you we Transomes will not contend for what is not our own."

"And this is what I have come to beg of you," said Mrs. Transome. "It is that you will come to Transome Court — and let us take full time to rrange matters. Do oblige me: you shall not be teazed more than you like by an old woman: you shall do just as you please, and become acquainted with your future home, since it is to be yours. I can tell you a world of things that you will want to know; and the business can proceed properly."

"Do consent," said Harold, with winning brevity.

Esther was flushed, and her eyes were bright. It was impossible for her not to feel that the proposal was a more tempting step towards her change of condition than she could have thought of beforehand. She had forgotten that she was in any trouble. But she looked towards her father, who was again stroking his chin, as was his habit when he was doubting and deliberating.

"I hope you do not disapprove of Miss Lyon's granting us this favour?" said Harold to the minister.

"I have nothing to oppose to it, sir, if my daughter's own mind is clear as to her course."

"You will come — now — with us," said Mrs. Transome, persuasively. "You will go back with us in the carriage."

Harold was highly gratified with the perfection of his mother's manner on this occasion, which he had looked forward to as difficult. Since he had come home again, he had never seen her so much at her ease, or with so much benignancy in her face. The secret lay in the charm of Esther's sweet young deference, a sort of charm that had not before entered into Mrs. Transome's elderly life. Esther's pretty behaviour, it must be confessed, was not fed entirely from lofty moral sources: over and above her really generous feeling, she enjoyed Mrs. Transome's accent, the high-bred quietness of her speech, the delicate odour of her drapery. She had always thought that life must be particularly easy if one could pass it among refined people; and so it seemed at this moment. She wished, unmixedly, to go to Transome Court.

"Since my father has no objection," she said, "and you urge me so kindly. But I must beg for time to pack up a few clothes."

"By all means," said Mrs. Transome. "We are not at all pressed."

When Esther had left the room, Harold said, "Apart from our immediate reason for coming, Mr. Lyon, I could have wished to see you about these unhappy consequences of the election contest. But you will understand that I have been much preoccupied with private affairs."

"You have well said that the consequences are unhappy, sir. And but for a reliance on something more than human calculation, I know not which I should most bewail — the scandal which wrong-dealing has brought on right principles, or the snares which it laid for the feet of a young man who is dear to me. 'One soweth, and another reapeth,' is a verity that applies to evil as well as good."

"You are referring to Felix Holt. I have not neglected steps to secure the best legal help for the prisoners; but I am given to understand that Holt refuses any aid from me. I hope he will not go rashly to work in speaking in his own defence without any legal instruction. It is an opprobrium of our law that no counsel is allowed to plead for the prisoner in cases of felony. A ready tongue may do a man as much harm as good in a court of justice. He piques himself on making a display, and displays a little too much."

"Sir, you know him not," said the little minister, in his deeper tone. "He would not accept, even if it were accorded, a defence wherein the truth was screened or avoided, — not from a vainglorious spirit of self-exhibition, for he hath a singular directness and simplicity of speech; but from an averseness to a profession wherein a man may without shame seek to justify the wicked for reward, and take away the righteousness of the righteous from him."

"It's a pity a fine young fellow should do himself harm by fanatical notions of that sort. I could at least have procured the advantage of first-rate consultation. He didn't look to me like a dreamy personage."

"Nor is he dreamy; rather, his excess lies in being too practical."

"Well, I hope you will not encourage him in such

irrationality: the question is not one of misrepresentation, but of adjusting fact, so as to raise it to the power of evidence. Don't you see that?"

"I do, I do. But I distrust not Felix Holt's discernment in regard to his own case. He builds not on doubtful things, and hath no illusory hopes; on the contrary, he is of a too-scornful incredulity where I would fain see a more childlike faith. But he will hold no belief without action corresponding thereto; and the occasion of his return to this his native place at a time which has proved fatal, was no other than his resolve to hinder the sale of some drugs, which had chiefly supported his mother, but which his better knowledge showed him to be pernicious to the human frame. He undertook to support her by his own labour: but, sir, I pray you to mark — and old as I am, I will not deny that this young man instructs me herein — I pray you to mark the poisonous confusion of good and evil which is the wide-spreading effect of vicious practices. Through the use of undue electioneering means — concerning which, however, I do not accuse you farther than of having acted the part of him who washes his hands when he delivers up to others the exercise of an iniquitous power — Felix Holt is, I will not scruple to say, the innocent victim of a riot; and that deed of strict honesty, whereby he took on himself the charge of his aged mother, seems now to have deprived her of sufficient bread, and is even an occasion of reproach to him from the weaker brethren."

"I shall be proud to supply her as amply as you think desirable," said Harold, not enjoying this lecture.

"I will pray you to speak of this question with my daughter, who, it appears, may herself have large means at command, and would desire to minister to Mistress Holt's needs with all friendship and delicacy. For the present, I can take care that she lacks nothing essential."

As Mr. Lyon was speaking, Esther re-entered, equipped for her drive. She laid her hand on her father's arm, and said, "You will let my pupils know at once, will you, father?"

"Doubtless, my dear," said the old man, trembling a little under the feeling that this departure of Esther's was a crisis. Nothing again would be as it had been in their mutual life. But he feared that he was being mastered by a too-tender self-regard, and struggled to keep himself calm.

Mrs. Transome and Harold had both risen.

"If you are quite ready, Miss Lyon," said Harold, divining that the father and daughter would like to have an unobserved moment, "I will take my mother to the carriage, and come back for you."

When they were alone, Esther put her hands on her father's shoulders, and kissed him.

"This will not be a grief to you, I hope, father? You think it is better that I should go?"

"Nay, child, I am weak. But I would fain be capable of a joy quite apart from the accidents of my aged earthly existence, which, indeed, is a petty and almost dried-up fountain — whereas to the receptive soul the river of life pauseth not, nor is diminished."

"Perhaps you will see Felix Holt again, and tell him everything?"

"Shall I say aught to him for you?"

"O no; only that Job Tudge has a little flannel shirt and a box of lozenges," said Esther, smiling. "Ah, I hear Mr. Transome coming back. I must say good-bye to Lyddy, else she will cry over my hard heart."

In spite of all the grave thoughts that had been, Esther felt it a very pleasant as well as new experience to be led to the carriage by Harold Transome, to be seated on soft cushions, and bowled along, looked at admiringly and deferentially by a person opposite, whom it was agreeable to look at in return, and talked to with suavity and liveliness. Towards what prospect was that easy carriage really leading her? She could not be always asking herself Mentor-like questions. Her young bright nature was rather weary of the sadness that had grown heavier in these last weeks, like a chill white mist hopelessly veiling the day. Her fortune was beginning to appear worthy of being called good fortune. She had come to a new stage in her journey; a new day had arisen on new scenes, and her young untired spirit was full of curiosity.

CHAPTER XV.

No man believes that many-textured knowledge and skill — as a just idea of the solar system, or the power of painting flesh, or of reading written harmonies — can come late and of a sudden; yet many will not stick at believing that happiness can come at any day and hour solely by a new disposition of events; though there is nought less capable of a magical production than a mortal's happiness, which is mainly a complex of habitual relations and dispositions not to be wrought by news from foreign parts, or any whirling of fortune's wheel for one on whose brow Time has written legibly.

SOME days after Esther's arrival at Transome Court, Denner, coming to dress Mrs. Transome before dinner — a labour of love for which she had ample leisure now — found her mistress seated with more than ever of that marble aspect of self-absorbed suffering, which to the waiting-woman's keen observation had been gradually intensifying itself during the past week. She had tapped at the door without having been summoned, and she had ventured to enter though she had heard no voice saying "Come in."

Mrs. Transome had on a dark warm dressing-gown, hanging in thick folds about her, and she was seated before a mirror which filled a panel from the floor to the ceiling. The room was bright with the light of the fire and of wax candles. For some reason, contrary to her usual practice, Mrs. Transome had herself unfastened her abundant grey hair, which rolled backward in a pale sunless stream over her dark dress. She was seated before the mirror apparently looking at herself, her brow knit in one deep furrow, and her jewelled hands laid one above the other on her knee.

Probably she had ceased to see the reflection in the mirror, for her eyes had the fixed wide-open look that belongs not to examination, but to reverie. Motionless in that way, her clear-cut features keeping distinct record of past beauty, she looked like an image faded, dried, and bleached by uncounted suns, rather than a breathing woman who had numbered the years as they passed, and had a consciousness within her which was the slow deposit of those ceaseless rolling years.

Denner, with all her ingrained and systematic reserve, could not help showing signs that she was startled, when, peering from between her half-closed eyelids, she saw the motionless image in the mirror opposite to her as she entered. Her gentle opening of the door had not roused her mistress, to whom the sensations produced by Denner's presence were as little disturbing as those of a favourite cat. But the slight cry, and the start reflected in the glass, were unusual enough to break the reverie: Mrs. Transome moved, leaned back in her chair, and said,

"So you're come at last, Denner?"

"Yes, madam; it is not late. I'm sorry you should have undone your hair yourself."

"I undid it to see what an old hag I am. These fine clothes you put on me, Denner, are only a smart shroud."

"Pray don't talk so, madam. If there's anybody doesn't think it pleasant to look at you, so much the worse for them. For my part, I've seen no young ones fit to hold up your train. Look at your likeness down below; and though you're older now, what signifies? I wouldn't be Letty in the scullery because she's got red cheeks. She mayn't know she's a poor creature, but I know it, and that's enough for me: I know what sort of a dowdy draggletail she'll be in ten years' time. I would change with nobody, madam. And if troubles were put up to market, I'd sooner buy old than new. It's something to have seen the worst."

"A woman never has seen the worst till she is old, Denner," said Mrs. Transome, bitterly.

The keen little waiting-woman was not clear as to the cause of her mistress's added bitterness; but she rarely brought herself to ask questions, when Mrs. Transome did not authorise them by beginning to give her information. Banks the bailiff and the head-servant had nodded and winked a good deal over the certainty that Mr. Harold was "none so fond" of Jermyn, but this was a subject on which Mrs. Transome had never made up her mind to speak, and Denner knew nothing definite. Again, she felt quite sure that there was some important secret connected with Esther's presence in the house; she suspected that the close Dominic knew the secret, and was more trusted than she was, in spite of her forty years' service; but any resentment on this ground would have been an entertained reproach against her mistress, inconsistent with Denner's creed and character. She inclined to the belief that Esther was the immediate cause of the new discontent.

"If there's anything worse coming to you, I should like to know what it is, madam," she said, after a moment's silence, speaking always in the same low quick way, and keeping up her quiet labours. "When I awake at cock-crow, I'd sooner have one real grief on my mind than twenty false. It's better to know one's robbed than to think one's going to be murdered."

"I believe you are the creature in the world that loves me best, Denner; yet you will never understand what I suffer. It's of no use telling you. There's no folly in you, and no heartache. You are made of iron. You have never had any trouble."

"I've had some of your trouble, madam."

"Yes, you good thing. But as a sick-nurse, that never caught the fever. You never even had a child."

"I can feel for things I never went through. I used to be sorry for the poor French Queen when I was young: I'd have lain cold for her to lie warm. I know people have feelings according to their birth and station. And you always took things to heart, madam, beyond anybody else. But I hope there's nothing new, to make you talk of the worst."

"Yes, Denner, there is — there is," said Mrs. Transome, speaking in a low tone of misery, while she bent for her head-dress to be pinned on.

"Is it this young lady?"

"Why, what do you think about her, Denner?" said Mrs. Transome, in a tone of more spirit, rather curious to hear what the old woman would say.

"I don't deny she's graceful, and she has a pretty smile and very good manners: it's quite unaccountable by what Banks says about her father. I know nothing of those Treby townsfolk myself, but for my part I'm puzzled. I'm fond of Mr. Harold. I always shall be, madam. I was at his bringing into the world, and nothing but his doing wrong by you would turn me against him. But the servants all say he's in love with Miss Lyon."

"I wish it were true, Denner," said Mrs. Transome, energetically. "I wish he were in love with her, so that she could master him, and make him do what she pleased."

"Then it is not true — what they say?"

"Not true that she will ever master him. No woman ever will. He will make her fond of him, and afraid of him. That's one of the things you have never gone through, Denner. A woman's love is always freezing into fear. She wants everything, she is secure of nothing. This girl has a fine spirit — plenty of fire and pride and wit. Men like such captives, as they like horses that champ the bit and paw the ground: they feel more triumph in their mastery. What is the use of a woman's will? — if she tries, she doesn't get it, and she ceases to be loved. God was cruel when he made women."

Denner was used to such outbursts as this. Her mistress's rhetoric and temper belonged to her superior rank, her grand person, and her piercing black eyes. Mrs. Transome had a sense of impiety in her words which made them all the more tempting to her impotent anger. The waiting-woman had none of that awe which could be turned into defiance: the Sacred Grove was a common thicket to her.

"It mayn't be good-luck to be a woman," she said. "But one begins with it from a baby: one gets used to it. And I shouldn't like to be a man — to cough so loud, and stand straddling about on a wet day, and be so wasteful with meat and drink. They're a coarse lot, I think. Then I needn't make a trouble of this young lady, madam," she added, after a moment's pause.

"No, Denner. I like her. If that were all — I should like Harold to marry her. It would be the best thing. If the truth were known — and it will be known soon — the estate is hers by law — such law as it is. It's a strange story: she's a Bycliffe really."

Denner did not look amazed, but went on fastening her mistress's dress, as she said,

"Well, madam, I was sure there was something wonderful at the bottom of it. And turning the old lawsuits and everything else over in my mind, I thought the law might have something to do with it. Then she is a born lady?"

"Yes; she has good blood in her veins."

"We talked that over in the housekeeper's room — what a hand and an instep she has, and how her head is set on her shoulders — almost like your own, madam. But her lightish complexion spoils her, to my thinking. And Dominic said Mr. Harold never admired that sort of woman before. There's nothing that smooth fellow couldn't tell you if he would: he knows the answers to riddles before they're made. However, he knows how to hold his tongue; I'll say that for him. And so do I, madam."

"Yes, yes; you will not talk of it till other people are talking of it."

"And so, if Mr. Harold married her, it would save all fuss and mischief?"

"Yes — about the estate."

"And he seems inclined; and she'll not refuse him, I'll answer for it. And you like her, madam. There's everything to set your mind at rest."

Denner was putting the finishing-touch to Mrs. Transome's dress by throwing an Indian scarf over her shoulders, and so completing the contrast between the majestic lady in costume and the dishevelled Hecuba-like woman whom she had found half an hour before.

"I am not at rest!" Mrs. Transome said, with slow distinctness, moving from the mirror to the window, where the blind was not drawn down, and she could see the chill white landscape and the far-off unheeding stars.

Denner, more distressed by her mistress's suffering than she could have been by anything else, took up with the instinct of affection a gold vinaigrette which Mrs. Transome often liked to carry with her, and going up to her put it into her hand gently. Mrs. Transome grasped the little woman's hand hard, and held it so.

"Denner," she said, in a low tone, "if I could choose at this moment, I would choose that Harold should never have been born."

"Nay, my dear" (Denner had only once before in her life said "my dear" to her mistress), "it was a happiness to you then."

"I don't believe I felt the happiness then as I feel the misery now. It is foolish to say people can't feel much when they are getting old. Not pleasure, perhaps — little comes. But they can feel they are forsaken — why, every fibre in me seems to be a memory that makes a pang. They can feel that all the love in their lives is turned to hatred or contempt."

"Not mine, madam, not mine. Let what would be, I should want to live for your sake, for fear you should have nobody to do for you as I would."

"Ah, then, you are a happy woman, Denner; you have loved somebody for forty years who is old and weak now, and can't do without you."

The sound of the dinner-gong resounded below, and Mrs. Transome let the faithful hand fall again.

CHAPTER XVI.

*"She's beautiful; and therefore to be wooed;
She is a woman; therefore to be won."* — *Henry VI.*

If Denner had had a suspicion that Esther's presence at Transome Court was not agreeable to her mistress, it was impossible to entertain such a suspicion with regard to the other members of the family. Between her and little Harry there was an extraordinary fascination. This creature, with the soft broad brown cheeks, low forehead, great black eyes, tiny well-defined nose, fierce biting tricks towards every person and thing he disliked, and insistance on entirely occupying those he liked, was a human specimen such as Esther had never seen before, and she seemed to be equally original in Harry's experience. At first sight her light complexion and her blue gown, probably also her sunny smile and her hands stretched out towards him, seemed to make a show for him as of a new sort of bird: he threw himself backward against his "Gappa," as he called old Mr. Transome, and stared at this new-comer with the gravity of a wild animal. But she had no sooner sat down on the sofa in the library than he climbed up to her, and began to treat her as an attractive object in natural history, snatched up her curls with his brown fist, and, discovering that there was a little ear under them, pinched it and blew into it, pulled at her coronet of plaits, and seemed to discover with satisfaction that it did not grow at the summit of her head, but could be dragged down and altogether undone. Then finding that she laughed, tossed him back, kissed, and pretended to bite him — in fact was an animal that understood fun — he rushed off and made Dominic bring a small menagerie of white mice, squirrels, and birds, with Moro, the black spaniel, to make her acquaintance. Whomsoever Harry liked, it followed that Mr. Transome must like: "Gappa," along with Nimrod the retriever, was part of the menagerie, and perhaps endured more than all the other live creatures in the way of being tumbled about. Seeing that Esther bore having her hair pulled down quite merrily, and that she was willing to be harnessed and beaten, the old man began to confide to her, in his feeble, smiling, and rather jerking fashion, Harry's remarkable feats: how he had one day, when Gappa was asleep, unpinned a whole drawerful of beetles, to see if they would fly away; then, disgusted with their stupidity, was about to throw them all on the ground and stamp on them, when Dominic came in and rescued these valuable specimens; also, how he had subtly watched Mrs. Transome at the cabinet where she kept her medicines, and, when she had left it for a little while without locking it, had gone to the drawers and scattered half the contents on the floor. But what old Mr. Transome thought the most wonderful proof of an almost preternatural cleverness was, that Harry would hardly ever talk, but preferred making inarticulate noises, or combining syllables after a method of his own.

"He can talk well enough if he likes," said Gappa, evidently thinking that Harry, like the monkeys, had deep reasons for his reticence.

"You mind him," he added, nodding at Esther, and shaking with low-toned laughter. "You'll hear: he knows the right names of things well enough, but he likes to make his own. He'll give you one all to yourself before long."

And when Harry seemed to have made up his mind distinctly that Esther's name was "Boo," Mr. Transome nodded at her with triumphant satisfaction, and then told her in a low whisper, looking round cautiously beforehand, that Harry would never call Mrs. Transome "Gamma," but always "Bite."

"It's wonderful!" said he, laughing slyly.

The old man seemed so happy now in the new world created for him by Dominic and Harry, that he would perhaps have made a holocaust of his flies and beetles if it had been necessary in order to keep this living, lively kindness about him. He no longer confined himself to the library, but shuffled along from room to room, staying and looking on at what was going forward wherever he did not find Mrs. Transome alone.

To Esther the sight of this feeble-minded, timid, paralytic man, who had long abdicated all mastery over the things that were his, was something piteous. Certainly this had never been part of the furniture she had imagined for the delightful aristocratic dwelling in her Utopia; and the sad irony of such a lot impressed her the more because in her father she was accustomed to age accompanied with mental acumen and activity. Her thoughts went back in conjecture over the past life of Mr. and Mrs. Transome, a couple so strangely different from each other. She found it impossible to arrange their existence in the seclusion of this fine park and in this lofty large-roomed house, where it seemed quite ridiculous to be anything so small as a human being, without finding it rather dull. Mr. Transome had always had his beetles, but Mrs. Transome ——? It was not easy to conceive that the husband and wife had ever been very fond of each other.

Esther felt at her ease with Mrs. Transome: she was gratified by the consciousness — for on this point Esther was very quick — that Mrs. Transome admired her, and looked at her with satisfied eyes. But when they were together in the early days of her stay, the conversation turned chiefly on what happened in Mrs. Transome's youth — what she wore when she was presented at Court — who were the most distinguished and beautiful women at that time — the terrible excitement of the French Revolution — the emigrants she had known, and the history of various titled members of the Lingon family. And Esther, from native delicacy, did not lead to more recent topics of a personal kind. She was copiously instructed that the Lingon family was better than that even of the elder Transomes, and was privileged with an explanation of the various quarterings, which proved that the Lingon blood had been continually enriched. Poor Mrs. Transome, with her secret bitterness and dread, still found a flavour in this sort of pride; none the less because certain deeds of her own life had been in fatal inconsistency with it. Besides, genealogies entered into her stock of ideas, and her talk on such subjects was as necessary as the notes of the linnet or the blackbird. She had no ultimate analysis of things that went beyond blood and family — the Herons of Fenshore or the Badgers of Hillbury. She had never seen behind

the canvas with which her life was hung. In the dim
background there was the burning mount and the
tables of the law; in the foreground there was Lady
Debarry privately gossiping about her, and Lady Wy-
vern finally deciding not to send her invitations to
dinner. Unlike that Semiramis who made laws to suit
her practical licence, she lived, poor soul, in the midst
of desecrated sanctities, and of honours that looked
tarnished in the light of monotonous and weary suns.
Glimpses of the Lingon heraldry in their freshness
were interesting to Esther; but it occurred to her that
when she had known about them a good while they
would cease to be succulent themes of converse or meditation, and Mrs. Transome, having known them all
along, might have felt a vacuum in spite of them.

Nevertheless it was entertaining at present to be
seated on soft cushions with her netting before her,
while Mrs. Transome went on with her embroidery,
and told in that easy phrase, and with that refined
high-bred tone and accent which she possessed in perfection, family stories that to Esther were like so many
novelettes: what diamonds were in the Earl's family,
own cousins to Mrs. Transome; how poor Lady Sara's
husband went off into jealous madness only a month
after their marriage, and dragged that sweet blue-eyed
thing by the hair; and how the brilliant Fanny, having
married a country parson, became so niggardly that
she had gone about almost begging for fresh eggs from
the farmers' wives, though she had done very well
with her six sons, as there was a bishop and no end
of interest in the family, and two of them got appoint-
ments in India.

At present Mrs. Transome did not touch at all on

her own time of privation, or her troubles with her eldest son, or on anything that lay very close to her heart. She conversed with Esther, and acted the part of hostess as she performed her toilette and went on with her embroidery: these things were to be done whether one were happy or miserable. Even the patriarch Job, if he had been a gentleman of the modern West, would have avoided picturesque disorder and poetical laments; and the friends who called on him, though not less disposed than Bildad the Shuhite to hint that their unfortunate friend was in the wrong, would have sat on chairs and held their hats in their hands. The harder problems of our life have changed less than our manners; we wrestle with the old sorrows, but more decorously. Esther's inexperience prevented her from divining much about this fine grey-haired woman, whom she could not help perceiving to stand apart from the family group, as if there were some cause of isolation for her both within and without. To her young heart there was a peculiar interest in Mrs. Transome. An elderly woman, whose beauty, position, and graceful kindness towards herself, made deference to her spontaneous, was a new figure in Esther's experience. Her quick light movement was always ready to anticipate what Mrs. Transome wanted; her bright apprehension and silvery speech were always ready to cap Mrs. Transome's narratives or instructions even about doses and liniments, with some lively commentary. She must have behaved charmingly; for one day when she had tripped across the room to put the screen just in the right place, Mrs. Transome said, taking her hand, "My dear, you make me wish I had a daughter!"

That was pleasant; and so it was to be decked by Mrs. Transome's own hands in a set of turquoise ornaments, which became her wonderfully, worn with a white Cashmere dress, which was also insisted on. Esther never reflected that there was a double intention in these pretty ways towards her; with young generosity, she was rather preoccupied by the desire to prove that she herself entertained no low triumph in the fact that she had rights prejudicial to this family whose life she was learning. And besides, through all Mrs. Transome's perfect manners there pierced some indefinable indications of a hidden anxiety much deeper than anything she could feel about this affair of the estate — to which she often alluded slightly as a reason for informing Esther of something. It was impossible to mistake her for a happy woman; and young speculation is always stirred by discontent for which there is no obvious cause. When we are older, we take the uneasy eyes and the bitter lips more as a matter of course.

But Harold Transome was more communicative about recent years than his mother was. He thought it well that Esther should know how the fortune of his family had been drained by law expenses, owing to suits mistakenly urged by her family; he spoke of his mother's lonely life and pinched circumstances, of her lack of comfort in her elder son, and of the habit she had consequently acquired of looking at the gloomy side of things. He hinted that she had been accustomed to dictate, and that, as he had left her when he was a boy, she had perhaps indulged the dream that he would come back a boy. She was still sore on the point of his politics. These things could not be helped, but, so far as he could, he wished to make the rest of her life as cheerful as possible.

Esther listened eagerly, and took these things to heart. The claim to an inheritance, the sudden discovery of a right to a fortune held by others, was acquiring a very distinct and unexpected meaning for her. Every day she was getting more clearly into her imagination what it would be to abandon her own past, and what she would enter into in exchange for it; what it would be to disturb a long possession, and how difficult it was to fix a point at which the disturbance might begin, so as to be contemplated without pain.

Harold Transome's thoughts turned on the same subject, but accompanied by a different state of feeling and with more definite resolutions. He saw a mode of reconciling all difficulties, which looked pleasanter to him the longer he looked at Esther. When she had been hardly a week in the house, he had made up his mind to marry her; and it had never entered into that mind that the decision did not rest entirely with his inclination. It was not that he thought slightly of Esther's demands; he saw that she would require considerable attractions to please her, and that there were difficulties to be overcome. She was clearly a girl who must be wooed; but Harold did not despair of presenting the requisite attractions, and the difficulties gave more interest to the wooing than he could have believed. When he had said that he would not marry an Englishwoman, he had always made a mental reservation in favour of peculiar circumstances; and now the peculiar circumstances were come. To be deeply in love was a catastrophe not likely to happen to him;

but he was readily amorous. No woman could make him miserable, but he was sensitive to the presence of women, and was kind to them; not with grimaces, like a man of mere gallantry, but beamingly, easily, like a man of genuine good-nature. And each day that he was near Esther, the solution of all difficulties by marriage became a more pleasing prospect; though he had to confess to himself that the difficulties did not diminish on a nearer view, in spite of the flattering sense that she brightened at his approach.

Harold was not one to fail in a purpose for want of assiduity. After an hour or two devoted to business in the morning, he went to look for Esther, and if he did not find her at play with Harry and old Mr. Transome, or chatting with his mother, he went into the drawing-room, where she was usually either seated with a book on her knee and "making a bed for her cheek" with one little hand, while she looked out of the window, or else standing in front of one of the full-length family portraits with an air of rumination. Esther found it impossible to read in these days; her life was a book which she seemed herself to be constructing — trying to make character clear before her, and looking into the ways of destiny.

The active Harold had almost always something definite to propose by way of filling the time: if it were fine, she must walk out with him and see the grounds; and when the snow melted and it was no longer slippery, she must get on horseback and learn to ride. If they stayed indoors, she must learn to play at billiards, or she must go over the house and see the pictures he had had hung anew, or the costumes he had brought from the East, or come into his study and look at the map of the estate, and hear what — if it had remained in his family — he had intended to do in every corner of it in order to make the most of its capabilities.

About a certain time in the morning Esther had learned to expect him. Let every wooer make himself strongly expected; he may succeed by dint of being absent, but hardly in the first instance. One morning Harold found her in the drawing-room, leaning against a consol table, and looking at the full-length portrait of a certain Lady Betty Transome, who had lived a century and a half before, and had the usual charm of ladies in Sir Peter Lely's style.

"Don't move, pray," he said on entering; "you look as if you were standing for your own portrait."

"I take that as an insinuation," said Esther, laughing, and moving towards her seat on an ottoman near the fire, "for I notice almost all the portraits are in a conscious, affected attitude. That fair Lady Betty looks as if she had been drilled into that posture, and had not will enough of her own ever to move again unless she had a little push given to her."

"She brightens up that panel well with her long satin skirt," said Harold, as he followed Esther, "but alive I daresay she would have been less cheerful company."

"One would certainly think that she had just been unpacked from silver paper. Ah, how chivalrous you are!" said Esther, as Harold, kneeling on one knee, held her silken netting-stirrup for her to put her foot through. She had often fancied pleasant scenes in which such homage was rendered to her, and the homage was not disagreeable now it was really come; but, strangely enough, a little darting sensation at that moment was accompanied by the vivid remembrance of some one who had never paid the least attention to her foot. There had been a slight blush, such as often came and went rapidly, and she was silent a moment. Harold naturally believed that it was he himself who was filling the field of vision. He would have liked to place himself on the ottoman near Esther, and behave very much more like a lover; but he took a chair opposite to her at a circumspect distance. He dared not do otherwise. Along with Esther's playful charm she conveyed an impression of personal pride and high spirit which warned Harold's acuteness that in the delicacy of their present position he might easily make a false move and offend her. A woman was likely to be credulous about adoration, and to find no difficulty in referring it to her intrinsic attractions; but Esther was too dangerously quick and critical not to discern the least awkwardness that looked like offering her marriage as a convenient compromise for himself. Beforehand he might have said that such characteristics as hers were not lovable in a woman; but, as it was, he found that the hope of pleasing her had a piquancy quite new to him.

"I wonder," said Esther, breaking her silence in her usual light silvery tones — "I wonder whether the women who looked in that way ever felt any troubles. I see there are two old ones up-stairs in the billiard-room who have only got fat; the expression of their faces is just of the same sort."

"A woman ought never to have any trouble There should always be a man to guard her from it." (Harold Transome was masculine and fallible; he had incautiously sat down this morning to pay his addresses by talk about nothing in particular; and, clever experienced man as he was, he fell into nonsense.)

"But suppose the man himself got into trouble — you would wish her to mind about that. Or suppose," added Esther, suddenly looking up merrily at Harold, "the man himself was troublesome?"

"O you must not strain probabilities in that way. The generality of men are perfect. Take me, for example."

"You are a perfect judge of sauces," said Esther, who had her triumphs in letting Harold know that she was capable of taking notes.

"That is perfection number one. Pray go on."

"O, the catalogue is too long — I should be tired before I got to your magnificent ruby ring and your gloves always of the right colour."

"If you would let me tell you your perfections, I should not be tired."

"That is not complimentary; it means that the list is short."

"No; it means that the list is pleasant to dwell upon."

"Pray don't begin," said Esther, with her pretty toss of the head; "it would be dangerous to our good understanding. The person I liked best in the world was one who did nothing but scold me and tell me of my faults."

When Esther began to speak, she meant to do no more than make a remote unintelligible allusion, feeling, it must be owned, a naughty will to flirt and be saucy, and thwart Harold's attempts to be felicitous in compliment. But she had no sooner uttered the words than they seemed to her like a confession. A deep flush spread itself over her face and neck, and the sense that she was blushing went on deepening her colour. Harold felt himself unpleasantly illuminated as to a possibility that had never yet occurred to him. His surprise made an uncomfortable pause, in which Esther had time to feel much vexation.

"You speak in the past tense," said Harold, at last; "yet I am rather envious of that person. I shall never be able to win your regard in the same way. Is it any one at Treby? Because in that case I can inquire about your faults."

"O you know I have always lived among grave people," said Esther, more able to recover herself now she was spoken to. "Before I came home to be with my father I was nothing but a school-girl first, and then a teacher in different stages of growth. People in those circumstances are not usually flattered. But there are varieties in fault-finding. At our Paris school the master I liked best was an old man who stormed at me terribly when I read Racine, but yet showed that he was proud of me."

Esther was getting quite cool again. But Harold was not entirely satisfied; if there was any obstacle in his way, he wished to know exactly what it was.

"That must have been a wretched life for you at Treby," he said, — "a person of your accomplishments."

"I used to be dreadfully discontented," said Esther, much occupied with mistakes she had made in her netting. "But I was becoming less so. I have had time to get rather wise, you know; I am two-and-twenty."

"Yes," said Harold, rising and walking a few paces backwards and forwards, "you are past your majority; you are empress of your own fortunes — and more besides."

"Dear me," said Esther, letting her work fall, and leaning back against the cushions; "I don't think I know very well what to do with my empire."

"Well," said Harold, pausing in front of her, leaning one arm on the mantelpiece, and speaking very gravely, "I hope that in any case, since you appear to have no near relative who understands affairs, you will confide in me, and trust me with all your intentions as if I had no other personal concern in the matter than a regard for you. I hope you believe me capable of acting as the guardian of your interest, even where it turns out to be inevitably opposed to my own."

"I am sure you have given me reason to believe it," said Esther, with seriousness, putting out her hand to Harold. She had not been left in ignorance that he had had opportunities twice offered of stifling her claims.

Harold raised the hand to his lips, but dared not retain it more than an instant. Still the sweet reliance in Esther's manner made an irresistible temptation to him. After standing still a moment or two, while she bent over her work, he glided to the ottoman and seated himself close by her, looking at her busy hands.

"I see you have made mistakes in your work," he said, bending still nearer, for he saw that she was conscious, yet not angry.

"Nonsense! you know nothing about it," said Esther,

laughing, and crushing up the soft silk under her palms. "Those blunders have a design in them."

She looked round, and saw a handsome face very near her. Harold was looking, as he felt, thoroughly enamoured of this bright woman, who was not at all to his preconceived taste. Perhaps a touch of hypothetic jealousy now helped to heighten the effect. But he mastered all indiscretion, and only looked at her as he said,

"I am wondering whether you have any deep wishes and secrets that I can't guess."

"Pray don't speak of my wishes," said Esther, quite overmastered by this new and apparently involuntary manifestation in Harold; "I could not possibly tell you one at this moment — I think I shall never find them out again. O yes," she said, abruptly, struggling to relieve herself from the oppression of unintelligible feelings — "I do know one wish distinctly. I want to go and see my father. He writes me word that all is well with him, but still I want to see him."

"You shall be driven there when you like."

"May I go now — I mean as soon as it is convenient?" said Esther, rising.

"I will give the order immediately, if you wish it," said Harold, understanding that the audience was broken up.

CHAPTER XVII.

> He rates me as a merchant does the wares
> He will not purchase — "quality not high! —
> 'Twill lose its colour opened to the sun,
> Has no aroma, and, in fine, is naught —
> I barter not for such commodities —
> There is no ratio betwixt sand and gems."
> 'Tis wicked judgment! for the soul can grow,
> As embryos, that live and move but blindly,
> Burst from the dark, emerge regenerate,
> And lead a life of vision and of choice.

ESTHER did not take the carriage into Malthouse Lane, but left it to wait for her outside the town; and when she entered the house she put her finger on her lip to Lyddy and ran lightly up-stairs. She wished to surprise her father by this visit, and she succeeded. The little minister was just then almost surrounded by a wall of books, with merely his head peeping above them, being much embarrassed to find a substitute for tables and desks on which to arrange the volumes he kept open for reference. He was absorbed in mastering all those painstaking interpretations of the Book of Daniel, which are by this time well gone to the limbo of mistaken criticism; and Esther, as she opened the door softly, heard him rehearsing aloud a passage in which he declared, with some parenthetic provisoes, that he conceived not how a perverse ingenuity could blunt the edge of prophetic explicitness, or how an open mind could fail to see in the chronology of "the little horn" the resplendent lamp of an inspired symbol searching out the germinal growth of an antichristian power.

"You will not like me to interrupt you, father?" said Esther, slyly.

"Ah, my beloved child!" he exclaimed, upsetting a pile of books, and thus unintentionally making a convenient breach in his wall, through which Esther could get up to him and kiss him. "'Thy appearing is as a joy despaired of. I had thought of thee as the blinded think of the daylight — which indeed is a thing to rejoice in, like all other good, though we see it not nigh."

"Are you sure you have been as well and comfortable as you said you were in your letters?" said Esther, seating herself close in front of her father, and laying her hand on his shoulder.

"I wrote truly, my dear, according to my knowledge at the time. But to an old memory like mine the present days are but as a little water poured on the deep. It seems now that all has been as usual, except my studies, which have gone somewhat curiously into prophetic history. But I fear you will rebuke me for my negligent apparel," said the little man, feeling in front of Esther's brightness like a bat overtaken by the morning.

"That is Lyddy's fault, who sits crying over her want of Christian assurance instead of brushing your clothes and putting out your clean cravat. She is always saying her righteousness is filthy rags, and really I don't think that is a very strong expression for it. I'm sure it is dusty clothes and furniture."

"Nay, my dear, your playfulness glances too severely on our faithful Lyddy. Doubtless I am myself deficient, in that I do not aid her infirm memory by admonition. But now tell me aught that you have left untold about yourself. Your heart has gone out somewhat towards this family — the old man and the child, whom I had not reckoned of?"

"Yes, father. It is more and more difficult to me to see how I can make up my mind to disturb these people at all."

"Something should doubtless be devised to lighten the loss and the change to the aged father and mother. I would have you in any case seek to temper a vicissitude, which is nevertheless a providential arrangement not to be wholly set aside."

"Do you think, father — do you feel assured that a case of inheritance like this of mine is a sort of providential arrangement that makes a command?"

"I have so held it," said Mr. Lyon, solemnly; "in all my meditations I have so held it. For you have to consider, my dear, that you have been led by a peculiar path, and into experience which is not ordinarily the lot of those who are seated in high places; and what I have hinted to you already in my letters on this head, I shall wish on a future opportunity to enter into more at large."

Esther was uneasily silent. On this great question of her lot she saw doubts and difficulties, in which it seemed as if her father could not help her. There was no illumination for her in this theory of providential arrangement. She said suddenly (what she had not thought of at all suddenly),

"Have you been again to see Felix Holt, father? You have not mentioned him in your letters."

"I have been since I last wrote, my dear, and

I took his mother with me, who, I fear, made the time heavy to him with her plaints. But afterwards I carried her away to the house of a brother minister at Loamford, and returned to Felix, and then we had much discourse."

"Did you tell him of everything that has happened — I mean about me — about the Transomes?"

"Assuredly I told him, and he listened as one astonished. For he had much to hear, knowing nought of your birth, and that you had any other father than Rufus Lyon. 'Tis a narrative I trust I shall not be called on to give to others; but I was not without satisfaction in unfolding the truth to this young man, who hath wrought himself into my affection strangely — I would fain hope for ends that will be a visible good in his less way-worn life, when mine shall be no longer."

"And you told him how the Transomes had come, and that I was staying at Transome Court?"

"Yes, I told these things with some particularity, as is my wont concerning what hath imprinted itself on my mind."

"What did Felix say?"

"Truly, my dear, nothing desirable to recite," said Mr. Lyon, rubbing his hand over his brow.

"Dear father, he did say something, and you always remember what people say. Pray tell me; I want to know."

"It was a hasty remark, and rather escaped him than was consciously framed. He said, 'Then she will marry Transome; that is what Transome means.'"

"That was all?" said Esther, turning rather pale,

and biting her lip with the determination that the tears should not start.

"Yes, we did not go further into that branch of the subject. I apprehend there is no warrant for his seeming prognostic, and I should not be without disquiet if I thought otherwise. For I confess that in your accession to this great position and property, I contemplate with hopeful satisfaction your remaining attached to that body of congregational Dissent, which, as I hold, hath retained most of pure and primitive discipline. Your education and peculiar history would thus be seen to have coincided with a long train of events in making this family property a mean of honouring and illustrating a purer form of Christianity than that which hath unhappily obtained the pre-eminence in this land. I speak, my child, as you know, always in the hope that you will fully join our communion; and this dear wish of my heart — nay, this urgent prayer — would seem to be frustrated by your marriage with a man, of whom there is at least no visible indication that he would unite himself to our body."

If Esther had been less agitated, she would hardly have helped smiling at the picture her father's words suggested of Harold Transome "joining the church" in Malthouse Yard. But she was too seriously preoccupied with what Felix had said, which hurt her in a two-edged fashion that was highly significant. First, she was angry with him for daring to say positively whom she would marry; secondly, she was angry at the implication that there was from the first a cool deliberate design in Harold Transome to marry her. Esther said to herself that she was quite capable of discerning

Harold Transome's disposition, and judging of his conduct. She felt sure he was generous and open. It did not lower him in her opinion that since circumstances had brought them together he evidently admired her — was in love with her — in short, desired to marry her; and she thought that she discerned the delicacy which hindered him from being more explicit. There is no point on which young women are more easily piqued than this of their sufficiency to judge the men who make love to them. And Esther's generous nature delighted to believe in generosity. All these thoughts were making a tumult in her mind while her father was suggesting the radiance her lot might cast on the cause of congregational Dissent. She heard what he said, and remembered it afterwards, but she made no reply at present, and chose rather to start up in search of a brush — an action which would seem to her father quite a usual sequence with her. It served the purpose of diverting him from a lengthy subject.

"Have you yet spoken with Mr. Transome concerning Mistress Holt, my dear?" he said, as Esther was moving about the room. "I hinted to him that you would best decide how assistance should be tendered to her."

"No, father, we have not approached the subject. Mr. Transome may have forgotten it, and, for several reasons, I would rather not talk of this — of money matters to him at present. There is money due to me from the Lukyns and the Pendrells."

"They have paid it," said Mr. Lyon, opening his desk. "I have it here ready to deliver to you."

"Keep it, father, and pay Mrs. Holt's rent with it, and do anything else that is wanted for her. We must consider everything temporary now," said Esther, enveloping her father in a towel, and beginning to brush his auburn fringe of hair, while he shut his eyes in preparation for this pleasant passivity. "Everything is uncertain — what may become of Felix — what may become of us all. O dear!" she went on, changing suddenly to laughing merriment, "I am beginning to talk like Lyddy, I think."

"Truly," said Mr. Lyon, smiling, "the uncertainty of things is a text rather too wide and obvious for fruitful application; and to discourse of it is, as one may say, to bottle up the air, and make a present of it to those who are already standing out of doors."

"Do you think," said Esther, in the course of their chat, "that the Treby people know at all about the reasons of my being at Transome Court?"

"I have had no sign thereof; and indeed there is no one, as it appears, who could make the story public. The man Christian is away in London with Mr. Debarry, Parliament now beginning; and Mr. Jermyn would doubtless respect the confidence of the Transomes. I have not seen him lately. I know nothing of his movements. And so far as my own speech is concerned, and my strict command to Lyddy, I have withheld the means of information even as to your having returned to Transome Court in the carriage, not wishing to give any occasion to solicitous questioning till time hath somewhat inured me. But it hath got abroad that you are there, and is the subject of conjectures, whereof, I imagine, the chief is, that you are gone as companion to Mistress Transome; for some of our friends have already hinted a rebuke to me that I should permit your taking a position so little likely to further your spiritual welfare."

"Now, father, I think I shall be obliged to run away from you, not to keep the carriage too long," said Esther, as she finished her reforms in the minister's toilette. "You look beautiful now, and I must give Lyddy a little lecture before I go."

"Yes, my dear; I would not detain you, seeing that my duties demand me. But take with you this Treatise, which I have purposely selected. It concerns all the main questions between ourselves and the Establishment — government, discipline, State-support. It is seasonable that you should give a nearer attention to these polemics, lest you be drawn aside by the fallacious association of a State Church with elevated rank."

Esther chose to take the volume submissively, rather than to adopt the ungraceful sincerity of saying that she was unable at present to give her mind to the original functions of a bishop, or the comparative merit of Endowments and Voluntaryism. But she did not run her eyes over the pages during her solitary drive to get a foretaste of the argument, for she was entirely occupied with Felix Holt's prophecy that she would marry Harold Transome.

CHAPTER XVIII.

*Thou sayst it, and not I; for thou hast done
The ugly deed that made these ugly words.*
SOPHOCLES: *Electra.*

*Yes, it becomes a man
To cherish memory, where he had delight.
For kindness is the natural birth of kindness.
Whose soul records not the great debt of joy,
Is stamped for ever an ignoble man.*
SOPHOCLES: *Ajax.*

IT so happened that, on the morning of the day when Esther went to see her father, Jermyn had not yet heard of her presence at Transome Court. One fact conducing to keep him in this ignorance was, that some days after his critical interview with Harold — days during which he had been wondering how long it would be before Harold made up his mind to sacrifice the luxury of satisfied anger for the solid advantage of securing fortune and position — he was peremptorily called away by business to the south of England, and was obliged to inform Harold by letter of his absence. He took care also to notify his return; but Harold made no sign in reply. The days passed without bringing him any gossip concerning Esther's visit, for such gossip was almost confined to Mr. Lyon's congregation, her Church pupils, Miss Louisa Jermyn among them, having been satisfied by her father's written statement that she was gone on a visit of uncertain duration. But on this day of Esther's call in Malthouse Yard, the Miss Jermyns in their walk saw her getting into the Transomes' carriage, which they had previously observed to be waiting, and which they now saw bowled along on the road towards Little Treby. It followed that only a few hours later the news reached the astonished ears of Matthew Jermyn.

Entirely ignorant of those converging indications and small links of incident which had raised Christian's conjectures, and had gradually contributed to put him in possession of the facts; ignorant too of some busy motives in the mind of his obliged servant Johnson; Jermyn was not likely to see at once how the momentous information that Esther was the surviving Bycliffe could possibly have reached Harold. His daughters naturally leaped, as others had done, to the conclusion that the Transomes, seeking a governess for little Harry, had had their choice directed to Esther, and observed that they must have attracted her by a high salary to induce her to take charge of such a small pupil; though of course it was important that his English and French should be carefully attended to from the first. Jermyn, hearing this suggestion, was not without a momentary hope that it might be true, and that Harold was still safely unconscious of having under the same roof with him the legal claimant of the family estate.

But a mind in the grasp of a terrible anxiety is not credulous of easy solutions. The one stay that bears up our hopes is sure to appear frail, and if looked at long will seem to totter. Too much depended on that unconsciousness of Harold's; and although Jermyn did not see the course of things that could have disclosed and combined the various items of knowledge which he had imagined to be his own secret, and therefore his safeguard, he saw quite clearly what was likely to be the result of the disclosure. Not only would Harold Transome be no longer afraid of him, but also, by marrying Esther (and Jermyn at once felt sure of this issue), he would be triumphantly freed from any unpleasant consequences, and could pursue much at his ease the gratification of ruining Matthew Jermyn. The prevision of an enemy's triumphant ease is in any case sufficiently irritating to hatred, and there were reasons why it was peculiarly exasperating here; but Jermyn had not the leisure now for mere fruitless emotion: he had to think of a possible device which might save him from imminent ruin — not an indefinite adversity, but a ruin in detail, which his thoughts painted out with the sharpest, ugliest intensity. A man of sixty, with an unsuspicious wife and daughters capable of shrieking and fainting at a sudden revelation, and of looking at him reproachfully in their daily misery under a shabby lot to which he had reduced them — with a mind and with habits dried hard by the years — with no glimpse of an endurable standing-ground except where he could domineer and be prosperous according to the ambitions of pushing middle-class gentility, — such a man is likely to find the prospect of worldly ruin ghastly enough to drive him to the most uninviting means of escape. He will probably prefer any private scorn that will save him from public infamy or that will leave him money in his pocket, to the humiliation and hardship of new servitude in old age, a shabby hat, and a melancholy hearth, where the firing must be used charily and the women look sad. But though a man may be willing to escape through a sewer, a sewer with an outlet into the dry air is not always at hand. Running away, especially when spoken of as absconding, seems at a distance to offer a good modern substitute for the right of sanctuary; but seen closely, it is often found inconvenient and scarcely possible.

Jermyn, on thoroughly considering his position, saw that he had no very agreeable resources at command. But he soon made up his mind what he would do next. He wrote to Mrs. Transome requesting her to appoint an hour in which he could see her privately: he knew she would understand that it was to be an hour when Harold was not at home. As he sealed the letter, he indulged a faint hope that in this interview he might be assured of Esther's birth being unknown at Transome Court; but in the worst case, perhaps some help might be found in Mrs. Transome. To such uses may tender relations come when they have ceased to be tender! The Hazaels of our world who are pushed on quickly against their preconceived confidence in themselves to do doglike actions by the sudden suggestion of a wicked ambition, are much fewer than those who are led on through the years by the gradual demands of a selfishness which has spread its fibres far and wide through the intricate vanities and sordid cares of an everyday existence.

In consequence of that letter to Mrs. Transome, Jermyn was two days afterwards ushered into the smaller drawing-room at Transome Court. It was a charming little room in its refurbished condition: it had two pretty inlaid cabinets, great china vases with contents that sent forth odours of paradise, groups of flowers in oval frames on the walls, and Mrs. Transome's own portrait in the evening costume of 1800, with a garden in the background. That brilliant young woman looked smilingly down on Mr. Jermyn as he passed in front of the fire; and at present hers was the only gaze in the room. He could not help meeting the gaze as he waited, holding his hat behind him — could not help seeing many memories lit up by it; but the strong bent of his mind was to go on arguing each memory into a claim, and to see in the regard others had for him a merit of his own. There had been plenty of roads open to him when he was a young man; perhaps if he had not allowed himself to be determined (chiefly, of course, by the feelings of others, for of what effect would his own feelings have been without them?) into the road he actually took, he might have done better for himself. At any rate, he was likely at last to get the worst of it, and it was he who had most reason to complain. The fortunate Jason, as we know from Euripides, piously thanked the goddess, and saw clearly that he was not at all obliged to Medea: Jermyn was perhaps not aware of the precedent, but thought out his own freedom from obligation and the indebtedness of others towards him with a native faculty not inferior to Jason's.

Before three minutes had passed, however, as if by some sorcery, the brilliant smiling young woman above the mantelpiece seemed to be appearing at the doorway withered and frosted by many winters, and with lips and eyes from which the smile had departed. Jermyn advanced, and they shook hands, but neither of them said anything by way of greeting. Mrs. Transome seated herself, and pointed to a chair opposite and near her.

"Harold has gone to Loamford," she said, in a subdued tone. "You had something particular to say to me?"

"Yes," said Jermyn, with his soft and deferential air. "The last time I was here I could not take the opportunity of speaking to you. But I am anxious to know whether you are aware of what has passed between me and Harold?"

"Yes, he has told me everything."

"About his proceedings against me? and the reason he stopped them?"

"Yes: have you had notice that he has begun them again?"

"No," said Jermyn, with a very unpleasant sensation.

"Of course he will now," said Mrs. Transome. "There is no reason in his mind why he should not."

"Has he resolved to risk the estate then?"

"He feels in no danger on that score. And if there were, the danger doesn't depend on you. The most likely thing is, that he will marry this girl."

"He knows everything then?" said Jermyn, the expression of his face getting clouded.

"Everything. It's of no use for you to think of mastering him: you can't do it. I used to wish Harold to be fortunate — and he is fortunate," said Mrs. Transome, with intense bitterness. "It's not my star that he inherits."

"Do you know how he came by the information about this girl?"

"No; but she knew it all before we spoke to her. It's no secret."

Jermyn was confounded by this hopeless frustration to which he had no key. Though he thought of Christian, the thought shed no light; but the more fatal point was clear: he held no secret that could help him.

"You are aware that these Chancery proceedings may ruin me?"

"He told me they would. But if you are imagining that I can do anything, dismiss the notion. I have told him as plainly as I dare that I wish him to drop all public quarrel with you, and that you could make an arrangement without scandal. I can do no more. He will not listen to me; he doesn't mind about my feelings. He cares more for Mr. Transome than he does for me. He will not listen to me any more than if I were an old ballad-singer."

"It's very hard on *me*, I know," said Jermyn, in the tone with which a man flings out a reproach.

"I besought you three months ago to bear anything rather than quarrel with him."

"I have not quarrelled with him. It is he who has been always seeking a quarrel with me. I have borne a good deal — more than any one else would. He set his teeth against me from the first."

"He saw things that annoyed him; and men are not like women," said Mrs. Transome. There was a bitter innuendo in that truism.

"It's very hard on me — I know that," said Jermyn, with an intensification of his previous tone, rising and walking a step or two, then turning and laying his hand on the back of the chair. "Of course the law in this case can't in the least represent the justice of the matter. I made a good many sacrifices in times past.

I gave up a great deal of fine business for the sake of attending to the family affairs, and in that lawsuit they would have gone to rack and ruin if it hadn't been for me."

He moved away again, laid down his hat, which he had been previously holding, and thrust his hands into his pockets as he returned. Mrs. Transome sat motionless as marble, and almost as pale. Her hands lay crossed on her knees. This man, young, slim, and graceful, with a selfishness which then took the form of homage to her, had at one time kneeled to her and kissed those hands fervently; and she had thought there was a poetry in such passion beyond any to be found in everyday domesticity.

"I stretched my conscience a good deal in that affair of Bycliffe, as you know perfectly well. I told you everything at the time. I told you I was very uneasy about those witnesses, and about getting him thrown into prison. I know it's the blackest thing anybody could charge me with, if they knew my life from beginning to end; and I should never have done it, if I had not been under an infatuation such as makes a man do anything. What did it signify to me about the loss of the lawsuit? I was a young bachelor — I had the world before me."

"Yes," said Mrs. Transome, in a low tone. "It was a pity you didn't make another choice."

"What would have become of you?" said Jermyn, carried along a climax, like other self-justifiers. "I had to think of you. You would not have liked me to make another choice then."

"Clearly," said Mrs. Transome, with concentrated

bitterness, but still quietly; "the greater mistake was mine."

Egoism is usually stupid in a dialogue; but Jermyn's did not make him so stupid that he did not feel the edge of Mrs. Transome's words. They increased his irritation.

"I hardly see that," he replied, with a slight laugh of scorn. "You had an estate and a position to save, to go no farther. I remember very well what you said to me — 'A clever lawyer can do anything if he has the will; if it's impossible, he will make it possible. And the property is sure to be Harold's some day.' He was a baby then."

"I remember most things a little too well: you had better say at once what is your object in recalling them."

"An object that is nothing more than justice. With the relation I stood in, it was not likely I should think myself bound by all the forms that are made to bind strangers. I had often immense trouble to raise the money necessary to pay off debts and carry on the affairs; and, as I said before, I had given up other lines of advancement which would have been open to me if I had not stayed in this neighbourhood at a critical time when I was fresh to the world. Anybody who knew the whole circumstances would say that my being hunted and run down on the score of my past transactions with regard to the family affairs, is an abominably unjust and unnatural thing."

Jermyn paused a moment, and then added, "At my time of life . . . and with a family about me — and after what has passed . . . I should have thought there was nothing you would care more to prevent."

"I do care. It makes me miserable. That is the extent of my power — to feel miserable."

"No, it is not the extent of your power. You could save me if you would. It is not to be supposed that Harold would go on against me ... if he knew the whole truth."

Jermyn had sat down before he uttered the last words. He had lowered his voice slightly. He had the air of one who thought that he had prepared the way for an understanding. That a man with so much sharpness, with so much suavity at command — a man who piqued himself on his persuasiveness towards women, — should behave just as Jermyn did on this occasion, would be surprising, but for the constant experience that temper and selfish insensibility will defeat excellent gifts — will make a sensible person shout when shouting is out of place, and will make a polished man rude when his polish might be of eminent use to him.

As Jermyn, sitting down and leaning forward with an elbow on his knee, uttered his last words — "if he knew the whole truth" — a slight shock seemed to pass through Mrs. Transome's hitherto motionless body, followed by a sudden light in her eyes, as in an animal's about to spring.

"And you expect me to tell him?" she said, not loudly, but yet with a clear metallic ring in her voice.

"Would it not be right for him to know?" said Jermyn, in a more bland and persuasive tone than he had yet used.

Perhaps some of the most terrible irony of the human lot is this of a deep truth coming to be uttered by lips that have no right to it.

"I will never tell him!" said Mrs. Transome, starting up, her whole frame thrilled with a passion that seemed almost to make her young again. Her hands hung beside her clenched tightly, her eyes and lips lost the helpless repressed bitterness of discontent, and seemed suddenly fed with energy. "You reckon up your sacrifices for me: you have kept a good account of them, and it is needful; they are some of them what no one else could guess or find out. But you made your sacrifices when they seemed pleasant to you; when you told me they were your happiness; when you told me that it was I who stooped, and I who bestowed favours."

Jermyn rose too, and laid his hand on the back of the chair. He had grown visibly paler, but seemed about to speak.

"Don't speak!" Mrs. Transome said peremptorily. "Don't open your lips again. You have said enough; I will speak now. I have made sacrifices too, but it was when I knew that they were not my happiness. It was after I saw that I *had* stooped — after I saw that your tenderness had turned into calculation — after I saw that you cared for yourself only, and not for me. I heard your explanations — of your duty in life — of our mutual reputation — of a virtuous young lady attached to you. I bore it; I let everything go; I shut my eyes; I might almost have let myself starve, rather than have scenes of quarrel with the man I had loved, in which I must accuse him of turning my love into a good bargain." There was a slight tremor in Mrs. Transome's voice in the last words, and for a moment she paused; but when she spoke again it seemed as if the tremor had frozen into a cutting icicle. "I suppose if a lover picked one's pocket, there's no woman would like to own it. I don't say I was not afraid of you: I *was* afraid of you, and I know now I was right."

"Mrs. Transome," said Jermyn, white to the lips, "it is needless to say more. I withdraw any words that have offended you."

"You can't withdraw them. Can a man apologise for being a dastard? . . . And I have caused you to strain your conscience, have I? — it is I who have sullied your purity? I should think the demons have more honour — they are not so impudent to one another. I would not lose the misery of being a woman, now I see what can be the baseness of a man. One must be a man — first to tell a woman that her love has made her your debtor, and then ask her to pay you by breaking the last poor threads between her and her son."

"I do not ask it," said Jermyn, with a certain asperity. He was beginning to find this intolerable. The mere brute strength of a masculine creature rebelled. He felt almost inclined to throttle the voice out of this woman.

"You do ask it: it is what you would like. I have had a terror on me lest evil should happen to you. From the first, after Harold came home, I had a horrible dread. It seemed as if murder might come between you — I didn't know what. I felt the horror of his not knowing the truth. I might have been dragged at last, by my own feeling — by my own memory — to tell him all, and make him as well as myself miserable, to save you."

Again there was a slight tremor, as if at the remembrance of womanly tenderness and pity. But immediately she launched forth again.

"But now you have asked me, I will never tell him! Be ruined — no — do something more dastardly to save yourself. If I sinned, my judgment went beforehand — that I should sin for a man like you."

Swiftly upon those last words Mrs. Transome passed out of the room. The softly-padded door closed behind her making no noise, and Jermyn found himself alone.

For a brief space he stood still. Human beings in moments of passionate reproach and denunciation, especially when their anger is on their own account, are never so wholly in the right that the person who has to wince cannot possibly protest against some unreasonableness or unfairness in their outburst. And if Jermyn had been capable of feeling that he had thoroughly merited this infliction, he would not have uttered the words that drew it down on him. Men do not become penitent and learn to abhor themselves by having their backs cut open with the lash; rather, they learn to abhor the lash. What Jermyn felt about Mrs. Transome when she disappeared was, that she was a furious woman — who would not do what he wanted her to do. And he was supported as to his justifiableness by the inward repetition of what he had already said to her: it was right that Harold should know the truth. He did not take into account (how should he?) the exasperation and loathing excited by his daring to urge the plea of right. A man who had stolen the pyx, and got frightened when justice was at his heels, might feel the sort of penitence which would induce him to run back in the dark and lay the pyx where the sexton might find it; but if in doing so he whispered to the Blessed Virgin that he was moved by considering the sacredness of all property, and the peculiar sacredness of the pyx, it is not to be believed that she would like him the better for it. Indeed, one often seems to see why the saints should prefer candles to words, especially from penitents whose skin is in danger. Some salt of generosity would have made Jermyn conscious that he had lost the citizenship which authorised him to plead the right; still more, that his self-vindication to Mrs. Transome would be like the exhibition of a brand-mark, and only show that he was shame-proof. There is heroism even in the circles of hell for fellow-sinners who cling to each other in the fiery whirlwind and never recriminate. But these things, which are easy to discern when they are painted for us on the large canvas of poetic story, become confused and obscure even for well-read gentlemen when their affection for themselves is alarmed by pressing details of actual experience. If their comparison of instances is active at such times, it is chiefly in showing them that their own case has subtle distinctions from all other cases, which should free them from unmitigated condemnation.

And it was in this way with Matthew Jermyn. So many things were more distinctly visible to him, and touched him more acutely, than the effect of his acts or words on Mrs. Transome's feelings! In fact — he asked, with a touch of something that makes us all akin — was it not preposterous, this excess of feeling on points which he himself did not find powerfully moving? She had treated him most unreasonably. It would have been right for her to do what he had —

not asked, but only hinted at in a mild and interrogatory manner. But the clearest and most unpleasant result of the interview was, that this right thing which he desired so much would certainly not be done for him by Mrs. Transome.

As he was moving his arm from the chair-back, and turning to take his hat, there was a boisterous noise in the entrance-hall; the door of the small drawing-room, which had closed without latching, was pushed open, and old Mr. Transome appeared with a face of feeble delight, playing horse to little Harry, who roared and flogged behind him, while Moro yapped in a puppy voice at their heels. But when Mr. Transome saw Jermyn in the room he stood still in the doorway, as if he did not know whether entrance were permissible. The majority of his thoughts were but ravelled threads of the past. The attorney came forward to shake hands with due politeness, but the old man said, with a bewildered look, and in a hesitating way,

"Mr. Jermyn? — why — why — where is Mrs. Transome?"

Jermyn smiled his way out past the unexpected group; and little Harry, thinking he had an eligible opportunity, turned round to give a parting stroke on the stranger's coat-tails.

CHAPTER XIX.

*Whichever way my days decline,
I felt and feel, though left alone,
His being working in mine own,
The footsteps of his life in mine.*

. . . .
*Dear friend, far off, my lost desire,
So far, so near, in woe and weal;
O, loved the most when most I feel
There is a lower and a higher!*
— TENNYSON: *In Memoriam.*

AFTER that morning on which Esther found herself reddened and confused by the sense of having made a distant allusion to Felix Holt, she felt it impossible that she should even, as she had sometimes intended, speak of him explicitly to Harold, in order to discuss the probabilities as to the issue of his trial. She was certain she could not do it without betraying emotion, and there were very complex reasons in Esther's mind why she could not bear that Harold should detect her sensibility on this subject. It was not only all the fibres of maidenly pride and reserve, of a bashfulness undefinably peculiar towards this man, who, while much older than herself, and bearing the stamp of an experience quite hidden from her imagination, was taking strongly the aspect of a lover — it was not only this exquisite kind of shame which was at work within her: there was another sort of susceptibility in Esther, which her present circumstances tended to encourage, though she had come to regard it as not at all lofty, but rather as something which condemned her

to littleness in comparison with a mind she had learned
to venerate. She knew quite well that, to Harold
Transome, Felix Holt was one of the common people
who could come into question in no other than a public
light. She had a native capability for discerning that
the sense of ranks and degrees has its repulsions corresponding to the repulsions dependent on difference
of race and colour; and she remembered her own impressions too well not to foresee that it would come on
Harold Transome as a shock, if he suspected there had
been any love-passages between her and this young
man, who to him was of course no more than any
other intelligent member of the working class. "To
him," said Esther to herself, with a reaction of her
newer, better pride, "who has not had the sort of intercourse in which Felix Holt's cultured nature would
have asserted its superiority." And in her fluctuations
on this matter, she found herself mentally protesting
that, whatever Harold might think, there was a light
in which he was vulgar compared with Felix. Felix
had ideas and motives which she did not believe that
Harold could understand. More than all, there was
this test: she herself had no sense of inferiority and
just subjection when she was with Harold Transome;
there were even points in him for which she felt a
touch, not of angry, but of playful scorn; whereas with
Felix she had always a sense of dependence and possible illumination. In those large, grave, candid grey
eyes of his, love seemed something that belonged to
the high enthusiasm of life, such as might now be for
ever shut out from her.

All the same, her vanity winced at the idea that
Harold should discern what, from his point of view,

would seem like a degradation of her taste and refinement. She could not help being gratified by all the manifestations from those around her that she was thought thoroughly fitted for a high position — could not help enjoying, with more or less keenness, a rehearsal of that demeanour amongst luxuries and dignities which had often been a part of her daydreams, and the rehearsal included the reception of more and more emphatic attentions from Harold, and of an effusiveness in his manners, which, in proportion as it would have been offensive if it had appeared earlier, became flattering as the effect of a growing acquaintance and daily contact. It comes in so many forms in this life of ours — the knowledge that there is something sweetest and noblest of which we despair, and the sense of something present that solicits us with an immediate and easy indulgence. And there is a pernicious falsity in the pretence that a woman's love lies above the range of such temptations.

Day after day Esther had an arm offered her, had very beaming looks upon her, had opportunities for a great deal of light, airy talk, in which she knew herself to be charming, and had the attractive interest of noticing Harold's practical cleverness — the masculine ease with which he governed everybody and administered everything about him, without the least harshness, and with a facile good-nature which yet was not weak. In the background, too, there was the ever-present consideration, that if Harold Transome wished to marry her, and she accepted him, the problem of her lot would be more easily solved than in any other way. It was difficult by any theory of Providence, or consideration of results, to see a course which she could call duty: if something would come and urge itself strongly as pleasure, and save her from the effort to find a clue of principle amid the labyrinthine confusions of right and possession, the promise could not but seem alluring. And yet, this life at Transome Court was *not* the life of her day-dreams: there was dulness already in its ease, and in the absence of high demand; and there was the vague consciousness that the love of this not unfascinating man who hovered about her gave an air of moral mediocrity to all her prospects. She would not have been able perhaps to define this impression; but somehow or other by this elevation of fortune it seemed that the higher ambition which had begun to spring in her was for ever nullified. All life seemed cheapened; as it might seem to a young student who, having believed that to gain a certain degree he must write a thesis in which he would bring his powers to bear with memorable effect, suddenly ascertained that no thesis was expected, but the sum (in English money) of twenty-seven pounds ten shillings and sixpence.

After all, she was a woman, and could not make her own lot. As she had once said to Felix, "A woman must choose meaner things, because only meaner things are offered to her." Her lot is made for her by the love she accepts. And Esther began to think that her lot was being made for her by the love that was surrounding her with the influence of a garden on a summer morning.

Harold, on his side, was conscious that the interest of his wooing was not standing still. He was beginning to think it a conquest, in which it would be disappointing to fail, even if this fair nymph had no

claim to the estate. He would have liked — and yet
he would not have liked — that just a slight shadow
of doubt as to his success should be removed. There
was something about Esther that he did not altogether
understand. She was clearly a woman that could be
governed; she was too charming for him to fear that
she would ever be obstinate or interfering. Yet there
was a lightning that shot out of her now and then,
which seemed the sign of a dangerous judgment; as if
she inwardly saw something more admirable than Harold
Transome. Now, to be perfectly charming, a woman
should not see this.

One fine February day, when already the golden
and purple crocuses were out on the terrace — one of
those flattering days which sometimes precede the north-
east winds of March, and make believe that the coming
spring will be enjoyable — a very striking group, of
whom Esther and Harold made a part, came out at
mid-day to walk upon the gravel at Transome Court.
They did not, as usual, go towards the pleasure-grounds
on the eastern side, because Mr. Lingon, who was one
of them, was going home, and his road lay through the
stone gateway into the park.

Uncle Lingon, who disliked painful confidences,
and preferred knowing "no mischief of anybody," had
not objected to being let into the important secret
about Esther, and was sure at once that the whole
affair, instead of being a misfortune, was a piece of
excellent luck. For himself, he did not profess to be
a judge of women, but she seemed to have all the
"points," and to carry herself as well as Arabella did,
which was saying a good deal. Honest Jack Lingon's
first impressions quickly became traditions, which no

subsequent evidence could disturb. He was fond of
his sister, and seemed never to be conscious of any
change for the worse in her since their early time. He
considered that man a beast who said anything unpleasant about the persons to whom he was attached.
It was not that he winked; his wide-open eyes saw
nothing but what his easy disposition inclined him to
see. Harold was a good fellow; a clever chap; and
Esther's peculiar fitness for him, under all the circumstances, was extraordinary: it reminded him of something in the classics, though he couldn't think exactly
what — in fact, a memory was a nasty uneasy thing.
Esther was always glad when the old Rector came.
With an odd contrariety to her former niceties she
liked his rough attire and careless frank speech; they
were something not point device that seemed to connect
the life of Transome Court with that rougher, commoner
world where her home had been.

She and Harold were walking a little in advance
of the rest of the party, who were retarded by various
causes. Old Mr. Transome, wrapped in a cloth cloak
trimmed with sable, and with a soft warm cap also
trimmed with fur on his head, had a shuffling uncertain walk. Little Harry was dragging a toy-vehicle,
on the seat of which he had insisted on tying Moro,
with a piece of scarlet drapery round him, making him
look like a barbaric prince in a chariot. Moro, having
little imagination, objected to this, and barked with
feeble snappishness as the tyrannous lad ran forward,
then whirled the chariot round, and ran back to
"Gappa," then came to a dead stop, which overset the
chariot, that he might watch Uncle Lingon's water-
spaniel run for the hurled stick and bring it in his

mouth. Nimrod kept close to his old master's legs, glancing with much indifference at this youthful ardour about sticks — he had "gone through all that;" and Dominic walked by, looking on blandly, and taking care both of young and old. Mrs. Transome was not there.

Looking back and seeing that they were a good deal in advance of the rest, Esther and Harold paused.

"What do you think about thinning the trees over there?" said Harold, pointing with his stick. "I have a bit of a notion that if they were divided into clumps so as to show the oaks beyond, it would be a great improvement. It would give an idea of extent that is lost now. And there might be some very pretty clumps got out of those mixed trees. What do you think?"

"I should think it would be an improvement. One likes a 'beyond' everywhere. But I never heard you express yourself so dubiously," said Esther, looking at him rather archly: "you generally see things so clearly, and are so convinced, that I shall begin to feel quite tottering if I find you in uncertainty. Pray don't begin to be doubtful; it is so infectious."

"You think me a great deal too sure — too confident?" said Harold.

"Not at all. It is an immense advantage to know your own will, when you always mean to have it."

"But suppose I couldn't get it, in spite of meaning?" said Harold, with a beaming inquiry in his eyes.

"O then," said Esther, turning her head aside, carelessly, as if she were considering the distant birchstems, "you would bear it quite easily, as you did your not getting into Parliament. You would know you could get it another time — or get something else as good."

"The fact is," said Harold, moving on a little, as if he did not want to be quite overtaken by the others, "you consider me a fat, fatuous, self-satisfied fellow."

"O there are degrees," said Esther, with a silvery laugh; "you have just as much of those qualities as is becoming. There are different styles. You are perfect in your own."

"But you prefer another style, I suspect. A more submissive, tearful, devout worshipper, who would offer his incense with more trembling."

"You are quite mistaken," said Esther, still lightly. "I find I am very wayward. When anything is offered to me, it seems that I prize it less, and don't want to have it."

Here was a very baulking answer, but in spite of it Harold could not help believing that Esther was very far from objecting to the sort of incense he had been offering just then.

"I have often read that that is in human nature," she went on, "yet it takes me by surprise in myself. I suppose," she added, smiling, "I didn't think of myself as human nature."

"I don't confess to the same waywardness," said Harold. "I am very fond of things that I can get. And I never longed much for anything out of my reach. Whatever I feel sure of getting I like all the better. I think half those priggish maxims about human nature in the lump are no more to be relied on than universal remedies. There are different sorts of human nature. Some are given to discontent and longing, others to securing and enjoying. And let me tell you, the discontented longing style is unpleasant to live with."

Harold nodded with a meaning smile at Esther.

"O, I assure you I have abjured all admiration for it," she said, smiling up at him in return.

She was remembering the schooling Felix had given her about her Byronic heroes, and was inwardly adding a third sort of human nature to those varieties which Harold had mentioned. He naturally supposed that he might take the abjuration to be entirely in his own favour. And his face did look very pleasant; she could not help liking him, although he was certainly too particular about sauces, gravies, and wines; and had a way of virtually measuring the value of everything by the contribution it made to his own pleasure. His very good-nature was unsympathetic: it never came from any thorough understanding or deep respect for what was in the mind of the person he obliged or indulged; it was like his kindness to his mother — an arrangement of his for the happiness of others, which, if they were sensible, ought to succeed. And an inevitable comparison which haunted her, showed her the same quality in his political views: the utmost enjoyment of his own advantages was the solvent that blended pride in his family and position with the adhesion to changes that were to obliterate tradition and melt down enchased gold heirlooms into plating for the egg-spoons of "the people." It is terrible — the keen bright eye of a woman when it has once been turned with admiration on what is severely true; but then, the severely true rarely comes within its range of vision. Esther had had an unusual illumination; Harold did not know how, but he discerned enough of the effect to make him more cautious than he had ever been in his life before. That caution would have prevented him just then from following up the question as to the style of person Esther would think pleasant to live with, even if Uncle Lingon had not joined them, as he did, to talk about soughing tiles; saying presently that he should turn across the grass and get on to the Home Farm, to have a look at the improvements that Harold was making with such racing speed.

"But you know, lad," said the Rector, as they paused at the expected parting, "you can't do everything in a hurry. The wheat must have time to grow, even when you've reformed all us old Tories off the face of the ground. Dash it! now the election's over: I'm an old Tory again. You see, Harold, a Radical won't do for the county. At another election, you must be on the look-out for a borough where they want a bit of blood. I should have liked you uncommonly to stand for the county; and a Radical of good family squares well enough with a new-fashioned Tory like young Debarry; but you see, these riots — it's been a nasty business. I shall have my hair combed at the sessions for a year to come. But, heyday! What dame is this, with a small boy? — not one of my parishioners?"

Harold and Esther turned, and saw an elderly woman advancing with a tiny red-haired boy, scantily attired as to his jacket, which merged into a small sparrow-tail a little higher than his waist, but muffled as to his throat with a blue woollen comforter. Esther recognised the pair too well, and felt very uncomfortable. We are so pitiably in subjection to all sorts of vanity — even the very vanities we are practically renouncing! And in spite of the almost solemn memories connected with Mrs. Holt, Esther's first shudder was raised by the idea of what things this woman would say, and by the mortification of having Felix in any way represented by his mother.

As Mrs. Holt advanced into closer observation, it became more evident that she was attired with a view not to charm the eye, but rather to afflict it with all that expression of woe which belongs to very rusty bombazine and the limpest state of false hair. Still, she was not a woman to lose the sense of her own value, or become abject in her manners under any circumstances of depression; and she had a peculiar sense on the present occasion that she was justly relying on the force of her own character and judgment, in independence of anything that Mr. Lyon or the masterful Felix would have said, if she had thought them worthy to know of her undertaking. She curtsied once, as if to the entire group, now including even the dogs, who showed various degrees of curiosity, especially as to what kind of game the smaller animal Job might prove to be after due investigation; and then she proceeded at once towards Esther, who, in spite of her annoyance, took her arm from Harold's, said, "How do you do, Mrs. Holt?" very kindly, and stooped to pat little Job.

"Yes — you know him, Miss Lyon," said Mrs. Holt, in that tone which implies that the conversation is intended for the edification of the company generally; "you know the orphin child, as Felix brought home for me that am his mother to take care of. And it's what I've done — nobody more so — though it's trouble is my reward."

Esther had raised herself again, to stand in helpless endurance of whatever might be coming. But by this time young Harry, struck even more than the dogs by the appearance of Job Tudge, had come round dragging his chariot, and placed himself close to the pale child, whom he exceeded in height and breadth, as well as in depth of colouring. He looked into Job's eyes, peeped round at the tail of his jacket and pulled it a little, and then, taking off the tiny cloth-cap, observed with much interest the tight red curls which had been hidden underneath it. Job looked at his inspector with the round blue eyes of astonishment, until Harry, purely by way of experiment, took a bonbon from a fantastic wallet which hung over his shoulder, and applied the test to Job's lips. The result was satisfactory to both. Every one had been watching this small comedy, and when Job crunched the bonbon while Harry looked down at him inquiringly and patted his back, there was general laughter except on the part of Mrs. Holt, who was shaking her head slowly, and slapping the back of her left hand with the painful patience of a tragedian whose part is in abeyance to an ill-timed introduction of the humorous.

"I hope Job's cough has been better lately," said Esther, in mere uncertainty as to what it would be desirable to say or do.

"I daresay you hope so, Miss Lyon," said Mrs. Holt, looking at the distant landscape. "I've no reason to disbelieve but what you wish well to the child, and to Felix, and to me. I'm sure nobody has any occasion to wish me otherways. My character will bear inquiry, and what you, as are young, don't know, others can tell you. That was what I said to myself when I made up my mind to come here and see you, and ask you to get me the freedom to speak to Mr. Transome. I said, whatever Miss Lyon may be now, in the way of being lifted up among great people, she's our minister's daughter, and was not above coming to my house and walking with my son Felix — though I'll not deny he made that figure on the Lord's Day, that'll perhaps go against him with the judge, if anybody thinks well to tell him."

Here Mrs. Holt paused a moment, as with a mind arrested by the painful image it had called up.

Esther's face was glowing, when Harold glanced at her; and seeing this, he was considerate enough to address Mrs. Holt instead of her.

"You are then the mother of the unfortunate young man who is in prison?"

"Indeed, I am, sir," said Mrs. Holt, feeling that she was now in deep water. "It's not likely I should claim him if he wasn't my own; though it's not by my will, nor my advice, sir, that he ever walked; for I gave him none but good. But if everybody's son was guided by their mothers, the world 'ud be different; my son is not worse than many another woman's son, and that in Treby, whatever they may say as haven't got their sons in prison. And as to his giving up the doctoring, and then stopping his father's medicines, I know it's bad — that I know — but it's me has had to suffer, and it's me a king and Parliament 'ud consider, if they meant to do the right thing, and had anybody to make it known to 'em. And as for the rioting and killing the constable — my son said most plain to me he never meant it, and there was his bit of potato-pie for his dinner getting dry by the fire, the whole blessed time as I sat and never knew what was coming on me. And it's my opinion as if great people make elections to get themselves into Parliament, and there's riot and murder to do it, they ought to see as the widow and the widow's son doesn't suffer for it. I well know my duty: and I read my Bible; and I know in Jude where it's been stained with the dried tulip-leaves this many a year, as you're told not to rail at your betters if they was the devil himself; nor will I; but this I do say, if it's three Mr. Transomes instead of one as is listening to me, as there's them ought to go to the king and get him to let off my son Felix."

This speech, in its chief points, had been deliberately prepared. Mrs. Holt had set her face like a flint, to make the gentry know their duty as she knew hers: her defiant, defensive tone was due to the consciousness, not only that she was braving a powerful audience, but that she was daring to stand on the strong basis of her own judgment in opposition to her son's. Her proposals had been waived off by Mr. Lyon and Felix; but she had long had the feminine conviction that if she could "get to speak" in the right quarter, things might be different. The daring bit of impromptu about the three Mr. Transomes was immediately suggested by a movement of old Mr. Transome to the foreground in a line with Mr. Lingon and Harold; his furred and unusual costume appearing to indicate a mysterious dignity which she must hasten to include in her appeal.

And there were reasons that none could have foreseen, which made Mrs. Holt's remonstrance immediately effective. While old Mr. Transome stared, very much like a waxen image in which the expression is a failure, and the Rector, accustomed to female parishioners and complainants, looked on with a smile in his eyes, Harold said at once, with cordial kindness —

"I think you are quite right, Mrs. Holt. And for my part, I am determined to do my best for your son, both in the witness-box and elsewhere. Take comfort; if it is necessary, the king shall be appealed to. And rely upon it, I shall bear you in mind, as Felix Holt's mother."

Rapid thoughts had convinced Harold that in this way he was best commending himself to Esther.

"Well, sir," said Mrs. Holt, who was not going to pour forth disproportionate thanks, "I'm glad to hear you speak so becoming; and if you had been the king himself, I should have made free to tell you my opinion. For the Bible says, the king's favour is towards a wise servant; and it's reasonable to think he'd make all the more account of them as have never been in service, or took wage, which I never did, and never thought of my son doing; and his father left money, meaning otherways, so as he might have been a doctor on horseback at this very minute, instead of being in prison."

"What! was he regularly apprenticed to a doctor?" said Mr. Lingon, who had not understood this before.

"Sir, he was, and most clever, like his father before him, only he turned contrairy. But as for harming anybody, Felix never meant to harm anybody but himself and his mother, which he certainly did in respect of his clothes, and taking to be a low working man, and stopping my living respectable, more particular by the pills, which had a sale, as you may be sure they suited people's insides. And what folks can never have boxes enough of to swallow, I should think you have a right to sell. And there's many and many a text for it, as I've opened on without ever thinking; for if it's true, 'Ask, and you shall have,' I should think it's truer when you're willing to pay for what you have."

This was a little too much for Mr. Lingon's gravity; he exploded, and Harold could not help following him. Mrs. Holt fixed her eyes on the distance, and slapped the back of her left hand again: it might be that this kind of mirth was the peculiar effect produced by forcible truth on high and worldly people who were neither in the Independent nor the General Baptist connection.

"I'm sure you must be tired with your long walk, and little Job too," said Esther, by way of breaking this awkward scene. "Arn't you, Job?" she added, stooping to caress the child, who was timidly shrinking from Harry's invitation to him to pull the little chariot — Harry's view being that Job would make a good horse for him to beat, and would run faster than Gappa.

"It's well you can feel for the orphin child, Miss Lyon," said Mrs. Holt, choosing an indirect answer rather than to humble herself by confessing fatigue before gentlemen who seemed to be taking her too lightly. "I didn't believe but what you'd behave pretty, as you always did to me, though everybody used to say you held yourself high. But I'm sure you never did to Felix, for you let him sit by you at the

Free School before all the town, and him with never a bit of stock round his neck. And it shows you saw *that* in him worth taking notice of; — and it is but right, if you know my words are true, as you should speak for him to the gentlemen."

"I assure you, Mrs. Holt," said Harold, coming to the rescue — "I assure you that enough has been said to make me use my best efforts for your son. And now, pray, go on to the house with the little boy and take some rest. Dominic, show Mrs. Holt the way, and ask Mrs. Hickes to make her comfortable, and see that somebody takes her back to Treby in the buggy."

"I will go back with Mrs. Holt," said Esther, making an effort against herself.

"No, pray," said Harold, with that kind of entreaty which is really a decision. "Let Mrs. Holt have time to rest. We shall have returned, and you can see her before she goes. We will say good-bye for the present, Mrs. Holt."

The poor woman was not sorry to have the prospect of rest and food, especially for "the orphin child," of whom she was tenderly careful. Like many women who appear to others to have a masculine decisiveness of tone, and to themselves to have a masculine force of mind, and who come into severe collision with sons arrived at the masterful stage, she had the maternal cord vibrating strongly within her towards all tiny children. And when she saw Dominic pick up Job and hoist him on his arm for a little while, by way of making acquaintance, she regarded him with an approval which she had not thought it possible to extend to a foreigner. Since Dominic was going, Harry and old Mr. Transome chose to follow. Uncle Lingon shook hands and turned off across the grass, and thus Esther was left alone with Harold.

But there was a new consciousness between them. Harold's quick perception was least likely to be slow in seizing indications of anything that might affect his position with regard to Esther. Some time before, his jealousy had been awakened to the possibility that before she had known him she had been deeply interested in some one else. Jealousy of all sorts — whether for our fortune or our love — is ready at combinations, and likely even to outstrip the fact. And Esther's renewed confusion, united with her silence about Felix, which now first seemed noteworthy, and with Mrs. Holt's graphic details as to her walking with him and letting him sit by her before all the town, were grounds not merely for a suspicion, but for a conclusion in Harold's mind. The effect of this, which he at once regarded as a discovery, was rather different from what Esther had anticipated. It seemed to him that Felix was the least formidable person that he could have found out as an object of interest antecedent to himself. A young workman who had got himself thrown into prison, whatever recommendations he might have had for a girl at a romantic age in the dreariness of Dissenting society at Treby, could hardly be considered by Harold in the light of a rival. Esther was too clever and tasteful a woman to make a ballad heroine of herself, by bestowing her beauty and her lands on this lowly lover. Besides, Harold cherished the belief that, at the present time, Esther was more wisely disposed to bestow these things on another lover in every way eligible. But in two directions this discovery had a determining effect on him; his curiosity was stirred to know exactly what the relation with Felix had been, and he was solicitous that his behaviour with regard to this young man should be such as to enhance his own merit in Esther's eyes. At the same time he was not inclined to any euphemisms that would seem by any possibility to bring Felix into the lists with himself.

Naturally, when they were left alone, it was Harold who spoke first. "I should think there's a good deal of worth in this young fellow — this Holt, notwithstanding the mistakes he has made. A little queer and conceited, perhaps; but that is usually the case with men of his class when they are at all superior to their fellows."

"Felix Holt is a highly cultivated man; he is not at all conceited," said Esther. The different kinds of pride within her were coalescing now. She was aware that there had been a betrayal.

"Ah?" said Harold, not quite liking the tone of this answer. "This eccentricity is a sort of fanaticism, then? — this giving up being a doctor on horseback, as the old woman calls it, and taking to — let me see — watchmaking, isn't it?"

"If it is eccentricity to be very much better than other men, he is certainly eccentric; and fanatical too, if it is fanatical to renounce all small selfish motives for the sake of a great and unselfish one. I never knew what nobleness of character really was before I knew Felix Holt."

It seemed to Esther as if, in the excitement of this moment, her own words were bringing her a clearer revelation.

"God bless me!" said Harold, in a tone of surprised yet thorough belief, and looking in Esther's face. "I wish you had talked to me about this before."

Esther at that moment looked perfectly beautiful, with an expression which Harold had never hitherto seen. All the confusion which had depended on personal feeling had given way before the sense that she had to speak the truth about the man whom she felt to be admirable.

"I think I didn't see the meaning of anything fine — I didn't even see the value of my father's character, until I had been taught a little by hearing what Felix Holt said, and seeing that his life was like his words."

Harold looked and listened, and felt his slight jealousy allayed rather than heightened. "This is not like love," he said to himself, with some satisfaction. With all due regard to Harold Transome, he was one of those men who are liable to make the greater mistakes about a particular woman's feelings, because they pique themselves on a power of interpretation derived from much experience. Experience is enlightening, but with a difference. Experiments on live animals may go on for a long period, and yet the fauna on which they are made may be limited. There may be a passion in the mind of a woman which precipitates her, not along the path of easy beguilement, but into a great leap away from it. Harold's experience had not taught him this; and Esther's enthusiasm about Felix Holt did not seem to him to be dangerous.

"He's quite an apostolic sort of fellow, then," was the self-quieting answer he gave to her last words. "He didn't look like that; but I had only a short interview with him, and I was given to understand that he refused to see me in prison. I believe he's not very well inclined towards me. But you saw a great deal of him, I suppose; and your testimony to any one is enough for me," said Harold, lowering his voice rather tenderly. "Now I know what your opinion is, I shall spare no effort on behalf of such a young man. In fact, I had come to the same resolution before, but your wish would make difficult things easy."

After that energetic speech of Esther's, as often happens, the tears had just suffused her eyes. It was nothing more than might have been expected in a tender-hearted woman, considering Felix Holt's circumstances, and the tears only made more lovely the look with which she met Harold's when he spoke so kindly. She felt pleased with him; she was open to the fallacious delight of being assured that she had power over him to make him do what she liked, and quite forgot the many impressions which had convinced her that Harold had a padded yoke ready for the neck of every man, woman, and child that depended on him.

After a short silence, they were getting near the stone gateway, and Harold said, with an air of intimate consultation —

"What could we do for this young man, supposing he were let off? I shall send a letter with fifty pounds to the old woman to-morrow. I ought to have done it before, but it really slipped my memory, amongst the many things that have occupied me lately. But this young man — what do you think would be the best thing we could do for him, if he gets at large again? He should be put in a position where his qualities could be more telling."

Esther was recovering her liveliness a little, and was disposed to encourage it for the sake of veiling other feelings, about which she felt renewed reticence, now that the overpowering influence of her enthusiasm was past. She was rather wickedly amused and scornful at Harold's misconceptions and ill-placed intentions of patronage.

"You are hopelessly in the dark," she said, with a light laugh and toss of her head. "What would you offer Felix Holt? a place in the Excise? You might as well think of offering it to John the Baptist. Felix has chosen his lot. He means always to be a poor man."

"Means? Yes," said Harold, slightly piqued, "but what a man means usually depends on what happens. I mean to be a commoner; but a peerage might present itself under acceptable circumstances."

"O there is no sum in proportion to be done there," said Esther, again gaily. "As you are to a peerage, so is *not* Felix Holt to any offer of advantage that you could imagine for him."

"You must think him fit for any position — the first in the county."

"No, I don't," said Esther, shaking her head mischievously. "I think him too high for it."

"I see you can be ardent in your admiration."

"Yes, it is my champagne; you know I don't like the other kind."

"That would be satisfactory if one were sure of getting your admiration," said Harold, leading her up to the terrace, and amongst the crocuses, from whence they had a fine view of the park and river. They stood still near the east parapet, and saw the dash of light on the water, and the pencilled shadows of the trees on the grassy lawn.

"Would it do as well to admire you, instead of being worthy to be admired?" said Harold, turning his eyes from that landscape to Esther's face.

"It would be a thing to be put up with," said Esther, smiling at him rather roguishly. "But you are not in that state of self-despair."

"Well, I am conscious of not having those severe virtues that you have been praising."

"That is true. You are quite in another *genre.*"

"A woman would not find me a tragic hero."

"O, no! She must dress for genteel comedy — such as your mother once described to me — where the most thrilling event is the drawing of a handsome cheque."

"You are a naughty fairy," said Harold, daring to press Esther's hand a little more closely to him, and drawing her down the eastern steps into the pleasure-ground, as if he were unwilling to give up the conversation. "Confess that you are disgusted with my want of romance."

"I shall not confess to being disgusted. I shall ask you to confess that you are not a romantic figure."

"I am a little too stout."

"For romance — yes. At least you must find security for not getting stouter."

"And I don't look languishing enough?"

"O yes — rather too much so — at a fine cigar."

"And I am not in danger of committing suicide?"

"No; you are a widower."

Harold did not reply immediately to this last thrust of Esther's. She had uttered it with innocent thoughtlessness from the playful suggestions of the moment; but it was a fact that Harold's previous married life had entered strongly into her impressions about him. The presence of Harry made it inevitable. Harold took this allusion of Esther's as an indication that his quality of widower was a point that made against him; and after a brief silence he said, in an altered, more serious tone —

"You don't suppose, I hope, that any other woman has ever held the place that you could hold in my life?"

Esther began to tremble a little, as she always did when the love-talk between them seemed getting serious. She only gave the rather stumbling answer, "How so?"

"Harry's mother had been a slave — was bought, in fact."

It was impossible for Harold to preconceive the effect this had on Esther. His natural disqualification for judging of a girl's feelings was heightened by the blinding effect of an exclusive object — which was to assure her that her own place was peculiar and supreme. Hitherto Esther's acquaintance with Oriental love was derived chiefly from Byronic poems, and this had not sufficed to adjust her mind to a new story, where the Giaour concerned was giving her his arm. She was unable to speak; and Harold went on —

"Though I am close on thirty-five, I never met with a woman at all like you before. There are new eras in one's life that are equivalent to youth — are something better than youth. I was never an aspirant till I knew you."

Esther was still silent.

"Not that I dare to call myself that. I am not so confident a personage as you imagine. I am necessarily in a painful position for a man who has any feeling."

Here at last Harold had stirred the right fibre. Esther's generosity seized at once the whole meaning implied in that last sentence. She had a fine sensibility to the line at which flirtation must cease; and she was now pale, and shaken with feelings she had not yet defined for herself.

"Do not let us speak of difficult things any more now," she said, with gentle seriousness. "I am come into a new world of late, and have to learn life all over again. Let us go in. I must see poor Mrs. Holt again, and my little friend Job."

She paused at the glass door that opened on the terrace, and entered there, while Harold went round to the stables.

When Esther had been up-stairs and descended again into the large entrance-hall, she found its stony spaciousness made lively by human figures extremely unlike the statues. Since Harry insisted on playing with Job again, Mrs. Holt and her orphan, after dining, had just been brought to this delightful scene for a game at hide-and-seek, and for exhibiting the climbing powers of the two pet-squirrels. Mrs. Holt sat on a stool, in singular relief against the pedestal of the Apollo, while Dominic and Denner (otherwise Mrs. Hickes) bore her company; Harry, in his bright red and purple, flitted about like a great tropic bird after the sparrow-tailed Job, who hid himself with much intelligence behind the scagliola pillars and the pedestals, while one of the squirrels perched itself on the head of the tallest statue, and the other was already peeping down from among the heavy stuccoed angels on the ceiling, near the summit of a pillar.

Mrs. Holt held on her lap a basket filled with good things for Job, and seemed much soothed by pleasant company and excellent treatment. As Esther, descending softly and unobserved, leaned over the stone bannisters and looked at the scene for a minute or two, she saw that Mrs. Holt's attention, having been directed to the squirrel which had scampered on to the head of the Silenus carrying the infant Bacchus, had been drawn downward to the tiny babe looked at with so much affection by the rather ugly and hairy gentleman, of whom she nevertheless spoke with reserve as of one who possibly belonged to the Transome family.

"It's most pretty to see its little limbs, and the gentleman holding it. I should think he was amiable by his look; but it was odd he should have his likeness took without any clothes. Was he Transome by name?" (Mrs. Holt suspected that there might be a mild madness in the family.)

Denner, peering and smiling quietly, was about to reply, when she was prevented by the appearance of old Mr. Transome, who since his walk had been having "forty winks" on the sofa in the library, and now came out to look for Harry. He had doffed his furred cap and cloak, but in lying down to sleep he had thrown over his shoulders a soft Oriental scarf which Harold had given him, and this still hung over his scanty white hair and down to his knees, held fast by his wooden-looking arms and laxly clasped hands, which fell in front of him.

This singular appearance of an undoubted Transome fitted exactly into Mrs. Holt's thought at the moment. It lay in the probabilities of things that gentry's intellects should be peculiar: since they had not to get their own living, the good Lord might have economised in their case that common sense which others were so much more in need of; and in the shuffling figure before her she saw a descendant of the gentleman who had chosen to be represented without his clothes — all the more eccentric where there were the means of buying the best. But these oddities "said nothing" in great folks, who were powerful in high quarters all the same. And Mrs. Holt rose and curtsied with a proud respect, precisely as she would have done if Mr. Transome had looked as wise as Lord Burleigh.

"I hope I'm in no ways taking a liberty, sir," she began, while the old gentleman looked at her with bland feebleness; "I'm not that woman to sit anywhere out of my own home without inviting, and pressing too. But I was brought here to wait, because the little gentleman wanted to play with the orphin child."

"Very glad, my good woman — sit down — sit down," said Mr. Transome, nodding and smiling between his clauses. "Nice little boy. Your grandchild?"

"Indeed, sir, no," said Mrs. Holt, continuing to stand. Quite apart from any awe of Mr. Transome — sitting down, she felt, would be a too great familiarity with her own pathetic importance on this extra and unlooked-for occasion. "It's not me has any grandchild, nor ever shall have, though most fit. But with my only son saying he'll never be married, and in prison besides, and some saying he'll be transported, you may see yourself — though a gentleman — as there isn't much chance of my having grandchildren of my own. And this is old Master Tudge's grandchild, as my own Felix took to for pity because he was sickly and clemm'd, and I was noways against it, being of a tender heart. For I'm a widow myself, and my son Felix, though big, is fatherless, and I know my duty in consequence. And it's to be wished, sir, as others should know it as are more in power and live in great houses, and can ride in a carriage where they will. And if you're the gentleman as is the head of everything — and it's not to be thought you'd give up to your son as a poor widow's been forced to do — it behoves you to take the part of them as are deserving; for the Bible says, grey hairs should speak."

"Yes, yes — poor woman — what shall I say?" said old Mr. Transome, feeling himself scolded, and as usual desirous of mollifying displeasure.

"Sir, I can tell you what to say fast enough; for it's what I should say myself if I could get to speak to the King. For I've asked them that know, and they say it's the truth both out of the Bible and in, as the King can pardon anything and anybody. And judging by his countenance on the new signs, and the talk there was a while ago about his being the people's friend, as the minister once said it from the very pulpit — if there's any meaning in words, he'll do the right thing by me and my son, if he's asked proper."

"Yes — a very good man — he'll do anything right," said Mr. Transome, whose own ideas about the King just then were somewhat misty, consisting chiefly in broken reminiscences of George the Third. "I'll ask him anything you like," he added, with a pressing desire to satisfy Mrs. Holt, who alarmed him slightly.

"Then, sir, if you'll go in your carriage and say, This young man, Felix Holt by name, as his father was known the country round, and his mother most respectable — he never meant harm to anybody, and so far from bloody murder and fighting, would part with his victual to them that needed it more — and if you'd get other gentlemen to say the same, and if they're not satisfied, to inquire — I'll not believe but what the King 'ud let my son out of prison. Or if it's true he must stand his trial, the King 'ud take care no mischief happened to him. I've got my senses, and I'll never believe as in a country where there's a God above and a king below, the right thing can't be done if great people was willing to do it."

Mrs. Holt, like all orators, had waxed louder and more energetic, ceasing to propel her arguments, and being propelled by them. Poor old Mr. Transome, getting more and more frightened at this severe-spoken woman, who had the horrible possibility to his mind of being a novelty that was to become permanent, seemed to be fascinated by fear, and stood helplessly forgetful that if he liked he might turn round and walk away.

Little Harry, alive to anything that had relation to "Gappa," had paused in his game, and, discerning what he thought a hostile aspect in this naughty black old woman, rushed towards her and proceeded first to beat her with his mimic jockey's whip, and then, suspecting that her bombazine was not sensitive, to set his teeth in her arm. While Dominic rebuked him and pulled him off, Nimrod began to bark anxiously, and the scene was become alarming even to the squirrels, which scrambled as far off as possible.

Esther, who had been waiting for an opportunity of intervention, now came up to Mrs. Holt to speak some soothing words; and old Mr. Transome, seeing a sufficient screen between himself and his formidable suppliant, at last gathered courage to turn round and shuffle away with unusual swiftness into the library.

"Dear Mrs. Holt," said Esther, "do rest comforted. I assure you, you have done the utmost that can be done by your words. Your visit has not been thrown away. See how the children have enjoyed it! I saw little Job actually laughing. I think I never saw him do more than smile before." Then, turning round to Dominic, she said, "Will the buggy come round to this door?"

This hint was sufficient. Dominic went to see if the vehicle was ready, and Denner, remarking that Mrs. Holt would like to mount it in the inner court, invited her to go back into the housekeeper's room. But there was a fresh resistance raised in Harry by the threatened departure of Job, who had seemed an invaluable addition to the menagerie of tamed creatures; and it was barely in time that Esther had the relief of seeing the entrance-hall cleared so as to prevent any further encounter of Mrs. Holt with Harold, who was now coming up the flight of steps at the entrance.

CHAPTER XX.

*I'm sick at heart. The eye of day,
The insistent summer noon, seems pitiless,
Shining in all the barren crevices
Of weary life, leaving no shade, no dark,
Where I may dream that hidden waters lie.*

SHORTLY after Mrs. Holt's striking presentation of herself at Transome Court, Esther went on a second visit to her father. The Loamford Assizes were approaching; it was expected that in about ten days Felix Holt's trial would come on, and some hints in her father's letters had given Esther the impression that he was taking a melancholy view of the result. Harold Transome had once or twice mentioned the subject with a facile hopefulness as to "the young fellow's coming off easily," which, in her anxious mind, was not a counterpoise to disquieting suggestions, and she had not chosen to introduce another conversation about Felix Holt, by questioning Harold concerning the probabilities he relied on. Since those moments on the terrace, Harold had daily become more of the solicitous and indirectly beseeching lover; and Esther, from the very fact that she was weighed on by thoughts that were painfully bewildering to her—by thoughts which, in their newness to her young mind, seemed to shake her belief that life could be anything else than a compromise with things repugnant to the moral taste—had become more passive to his attentions at the very time that she had begun to feel more profoundly that in accepting Harold

Transome she left the high mountain air, the passionate serenity of perfect love for ever behind her, and must adjust her wishes to a life of middling delights, overhung with the languorous haziness of motiveless ease, where poetry was only literature, and the fine ideas had to be taken down from the shelves of the library when her husband's back was turned. But it seemed as if all outward conditions concurred, along with her generous sympathy for the Transomes, and with those native tendencies against which she had once begun to struggle, to make this middling lot the best she could attain to. She was in this half-sad half-satisfied resignation to something like what is called worldly wisdom, when she went to see her father, and learn what she could from him about Felix.

The little minister was much depressed, unable to resign himself to the dread which had begun to haunt him, that Felix might have to endure the odious penalty of transportation for the manslaughter, which was the offence that no evidence in his favour could disprove.

"I had been encouraged by the assurances of men instructed in this regard," said Mr. Lyon, while Esther sat on the stool near him, and listened anxiously, "that though he were pronounced guilty in regard to this deed whereinto he hath calamitously fallen, yet that a judge mildly disposed, and with a due sense of that invisible activity of the soul whereby the deeds which are the same in the outward appearance and effect, yet differ as the knife-stroke of the surgeon, even though it kill, differs from the knife-stroke of a wanton mutilator, might use his discretion in tempering the punishment, so that it would not be very evil to bear. But now it is said that the judge who cometh is a severe man, and one nourishing a prejudice against the bolder spirits who stand not in the old paths."

"I am going to be present at the trial, father," said Esther, who was preparing the way to express a wish, which she was timid about even with her father. "I mentioned to Mrs. Transome that I should like to do so, and she said that she used in old days always to attend the assizes, and that she would take me. You will be there, father?"

"Assuredly I shall be there, having been summoned to bear witness to Felix's character, and to his having uttered remonstrances and warnings long beforehand whereby he proved himself an enemy to riot. In our ears, who know him, it sounds strangely that aught else should be credible; but he hath few to speak for him, though I trust that Mr. Harold Transome's testimony will go far, if, as you say, he is disposed to set aside all minor regards, and not to speak the truth grudgingly and reluctantly. For the very truth hath a colour from the disposition of the utterer."

"He is kind; he is capable of being generous," said Esther.

"It is well. For I verily believe that evil-minded men have been at work against Felix. The *Duffield Watchman* hath written continually in allusion to him as one of those mischievous men who seek to elevate themselves through the dishonour of their party; and as one of those who go not heart and soul with the needs of the people, but seek only to get a hearing for themselves by raising their voices in crotchety discord. It is these things that cause me heaviness of spirit: the dark secret of this young man's lot is a cross I carry daily."

"Father," said Esther, timidly, while the eyes of both were filling with tears, "I should like to see him again, before his trial. Might I? Will you ask him? Will you take me?"

The minister raised his suffused eyes to hers, and did not speak for a moment or two. A new thought had visited him. But his delicate tenderness shrank even from an inward inquiry that was too curious—that seemed like an effort to peep at sacred secrets.

"I see nought against it, my dear child, if you arrived early enough, and would take the elderly lady into your confidence, so that you might descend from the carriage at some suitable place—the house of the Independent minister, for example—where I could meet and accompany you. I would forewarn Felix, who would doubtless delight to see your face again; seeing that he may go away, and be, as it were, buried from you, even though it may be only in prison, and not—"

This was too much for Esther. She threw her arms round her father's neck and sobbed like a child. It was an unspeakable relief to her after all the pent-up stifling experience, all the inward incommunicable debate of the last few weeks. The old man was deeply moved too, and held his arm close round the dear child, praying silently.

No word was spoken for some minutes, till Esther raised herself, dried her eyes, and with an action that seemed playful, though there was no smile on her face, pressed her handkerchief against her father's cheeks. Then, when she had put her hand in his, he said, solemnly,

"'Tis a great and mysterious gift, this clinging of the heart, my Esther, whereby it hath often seemed to

me that even in the very moment of suffering our souls
have the keenest foretaste of heaven. I speak not
lightly, but as one who hath endured. And 'tis a
strange truth that only in the agony of parting we look
into the depths of love."

So the interview ended, without any question from
Mr. Lyon concerning what Esther contemplated as the
ultimate arrangement between herself and the Transomes.

After this conversation, which showed him that what
happened to Felix touched Esther more closely than
he had supposed, the minister felt no impulse to raise
the images of a future so unlike anything that Felix
would share. And Esther would have been unable to
answer any such questions. The successive weeks, instead of bringing her nearer to clearness and decision,
had only brought that state of disenchantment belonging
to the actual presence of things which have long dwelt
in the imagination with all the factitious charms of
arbitrary arrangement. Her imaginary mansion had
not been inhabited just as Transome Court was; her
imaginary fortune had not been attended with circumstances which she was unable to sweep away. She herself, in her Utopia, had never been what she was now — a
woman whose heart was divided and oppressed. The
first spontaneous offering of her woman's devotion, the
first great inspiration of her life, was a sort of vanished
ecstasy which had left its wounds. It seemed to her a
cruel misfortune of her young life that her best feeling,
her most precious dependence, had been called forth
just where the conditions were hardest, and that all
the easy invitations of circumstance were towards something which that previous consecration of her longing

had made a moral descent for her. It was characteristic of her that she scarcely at all entertained the alternative of such a compromise as would have given her the larger portion of the fortune to which she had a legal claim, and yet have satisfied her sympathy by leaving the Transomes in possession of their old home. Her domestication with this family had brought them into the foreground of her imagination; the gradual wooing of Harold had acted on her with a constant immediate influence that predominated over all indefinite prospects; and a solitary elevation to wealth, which out of Utopia she had no notion how she should manage, looked as chill and dreary as the offer of dignities in an unknown country.

In the ages since Adam's marriage, it has been good for some men to be alone, and for some women also. But Esther was not one of these women: she was intensely of the feminine type, verging neither towards the saint nor the angel. She was "a fair divided excellence, whose fulness of perfection" must be in marriage. And, like all youthful creatures, she felt as if the present conditions of choice were final. It belonged to the freshness of her heart that, having had her emotions strongly stirred by real objects, she never speculated on possible relations yet to come. It seemed to her that she stood at the first and last parting of the ways. And, in one sense, she was under no illusion. It is only in that freshness of our time that the choice is possible which gives unity to life, and makes the memory a temple where all relics and all votive offerings, all worship and all grateful joy, are an unbroken history sanctified by one religion.

CHAPTER XXI.

*We may not make this world a paradise
By walking it together with clasped hands
And eyes that meeting feed a double strength.
We must be only joined by pains divine,
Of spirits blent in mutual memories.*

It was a consequence of that interview with her father, that when Esther stepped early on a grey March morning into the carriage with Mrs. Transome, to go to the Loamford Assizes, she was full of an expectation that held her lips in trembling silence, and gave her eyes that sightless beauty which tells that the vision is all within.

Mrs. Transome did not disturb her with unnecessary speech. Of late, Esther's anxious observation had been drawn to a change in Mrs. Transome, shown in many small ways which only women notice. It was not only that when they sat together the talk seemed more of an effort to her: that might have come from the gradual draining away of matter for discourse pertaining to most sorts of companionship, in which repetition is not felt to be as desirable as novelty. But while Mrs. Transome was dressed just as usual, took her seat as usual, trifled with her drugs and had her embroidery before her as usual, and still made her morning greetings with that finished easy politeness and consideration of tone which to rougher people seems like affection, Esther noticed a strange fitfulness in her movements. Sometimes the stitches of her embroidery went on with silent unbroken swiftness for a quarter of an hour as if she had to work out her deliverance from bondage by finishing a scroll-patterned border; then her hands dropt suddenly and her gaze fell blankly on the table before her, and she would sit in that way motionless as a seated statue, apparently unconscious of Esther's presence, till some thought darting within her seemed to have the effect of an external shock and rouse her with a start, when she looked round hastily like a person ashamed of having slept. Esther, touched with wondering pity at signs of unhappiness that were new in her experience, took the most delicate care to appear inobservant, and only tried to increase the gentle attention that might help to soothe or gratify this uneasy woman. But, one morning, Mrs. Transome had said, breaking rather a long silence,

"My dear, I shall make this house dull for you. You sit with me like an embodied patience. I am unendurable; I am getting into a melancholy dotage. A fidgety old woman like me is as unpleasant to see as a rook with its wing broken. Don't mind me, my dear. Run away from me without ceremony. Every one else does, you see. I am part of the old furniture with new drapery."

"Dear Mrs. Transome," said Esther, gliding to the low ottoman close by the basket of embroidery, "do you dislike my sitting with you?"

"Only for your own sake, my fairy," said Mrs. Transome, smiling faintly, and putting her hand under Esther's chin. "Doesn't it make you shudder to look at me?"

"Why will you say such naughty things?" said

Esther, affectionately. "If you had had a daughter, she would have desired to be with you most when you most wanted cheering. And surely every young woman has something of a daughter's feeling towards an elder one who has been kind to her."

"I should like you to be really my daughter," said Mrs. Transome, rousing herself to look a little brighter. "That is something still for an old woman to hope for."

Esther blushed: she had not foreseen this application of words that came from pitying tenderness. To divert the train of thought as quickly as possible, she at once asked what she had previously had in her mind to ask. Before her blush had disappeared she said,

"O, you are so good; I shall ask you to indulge me very much. It is to let us set out very early to Loamford on Wednesday, and put me down at a particular house, that I may keep an engagement with my father. It is a private matter, that I wish no one to know about, if possible. And he will bring me back to you wherever you appoint."

In that way Esther won her end without needing to betray it; and as Harold was already away at Loamford, she was the more secure.

The Independent minister's house at which she was set down, and where she was received by her father, was in a quiet street not far from the jail. Esther had thrown a dark cloak over the handsomer coverings which Denner had assured her was absolutely required of ladies who sat anywhere near the judge at a great trial; and as the bonnet of that day did not throw the face into high relief, but rather into perspective, a veil drawn down gave her a sufficiently inconspicuous appearance.

"I have arranged all things, my dear," said Mr. Lyon, "and Felix expects us. We will lose no time."

They walked away at once, Esther not asking a question. She had no consciousness of the road along which they passed; she could never remember anything but a dim sense of entering within high walls and going along passages, till they were ushered into a larger space than she expected, and her father said, —

"It is here that we are permitted to see Felix, my Esther. He will presently appear."

Esther automatically took off her gloves and bonnet, as if she had entered the house after a walk. She had lost the complete consciousness of everything except that she was going to see Felix. She trembled. It seemed to her as if he too would look altered after her new life — as if even the past would change for her and be no longer a steadfast remembrance, but something she had been mistaken about, as she had been about the new life. Perhaps she was growing out of that childhood to which common things have rareness, and all objects look larger. Perhaps from henceforth the whole world was to be meaner for her. The dread concentrated in those moments seemed worse than anything she had known before. It was what the dread of a pilgrim might be who has it whispered to him that the holy places are a delusion, or that he will see them with a soul unstirred and unbelieving. Every minute that passes may be charged with some such crisis in the little inner world of man or woman.

But soon the door opened slightly; some one looked in; then it opened wide, and Felix Holt entered.

"Miss Lyon — Esther!" and her hand was in his grasp.

He was just the same — no, something inexpressibly better, because of the distance and separation, and the half-weary novelties, which made him like the return of morning.

"Take no heed of me, children," said Mr. Lyon. "I have some notes to make, and my time is precious. We may remain here only a quarter of an hour." And the old man sat down at a window with his back to them, writing with his head bent close to the paper.

"You are very pale; you look ill, compared with your old self," said Esther. She had taken her hand away, but they stood still near each other, she looking up at him.

"The fact is, I'm not fond of prison," said Felix, smiling; "but I suppose the best I can hope for is to have a good deal more of it."

"It is thought that in the worst case a pardon may be obtained," said Esther, avoiding Harold Transome's name.

"I don't rely on that," said Felix, shaking his head. "My wisest course is to make up my mind to the very ugliest penalty they can condemn me to. If I can face that, anything less will seem easy. But you know," he went on, smiling at her brightly, "I never went in for fine company and cushions. I can't be very heavily disappointed in that way."

"Do you see things just as you used to do?" said Esther, turning pale as she said it — "I mean — about poverty, and the people you will live among. Has all the misunderstanding and sadness left you just as obstinate?" She tried to smile, but could not succeed.

"What — about the sort of life I should lead if I were free again?" said Felix.

"Yes. I can't help being discouraged for you by all these things that have happened. See how you may fail!" Esther spoke timidly. She saw a peculiar smile, which she knew well, gathering in his eyes. "Ah, I daresay I am silly," she said, deprecatingly.

"No, you are dreadfully inspired," said Felix. "When the wicked Tempter is tired of snarling that word failure in a man's cell, he sends a voice like a thrush to say it for him. See now what a messenger of darkness you are!" He smiled, and took her two hands between his, pressed together as children hold them up in prayer. Both of them felt too solemnly to be bashful. They looked straight into each other's eyes, as angels do when they tell some truth. And they stood in that way while he went on speaking.

"But I'm proof against that word failure. I've seen behind it. The only failure a man ought to fear is failure in cleaving to the purpose he sees to be best. As to just the amount of result he may see from his particular work — that's a tremendous uncertainty: the universe has not been arranged for the gratification of his feelings. As long as a man sees and believes in some great good, he'll prefer working towards that in the way he's best fit for, come what may. I put effects at their minimum, but I'd rather have the minimum of effect, if it's of the sort I care for, than the maximum of effect I don't care for — a lot of fine things that are not to my taste — and if they were, the conditions of holding them while the world is what it is, are such as would jar on me like grating metal."

"Yes," said Esther, in a low tone, "I think I understand that now, better than I used to do." The words of Felix at last seemed strangely to fit her own experience. But she said no more, though he seemed to wait for it a moment or two, looking at her. But then he went on —

"I don't mean to be illustrious, you know, and make a new era, else it would be kind of you to get a raven and teach it to croak 'failure' in my ears. Where great things can't happen, I care for very small things, such as will never be known beyond a few garrets and workshops. And then, as to one thing I believe in, I don't think I can altogether fail. If there's anything our people want convincing of, it is, that there's some dignity and happiness for a man other than changing his station. That's one of the beliefs I choose to consecrate my life to. If anybody could demonstrate to me that I was a flat for it, I shouldn't think it would follow that I must borrow money to set up genteelly and order new clothes. That's not a rigorous consequence to my understanding."

They smiled at each other, with the old sense of amusement they had so often had together.

"You are just the same," said Esther.

"And you?" said Felix. "My affairs have been settled long ago. But yours — a great change has come in them — magic at work."

"Yes," said Esther, rather falteringly.

"Well," said Felix, looking at her gravely again, "it's a case of fitness that seems to give a chance sanction to that musty law. The first time I saw you, your birth was an immense puzzle to me. However, the appropriate conditions are come at last."

These words seemed cruel to Esther. But Felix could not know all the reasons for their seeming so. She could not speak; she was turning cold and feeling her heart beat painfully.

"All your tastes are gratified now," he went on innocently. "But you'll remember the old pedagogue and his lectures?"

One thought in the mind of Felix was, that Esther was sure to marry Harold Transome. Men readily believe these things of the women who love them. But he could not allude to the marriage more directly. He was afraid of this destiny for her, without having any very distinct knowledge by which to justify his fear to the mind of another. It did not satisfy him that Esther should marry Harold Transome.

"My children," said Mr. Lyon at this moment, not looking round, but only looking close at his watch, "we have just two minutes more." Then he went on writing.

Esther did not speak, but Felix could not help observing now that her hands had turned to a deathly coldness, and that she was trembling. He believed, he knew, that whatever prospects she had, this feeling was for his sake. An overpowering impulse from mingled love, gratitude, and anxiety, urged him to say —

"I had a horrible struggle, Esther. But you see I was right. There was a fitting lot in reserve for you. But remember you have cost a great price — don't throw what is precious away. I shall want the news that you have a happiness worthy of you."

Esther felt too miserable for tears to come. She looked helplessly at Felix for a moment, then took her hands from his, and, turning away mutely, walked dreamily towards her father, and said, "Father, I am ready — there is no more to say."

She turned back again, towards the chair where her bonnet lay, with a face quite corpse-like above her dark garment.

"Esther!"

She heard Felix say the word, with an entreating cry, and went towards him with the swift movement of a frightened child towards its protector. He clasped her, and they kissed each other.

She never could recall anything else that happened, till she was in the carriage again with Mrs. Transome.

CHAPTER XXII.

> Why, there are maidens of heroic touch.
> And yet they seem like things of gossamer
> You'd pinch the life out of, as out of moths.
> O, it is not loud tones and mouthingness,
> 'Tis not the arms akimbo and large strides,
> That make a woman's force. The tiniest birds,
> With softest downy breasts, have passions in them
> And are brave with love.

ESTHER was so placed in the Court, under Mrs. Transome's wing, as to see and hear everything without effort. Harold had received them at the hotel, and had observed that Esther looked ill, and was unusually abstracted in her manner, but this seemed to be sufficiently accounted for by her sympathetic anxiety about the result of a trial in which the prisoner at the bar was a friend, and in which both her father and himself were important witnesses. Mrs. Transome had no reluctance to keep a small secret from her son, and no betrayal was made of that previous "engagement" of Esther's with her father. Harold was particularly delicate and unobtrusive in his attentions to-day; he had the consciousness that he was going to behave in a way that would gratify Esther and win her admiration, and we are all of us made more graceful by the inward presence of what we believe to be a generous purpose; our actions move to a hidden music — "a melody that's sweetly pitched in tune."

If Esther had been less absorbed by supreme feelings, she would have been aware that she was an object of special notice. In the bare squareness of a

public hall, where there was not one jutting angle to
hang a guess or a thought upon, not an image or a
bit of colour to stir the fancy, and where the only objects of speculation, of admiration, or of any interest
whatever, were human beings, and especially the human
beings that occupied positions indicating some importance, the notice bestowed on Esther would not have
been surprising, even if it had been merely a tribute
to her youthful charm, which was well companioned
by Mrs. Transome's elderly majesty. But it was due
also to whisperings that she was an hereditary claimant
of the Transome estates, whom Harold Transome was
about to marry. Harold himself had of late not cared
to conceal either the fact or the probability: they both
tended rather to his honour than his dishonour. And
to-day, when there was a good proportion of Trebians
present, the whisperings spread rapidly.

The Court was still more crowded than on the
previous day, when our poor acquaintance Dredge and
his two collier companions were sentenced to a year's
imprisonment with hard labour, and the more en-
lightened prisoner, who stole the Debarry's plate, to
transportation for life. Poor Dredge had cried, had
wished he'd "never heared of a 'lection," and in spite
of sermons from the jail chaplain, fell back on the
explanation that this was a world in which Spratt and
Old Nick were sure to get the best of it; so that in
Dredge's case, at least, most observers must have had
the melancholy conviction that there had been no en-
hancement of public spirit and faith in progress from
that wave of political agitation which had reached the
Sproxton Pits.

But curiosity was necessarily at a higher pitch to-day, when the character of the prisoner and the circumstances of his offence were of a highly unusual kind. As soon as Felix appeared at the bar, a murmur rose and spread into a loud buzz, which continued until there had been repeated authoritative calls for silence in the Court. Rather singularly, it was now for the first time that Esther had a feeling of pride in him on the ground simply of his appearance. At this moment, when he was the centre of a multitudinous gaze, which seemed to act on her own vision like a broad unmitigated daylight, she felt that there was something pre-eminent in him, notwithstanding the vicinity of numerous gentlemen. No apple-woman would have admired him; not only to feminine minds like Mrs. Tiliot's, but to many minds in coat and waistcoat, there was something dangerous and perhaps unprincipled in his bare throat and great Gothic head; and his somewhat massive person would doubtless have come out very oddly from the hands of a fashionable tailor of that time. But as Esther saw his large grey eyes looking round calmly and undefiantly, first at the audience generally, and then with a more observant expression at the lawyers and other persons immediately around him, she felt that he bore the outward stamp of a distinguished nature. Forgive her if she needed this satisfaction: all of us — whether men or women — are liable to this weakness of liking to have our preference justified before others as well as ourselves. Esther said inwardly, with a certain triumph, that Felix Holt looked as worthy to be chosen in the midst of this large assembly, as he had ever looked in their *tête-à-tête* under the sombre light of the little parlour in Malthouse Yard.

Esther had felt some relief in hearing from her father that Felix had insisted on doing without his mother's presence; and since to Mrs. Holt's imagination, notwithstanding her general desire to have her character inquired into, there was no greatly consolatory difference between being a witness and a criminal, and an appearance of any kind "before the judge" could hardly be made to suggest anything definite that would overcome the dim sense of unalleviated disgrace, she had been less inclined than usual to complain of her son's decision. Esther had shuddered beforehand at the inevitable farce there would be in Mrs. Holt's testimony. But surely Felix would lose something for want of a witness who could testify to his behaviour in the morning before he became involved in the tumult?

"He is really a fine young fellow," said Harold, coming to speak to Esther after a colloquy with the prisoner's solicitor. "I hope he will not make a blunder in defending himself."

"He is not likely to make a blunder," said Esther. She had recovered her colour a little, and was brighter than she had been all the morning before.

Felix had seemed to include her in his general glance, but had avoided looking at her particularly. She understood how delicate feeling for her would prevent this, and that she might safely look at him, and towards her father, whom she could see in the same direction. Turning to Harold to make an observation, she saw that he was looking towards the same point, but with an expression on his face that surprised her.

"Dear me," she said, prompted to speak without any reflection; "how angry you look! I never saw you look so angry before. It is not my father you are looking at?"

"Oh no! I am angry at something I'm looking away from," said Harold, making an effort to drive back the troublesome demon who would stare out at window. "It's that Jermyn," he added, glancing at his mother as well as Esther. "He will thrust himself under my eyes everywhere since I refused him an interview and returned his letter. I'm determined never to speak to him directly again, if I can help it."

Mrs. Transome heard with a changeless face. She had for some time been watching, and had taken on her marble look of immobility. She said an inward bitter "Of course!" to everything that was unpleasant.

After this Esther soon became impatient of all speech: her attention was riveted on the proceedings of the Court, and on the mode in which Felix bore himself. In the case for the prosecution there was nothing more than a reproduction, with irrelevancies added by witnesses, of the facts already known to us. Spratt had retained consciousness enough, in the midst of his terror, to swear that, when he was tied to the finger-post, Felix was presiding over the actions of the mob. The landlady of the Seven Stars, who was indebted to Felix for rescue from pursuit by some drunken rioters, gave evidence that went to prove his assumption of leadership prior to the assault on Spratt, — remembering only that he had called away her pursuers to "better sport." Various respectable witnesses swore to Felix's "encouragement" of the rioters who were dragging Spratt in King Street; to his fatal assault on Tucker; and to his attitude in front of the drawing-room window at the Manor.

Three other witnesses gave evidence of expressions used by the prisoner, tending to show the character of the acts with which he was charged. Two were Treby tradesmen, the third was a clerk from Duffield. The clerk had heard Felix speak at Duffield; the Treby men had frequently heard him declare himself on public matters; and they all quoted expressions which tended to show that he had a virulent feeling against the respectable shop-keeping class, and that nothing was likely to be more congenial to him than the gutting of retailers' shops. No one else knew — the witnesses themselves did not know fully — how far their strong perception and memory on these points was due to a fourth mind, namely, that of Mr. John Johnson, the attorney, who was nearly related to one of the Treby witnesses, and a familiar acquaintance of the Duffield clerk. Man cannot be defined as an evidence-giving animal; and in the difficulty of getting up evidence on any subject, there is room for much unrecognised action of diligent persons who have the extra stimulus of some private motive. Mr. Johnson was present in court to-day, but in a modest, retired situation. He had come down to give information to Mr. Jermyn, and to gather information in other quarters, which was well illuminated by the appearance of Esther in company with the Transomes.

When the case for the prosecution closed, all strangers thought that it looked very black for the prisoner. In two instances only Felix had chosen to put a cross-examining question. The first was to ask Spratt if he did not believe that his having been tied to the post had saved him from a probably mortal injury? The second was to ask the tradesman who swore to his having heard Felix tell the rioters to leave Tucker alone and come along with him, whether he had not, shortly before, heard cries among the mob summoning to an attack on the wine-vaults and brewery.

Esther had hitherto listened closely but calmly. She knew that there would be this strong adverse testimony; and all her hopes and fears were bent on what was to come beyond it. It was when the prisoner was asked what he had to adduce in reply that she felt herself in the grasp of that tremor which does not disable the mind, but rather gives keener consciousness of a mind having a penalty of body attached to it.

There was a silence as of night when Felix Holt began to speak. His voice was firm and clear: he spoke with simple gravity, and evidently without any enjoyment of the occasion. Esther had never seen his face look so weary.

"My Lord, I am not going to occupy the time of the Court with unnecessary words. I believe the witnesses for the prosecution have spoken the truth as far as a superficial observation would enable them to do it; and I see nothing that can weigh with the jury in my favour, unless they believe my statement of my own motives, and the testimony that certain witnesses will give to my character and purposes as being inconsistent with my willingly abetting disorder. I will tell the Court in as few words as I can, how I got entangled in the mob, how I came to attack the constable, and how I was led to take a course which seems rather mad to myself, now I look back upon it."

Felix then gave a concise narrative of his motives and conduct on the day of the riot, from the moment when he was startled into quitting his work by the earlier uproar of the morning. He omitted, of course, his visit to Malthouse Yard, and merely said that he went out to walk again after returning to quiet his mother's mind. He got warmed by the story of his experience, which moved him more strongly than ever, now he recalled it in vibrating words before a large audience of his fellow-men. The sublime delight of truthful speech to one who has the great gift of uttering it, will make itself felt even through the pangs of sorrow.

"That is all I have to say for myself, my Lord. I pleaded 'Not guilty' to the charge of Manslaughter, because I know that word may carry a meaning which would not fairly apply to my act. When I threw Tucker down, I did not see the possibility that he would die from a sort of attack which ordinarily occurs in fighting without any fatal effect. As to my assaulting a constable, it was a quick choice between two evils: I should else have been disabled. And he attacked me under a mistake about my intentions. I'm not prepared to say I never would assault a constable where I had more chance of deliberation. I certainly should assault him if I saw him doing anything that made my blood boil: I reverence the law, but not where it is a pretext for wrong, which it should be the very object of law to hinder. I consider that I should be making an unworthy defence, if I let the Court infer from what I say myself, or from what is said by my witnesses, that because I am a man who hate drunken motiveless disorder, or any wanton harm, therefore I am a man who would never fight against authority. I hold it blasphemy to say that a man ought not to fight against authority: there is no great religion and no great freedom that has not done it, in the beginning. It would be impertinent for me to speak of this now, if I did not need to say in my own defence, that I should hold myself the worst sort of traitor if I put my hand either to fighting or disorder — which must mean injury to somebody — if I were not urged to it by what I hold to be sacred feelings, making a sacred duty either to my own manhood or to my fellow-man. And certainly," Felix ended with a strong ring of scorn in his voice, "I never held it a sacred duty to try and get a Radical candidate returned for Noth Loamshire, by willingly heading a drunken howling mob, whose public action must consist in breaking windows, destroying hard-got produce, and endangering the lives of men and women. I have no more to say, my Lord."

"I foresaw he would make a blunder," said Harold, in a low voice to Esther. Then, seeing her shrink a little, he feared she might suspect him of being merely stung by the allusion to himself. "I don't mean what he said about the Radical candidate," he added hastily, in correction. "I don't mean the last sentence. I mean that whole peroration of his, which he ought to have left unsaid. It has done him harm with the jury — they won't understand it, or rather will misunderstand it. And I'll answer for it, it has soured the judge. It remains to be seen what wo witnesses can say for him, to nullify the effect of what he has said for himself. I hope the attorney has done his best in collecting the evidence: I understand the expense of the witnesses is undertaken by some Liberals at Glasgow and in Lancashire, friends of Holt's. But I suppose your father has told you."

The first witness called for the defence was Mr. Lyon. The gist of his statements was, that from the beginning of September last until the day of election he was in very frequent intercourse with the prisoner; that he had become intimately acquainted with his character and views of life, and his conduct with respect to the election, and that these were totally inconsistent with any other supposition than that his being involved in the riot, and his fatal encounter with the constable, were due to the calamitous failure of a bold but good purpose. He stated further that he had been present when an interview had occurred in his own house between the prisoner and Mr. Harold Transome, who was then canvassing for the representation of North Loamshire. That the object of the prisoner in seeking this interview had been to inform Mr. Transome of treating given in his name to the workmen in the pits and on the canal at Sproxton, and to remonstrate against its continuance; the prisoner fearing that disturbance and mischief might result from what he believed to be the end towards which this treating was directed — namely, the presence of these men on the occasions of the nomination and polling. Several times after this interview, Mr. Lyon said, he had heard Felix Holt recur to the subject therein discussed with expressions of grief and anxiety. He himself was in the habit of visiting Sproxton in his ministerial capacity: he knew fully what the prisoner had done there in order to found a night-school, and was certain that the prisoner's interest in the working men of that district turned entirely on the possibility of converting them somewhat to habits of soberness and to a due care for the instruction of their children. Finally, he stated that the prisoner, in compliance with his request, had been present at Duffield on the day of the nomination, and had on his return expressed himself with strong indignation concerning the employment of the Sproxton men on that occasion, and what he called the wickedness of hiring blind violence.

The quaint appearance and manner of the little Dissenting minister could not fail to stimulate the peculiar wit of the bar. He was subjected to a troublesome cross-examination, which he bore with wide-eyed short-sighted quietude and absorption in the duty of truthful response. On being asked, rather sneeringly, if the prisoner was not one of his flock? he answered, in that deeper tone which made one of the most effective transitions of his varying voice,

"Nay — would to God he were! I should then feel that the great virtues and the pure life I have beheld in him were a witness to the efficacy of the faith I believe in and the discipline of the Church whereunto I belong."

Perhaps it required a larger power of comparison than was possessed by any of that audience to appreciate the moral elevation of an Independent minister who could utter those words. Nevertheless there was a murmur, which was clearly one of sympathy.

The next witness, and the one on whom the interest of the spectators was chiefly concentrated, was Harold Transome. There was a decided predominance of Tory feeling in the Court, and the human disposition to enjoy the infliction of a little punishment on an opposite party, was, in this instance, of a Tory complexion. Harold was keenly alive to this, and to everything else that might prove disagreeable to him in his having to appear in the witness-box. But he was not likely to lose his self-possession, or to fail in adjusting himself gracefully, under conditions which most men would find it difficult to carry without awkwardness. He had generosity and candour enough to bear Felix Holt's proud rejection of his advances without any petty resentment; he had all the susceptibilities of a gentleman; and these moral qualities gave the right direction to his acumen, in judging of the behaviour that would best secure his dignity. Everything requiring self-command was easier to him because of Esther's presence; for her admiration was just then the object which this well-tanned man of the world had it most at heart to secure.

When he entered the witness-box he was much admired by the ladies amongst the audience, many of whom sighed a little at the thought of his wrong course in politics. He certainly looked like a handsome portrait by Sir Thomas Lawrence, in which that remarkable artist had happily omitted the usual excess of honeyed blandness mixed with alert intelligence, which is hardly compatible with the state of man out of paradise. He stood not far off Felix; and the two Radicals certainly made a striking contrast. Felix might have come from the hands of a sculptor in the later Roman period, when the plastic impulse was stirred by the grandeur of barbaric forms — when rolled collars were not yet conceived, and satin stocks were not.

Harold Transome declared that he had had only one interview with the prisoner: it was the interview referred to by the previous witness, in whose presence and in whose house it was begun. The interview, however, was continued beyond the observation of Mr. Lyon. The prisoner and himself quitted the Dissenting minister's house in Malthouse Yard together, and proceeded to the office of Mr. Jermyn, who was then conducting electioneering business on his behalf. His object was to comply with Holt's remonstrance by inquiring into the alleged proceedings at Sproxton, and, if possible, to put a stop to them. Holt's language, both in Malthouse Yard and in the attorney's office, was strong: he was evidently indignant, and his indignation turned on the danger of employing ignorant men excited by drink on an occasion of popular concourse. He believed that Holt's sole motive was the prevention of disorder, and what he considered the demoralisation of the workmen by treating. The event had certainly justified his remonstrances. He had not had any subsequent opportunities of observing the prisoner; but if any reliance was to be placed on a rational conclusion, it must, he thought, be plain that the anxiety thus manifested by Holt was a guarantee of the statement he had made as to his motives on the day of the riot. His entire impression from Holt's manner in that single interview was, that he was a moral and political enthusiast, who, if he sought to coerce others, would seek to coerce them into a difficult, and perhaps impracticable, scrupulosity.

Harold spoke with as noticeable a directness and emphasis, as if what he said could have no reaction on himself. He had of course not entered unnecessarily into what occurred in Jermyn's office. But now he was subjected to a cross-examination on this subject, which gave rise to some subdued shrugs, smiles, and winks, among county gentlemen.

The questions were directed so as to bring out, if possible, some indication that Felix Holt was moved to his remonstrance by personal resentment against the political agents concerned in setting on foot the treating at Sproxton, but such questioning is a sort of target-shooting that sometimes hits about widely. The cross-examining counsel had close connections among the Tories of Loamshire, and enjoyed his business today. Under the fire of various questions about Jermyn and the agent employed by him at Sproxton, Harold got warm, and in one of his replies said, with his rapid sharpness,

"Mr. Jermyn was my agent then, not now: I have no longer any but hostile relations with him."

The sense that he had shown a slight heat would have vexed Harold more if he had not got some satisfaction out of the thought that Jermyn heard those words. He recovered his good temper quickly, and when, subsequently, the question came,

"You acquiesced in the treating of the Sproxton men, as necessary to the efficient working of the reformed constituency?" Harold replied, with quiet fluency,

"Yes; on my return to England, before I put up for North Loamshire, I got the best advice from practised agents, both Whig and Tory. They all agreed as to electioneering measures."

The next witness was Michael Brincey, otherwise Mike Brindle, who gave evidence of the sayings and doings of the prisoner amongst the Sproxton men. Mike declared that Felix went "uncommon again' drink, and pitch-and-toss, and quarrelling, and sich," and was "all for schooling and bringing up the little chaps;" but on being cross-examined, he admitted that he "couldn't give much account;" that Felix did talk again' idle folks, whether poor or rich, and that most like he meant the rich, who had "a rights to be idle," which was what he, Mike, liked himself sometimes, though for the most part he was "a hard-working butty." On being checked for this superfluous allegation of his own theory and practice, Mike became timidly conscious that answering was a great mystery beyond the reaches of a butty's soul, and began to err from defect instead of excess. However, he reasserted that what Felix most wanted was, "to get 'em to set up a school for the little chaps."

With the two succeeding witnesses, who swore to the fact that Felix had tried to lead the mob along Hobb's Lane instead of towards the Manor, and to the violently threatening character of Tucker's attack on him, the case for the defence was understood to close.

Meanwhile Esther had been looking on and listening with growing misery, in the sense that all had not been said which might have been said on behalf of Felix. If it was the jury who were to be acted on, she argued to herself, there might have been an impression made on their feeling which would determine their verdict. Was it not constantly said and seen that juries pronounced Guilty or Not Guilty from sympathy for or against the accused? She was too inexperienced to check her own argument by thoroughly representing to herself the course of things: how the counsel for the prosecution would reply, and how the judge would sum up, with the object of cooling down sympathy into deliberation. What she had painfully pressing on her inward vision was, that the trial was coming to an end, and that the voice of right and truth had not been strong enough.

When a woman feels purely and nobly, that ardour

of hers which breaks through formulas too rigorously urged on men by daily practical needs, makes one of her most precious influences: she is the added impulse that shatters the stiffening crust of cautious experience. Her inspired ignorance gives a sublimity to actions so incongruously simple, that otherwise they would make men smile. Some of that ardour which has flashed out and illuminated all poetry and history was burning to-day in the bosom of sweet Esther Lyon. In this, at least, her woman's lot was perfect: that the man she loved was her hero; that her woman's passion and her reverence for rarest goodness rushed together in an undivided current. And to-day they were making one danger, one terror, one irresistible impulse for her heart. Her feelings were growing into a necessity for action, rather than a resolve to act. She could not support the thought that the trial would come to an end, that sentence would be passed on Felix, and that all the while something had been omitted which might have been said for him. There had been no witness to tell what had been his behaviour and state of mind just before the riot. She must do it. It was possible. There was time. But not too much time. All other agitation became merged in eagerness not to let the moment escape. The last witness was being called. Harold Transome had not been able to get back to her on leaving the witness-box, but Mr. Lingon was close by her. With firm quickness she said to him —

"Pray tell the attorney that I have evidence to give for the prisoner — lose no time."

"Do you know what you are going to say, my dear?" said Mr. Lingon, looking at her in astonishment.

"Yes — I entreat you, for God's sake," said Esther, in that low tone of urgent beseeching which is equivalent to a cry; and with a look of appeal more penetrating still, "I would rather die than not do it."

The old Rector, always leaning to the good-natured view of things, felt chiefly that there seemed to be an additional chance for the poor fellow who had got himself into trouble. He disputed no farther, but went to the attorney.

Before Harold was aware of Esther's intention she was on her way to the witness-box. When she appeared there, it was as if a vibration, quick as light, had gone through the Court and had shaken Felix himself, who had hitherto seemed impassive. A sort of gleam seemed to shoot across his face, and any one close to him could have seen that his hand, which lay on the edge of the dock, trembled.

At the first moment Harold was startled and alarmed; the next, he felt delight in Esther's beautiful aspect, and in the admiration of the Court. There was no blush on her face: she stood, divested of all personal considerations whether of vanity or shyness. Her clear voice sounded as it might have done if she had been making a confession of faith. She began and went on without query or interruption. Every face looked grave and respectful.

"I am Esther Lyon, the daughter of Mr. Lyon, the Independent minister at Treby, who has been one of the witnesses for the prisoner. I know Felix Holt well. On the day of the election at Treby, when I had been much alarmed by the noises that reached me from the main street, Felix Holt came to call upon me. He knew that my father was away, and he thought that I should be alarmed by the sounds of disturbance. It was about the middle of the day, and he came to tell me that the disturbance was quieted, and that the streets were nearly emptied. But he said he feared that the men would collect again after drinking, and that something worse might happen later in the day. And he was in much sadness at this thought. He stayed a little while, and then he left me. He was very melancholy. His mind was full of great resolutions that came from his kind feeling towards others. It was the last thing he would have done to join in riot or to hurt any man, if he could have helped it. His nature is very noble; he is tender-hearted; he could never have had any intention that was not brave and good."

There was something so naive and beautiful in this action of Esther's, that it conquered every low or petty suggestion even in the commonest minds. The three men in that assembly who knew her best — even her father and Felix Holt — felt a thrill of surprise mingling with their admiration. This bright, delicate, beautiful-shaped thing that seemed most like a toy or ornament — some hand had touched the chords, and there came forth music that brought tears. Half a year before, Esther's dread of being ridiculous spread over the surface of her life; but the depth below was sleeping.

Harold Transome was ready to give her his hand and lead her back to her place. When she was there, Felix, for the first time, could not help looking towards her, and their eyes met in one solemn glance.

Afterwards Esther found herself unable to listen

so as to form any judgment on what she heard. The
acting out of that strong impulse had exhausted her
energy. There was a brief pause, filled with a murmur,
a buzz, and much coughing. The audience generally
felt as if dull weather was setting in again. And
under those auspices the counsel for the prosecution
got up to make his reply. Esther's deed had its effect
beyond the momentary one, but the effect was not
visible in the rigid necessities of legal procedure. The
counsel's duty of restoring all unfavourable facts to
due prominence in the minds of the jurors, had its
effect altogether reinforced by the summing-up of the
judge. Even the bare discernment of facts, much
more their arrangement with a view to inferences, must
carry a bias: human impartiality, whether judicial or
not, can hardly escape being more or less loaded. It
was not that the judge had severe intentions; it was
only that he saw with severity. The conduct of Felix
was not such as inclined him to indulgent consideration, and, in his directions to the jury, that mental
attitude necessarily told on the light in which he
placed the homicide. Even to many in the Court who
were not constrained by judicial duty, it seemed that
though this high regard felt for the prisoner by his
friends, and especially by a generous-hearted woman,
was very pretty, such conduct as his was not the less
dangerous and foolish, and assaulting and killing a
constable was not the less an offence to be regarded
without leniency.

Esther seemed now so tremulous, and looked so ill,
that Harold begged her to leave the Court with his
mother and Mr. Lingon. He would come and tell
her the issue. But she said, quietly, that she would

rather stay; she was only a little overcome by the
exertion of speaking. She was inwardly resolved to
see Felix to the last moment before he left the Court.

Though she could not follow the address of the
counsel or the judge, she had a keen ear for what was
brief and decisive. She heard the verdict, "Guilty of
manslaughter." And every word uttered by the judge
in pronouncing sentence fell upon her like an un-
forgetable sound that would come back in dreaming
and in waking. She had her eyes on Felix, and at
the words, "Imprisonment for four years," she saw his
lip tremble. But otherwise he stood firm and calm.

Esther gave a start from her seat. Her heart
swelled with a horrible sensation of pain; but, alarmed
lest she should lose her self-command, she grasped
Mrs. Transome's hand, getting some strength from that
human contact.

Esther saw that Felix had turned. She could no
longer see his face. "Yes," she said, drawing down
her veil, "let us go."

CHAPTER XXIII.

*The devil tempts us not — 'tis we tempt him,
Beckoning his skill with opportunity.*

THE more permanent effect of Esther's action in the trial was visible in a meeting which took place the next day in the principal room of the White Hart at Loamford. To the magistrates and other county gentlemen who were drawn together about noon, some of the necessary impulse might have been lacking but for that stirring of heart in certain just-spirited men and good fathers among them, which had been raised to a high pitch of emotion by Esther's maidenly fervour. Among these one of the foremost was Sir Maximus Debarry, who had come to the assizes with a mind, as usual, slightly rebellious under an influence which he never ultimately resisted — the influence of his son. Philip Debarry himself was detained in London, but in his correspondence with his father he had urged him, as well as his uncle Augustus, to keep eyes and interest awake on the subject of Felix Holt, whom, from all the knowledge of the case he had been able to obtain, he was inclined to believe peculiarly unfortunate rather than guilty. Philip had said he was the more anxious that his family should intervene benevolently in this affair, if it were possible, because he understood that Mr. Lyon took the young man's case particularly to heart, and he should always regard himself as obliged to the old preacher. At this super-

fineness of consideration Sir Maximus had vented a
few "pshaws!" and, in relation to the whole affair,
had grumbled that Phil was always setting him to
do he didn't know what — always seeming to turn
nothing into something by dint of words which hadn't
so much substance as a mote behind them. Nevertheless he was coerced; and in reality he was willing
to do anything fair or good-natured which had a
handle that his understanding could lay hold of. His
brother, the Rector, desired to be rigorously just; but
he had come to Loamford with a severe opinion concerning Felix, thinking that some sharp punishment
might be a wholesome check on the career of a young
man disposed to rely too much on his own crude devices.

Before the trial commenced, Sir Maximus had
naturally been one of those who had observed Esther
with curiosity, owing to the report of her inheritance,
and her probable marriage to his once welcome but
now exasperating neighbour, Harold Transome; and
he had made the emphatic comment — "A fine girl!
something thoroughbred in the look of her. Too good
for a Radical; that's all I have to say." But during
the trial Sir Maximus was wrought into a state of
sympathetic ardour that needed no fanning. As soon
as he could take his brother by the buttonhole, he
said,

"I tell you what, Gus! we must exert ourselves to
get a pardon for this young fellow. Confound it!
what's the use of mewing him up for four years?
Example? Nonsense. Will there be a man knocked
down the less for it? That girl made me cry. Depend upon it, whether she's going to marry Transome

or not, she's been fond of Holt — in her poverty, you know. She's a modest, brave, beautiful woman. I'd ride a steeplechase, old as I am, to gratify her feelings. Hang it! the fellow's a good fellow if she thinks so. And he threw out a fine sneer, I thought, at the Radical candidate. Depend upon it, he's a good fellow at bottom."

The Rector had not exactly the same kind of ardour, nor was he open to precisely that process of proof which appeared to have convinced Sir Maximus; but he had been so far influenced as to be inclined to unite in an effort on the side of mercy, observing, also, that he "knew Phil would be on that side." And by the co-operation of similar movements in the minds of other men whose names were of weight, a meeting had been determined on to consult about getting up a memorial to the Home Secretary on behalf of Felix Holt. His case had never had the sort of significance that could rouse political partisanship; and such interest as was now felt in him was still more unmixed with that inducement. The gentlemen who gathered in the room at the White Hart were — not as the large imagination of the *North Loamshire Herald* suggested, "of all shades of political opinion," but — of as many shades as were to be found among the gentlemen of that county.

Harold Transome had been energetically active in bringing about this meeting. Over and above the stings of conscience and a determination to act up to the level of all recognised honourableness, he had the powerful motive of desiring to do what would satisfy Esther. His gradually heightened perception that she had a strong feeling towards Felix Holt had not made him uneasy. Harold had a conviction that might have seemed like fatuity if it had not been that he saw the effect he produced on Esther by the light of his opinions about women in general. The conviction was, that Felix Holt could not be his rival in any formidable sense: Esther's admiration for this eccentric young man was, he thought, a moral enthusiasm, a romantic fervour, which was one among those many attractions quite novel in his own experience; her distress about the trouble of one who had been a familiar object in her former home, was no more than naturally followed from a tender woman's compassion. The place young Holt had held in her regard had necessarily changed its relations now that her lot was so widely changed. It is undeniable, that what most conduced to the quieting nature of Harold's conclusions was the influence on his imagination of the more or less detailed reasons that Felix Holt was a watchmaker, that his home and dress were of a certain quality, that his person and manners — that, in short (for Harold, like the rest of us, had many impressions which saved him the trouble of distinct ideas), Felix Holt was not the sort of man a woman would be likely to be in love with when she was wooed by Harold Transome.

Thus, he was sufficiently at rest on this point not to be exercising any painful self-conquest in acting as the zealous advocate of Felix Holt's cause with all persons worth influencing; but it was by no direct intercourse between him and Sir Maximus that they found themselves in co-operation, for the old baronet would not recognise Harold by more than the faintest bow, and Harold was not a man to expose himself to a re-

buff. Whatever he in his inmost soul regarded as
nothing more than a narrow prejudice, he could defy,
not with airs of importance, but with easy indifference.
He could bear most things good-humouredly where he
felt that he had the superiority. The object of the
meeting was discussed, and the memorial agreed upon
without any clashing. Mr. Lingon was gone home, but
it was expected that his concurrence and signature
would be given, as well as those of other gentlemen
who were absent. The business gradually reached that
stage at which the concentration of interest ceases —
when the attention of all but a few who are more practically concerned drops off and disperses itself in private
chat, and there is no longer any particular reason why
everybody stays except that everybody is there. The
room was rather a long one, and invited to a little
movement: one gentleman drew another aside to speak
in an under-tone about Scotch bullocks, another had
something to say about the North Loamshire Hunt to
a friend who was the reverse of good-looking, but who,
nevertheless, while listening, showed his strength of
mind by giving a severe attention also to his full-length
reflection in the handsome tall mirror that filled the
space between two windows. And in this way the groups
were continually shifting.

But in the mean time there were moving towards
this room at the White Hart the footsteps of a person
whose presence had not been invited, and who, very
far from being drawn thither by the belief that he would
be welcome, knew well that his entrance would, to
one person at least, be bitterly disagreeable. They
were the footsteps of Mr. Jermyn, whose appearance
that morning was not less comely and less carefully

tended than usual, but who was suffering the torment of a compressed rage, which, if not impotent to inflict pain on another, was impotent to avert evil from himself. After his interview with Mrs. Transome there had been for some reasons a delay of positive procedures against him by Harold, of which delay Jermyn had twice availed himself; first, to seek an interview with Harold, and then to send him a letter. The interview had been refused; and the letter had been returned, with the statement that no communication could take place except through Harold's lawyers. And yesterday Johnson had brought Jermyn the information that he would quickly hear of the proceedings in Chancery being resumed: the watch Johnson kept in town had given him secure knowledge on this head. A doomed animal, with every issue earthed up except that where its enemy stands, must, if it has teeth and fierceness, try its one chance without delay. And a man may reach a point in his life in which his impulses are not distinguished from those of a hunted brute by any capability of scruples. Our selfishness is so robust and many-clutching, that, well encouraged, it easily devours all sustenance away from our poor little scruples.

Since Harold would not give Jermyn access to him, that vigorous attorney was resolved to take it. He knew all about the meeting at the White Hart, and he was going thither with the determination of accosting Harold. He thought he knew what he should say, and the tone in which he should say it. It would be a vague intimation, carrying the effect of a threat, which should compel Harold to give him a private interview. To any counter-consideration that presented itself in his mind — to anything that an imagined voice might say — the imagined answer arose, "That's all very fine, but I'm not going to be ruined if I can help it — least of all, ruined in that way." Shall we call it degeneration or gradual development — this effect of thirty additional winters on the soft-glancing, versifying young Jermyn?

When Jermyn entered the room at the White Hart he did not immediately see Harold. The door was at the extremity of the room, and the view was obstructed by groups of gentlemen with figures broadened by overcoats. His entrance excited no peculiar observation: several persons had come in late. Only one or two, who knew Jermyn well, were not too much preoccupied to have a glancing remembrance of what had been chatted about freely the day before — Harold's irritated reply about his agent, from the witness-box. Receiving and giving a slight nod here and there, Jermyn pushed his way, looking round keenly, until he saw Harold standing near the other end of the room. The solicitor who had acted for Felix was just then speaking to him, but having put a paper into his hand turned away; and Harold, standing isolated, though at no great distance from others, bent his eyes on the paper. He looked brilliant that morning; his blood was flowing prosperously. He had come in after a ride, and was additionally brightened by rapid talk and the excitement of seeking to impress himself favourably, or at least powerfully, on the minds of neighbours nearer or more remote. He had just that amount of flush which indicates that life is more enjoyable than usual; and as he stood with his left hand caressing his whisker, and his right holding the paper and his riding whip, his

dark eyes running rapidly along the written lines, and
his lips reposing in a curve of good-humour which had
more happiness in it than a smile, all beholders might
have seen that his mind was at ease.

Jermyn walked quickly and quietly close up to
him. The two men were of the same height, and before Harold looked round Jermyn's voice was saying,
close to his ear, not in a whisper, but in a hard, incisive, disrespectful and yet not loud tone,

"Mr. Transome, I must speak to you in private."

The sound jarred through Harold with a sensation
all the more insufferable because of the revulsion from
the satisfied, almost elated, state in which it had seized
him. He started and looked round into Jermyn's eyes.
For an instant, which seemed long, there was no sound
between them, but only angry hatred gathering in the
two faces. Harold felt himself going to crush this insolence: Jermyn felt that he had words within him that
were fangs to clutch this obstinate strength, and wring
forth the blood and compel submission. And Jermyn's
impulse was the more urgent. He said, in a tone that
was rather lower, but yet harder and more biting,

"You will repent else — for your mother's sake."

At that sound, quick as a leaping flame, Harold
had struck Jermyn across the face with his whip. The
brim of the hat had been a defence. Jermyn, a powerful man, had instantly thrust out his hand and clutched
Harold hard by the clothes just below the throat, pushing him slightly so as to make him stagger.

By this time everybody's attention had been called
to this end of the room, but both Jermyn and Harold
were beyond being arrested by any consciousness of
spectators.

"Let me go, you scoundrel!" said Harold, fiercely, "or I'll be the death of you."

"Do," said Jermyn, in a grating voice; "*I am your father.*"

In the thrust by which Harold had been made to stagger backward a little, the two men had got very near the long mirror. They were both white; both had anger and hatred in their faces; the hands of both were upraised. As Harold heard the last terrible words he started at a leaping throb that went through him, and in the start turned his eyes away from Jermyn's face. He turned them on the same face in the glass with his own beside it, and saw the hated fatherhood reasserted.

The young strong man reeled with a sick faintness. But in the same moment Jermyn released his hold, and Harold felt himself supported by the arm. It was Sir Maximus Debarry who had taken hold of him.

"Leave the room, sir!" the Baronet said to Jermyn, in a voice of imperious scorn. "This is a meeting of gentlemen."

"Come, Harold," he said, in the old friendly voice, "come away with me."

CHAPTER XXIV.

*'Tis law as stedfast as the throne of Zeus —
Our days are heritors of days gone by.*
— *Æschylus: Agamemnon.*

A LITTLE after five o'clock that day, Harold arrived at Transome Court. As he was winding along the broad road of the park, some parting gleams of the March sun pierced the trees here and there, and threw on the grass a long shadow of himself and the groom riding, and illuminated a window or two of the home he was approaching. But the bitterness in his mind made these sunny gleams almost as odious as an artificial smile. He wished he had never come back to this pale English sunshine.

In the course of his eighteen miles' drive, he had made up his mind what he would do. He understood now, as he had never understood before, the neglected solitariness of his mother's life, the allusions and innuendoes which had come out during the election. But with a proud insurrection against the hardship of an ignominy which was not of his own making, he inwardly said, that if the circumstances of his birth were such as to warrant any man in regarding his character of gentleman with ready suspicion, that character should be the more strongly asserted in his conduct. No one should be able to allege with any show of proof that he had inherited meanness.

As he stepped from the carriage and entered the

hall, there were the voice and the trotting feet of little Harry as usual, and the rush to clasp his father's leg and make his joyful puppy-like noises. Harold just touched the boy's head, and then said to Dominic in a weary voice,

"Take the child away. Ask where my mother is."

Mrs. Transome, Dominic said, was up-stairs. He had seen her go up after coming in from her walk with Miss Lyon, and she had not come down again.

Harold, throwing off his hat and greatcoat, went straight to his mother's dressing-room. There was still a hope in his mind. He might be suffering simply from a lie. There is much misery created in the world by mere mistake or slander, and he might have been stunned by a lie suggested by such slander. He rapped at his mother's door.

Her voice said immediately, "Come in."

Mrs. Transome was resting in her easy-chair, as she often did between an afternoon walk and dinner. She had taken off her walking-dress and wrapped herself in a soft dressing-gown. She was neither more nor less empty of joy than usual. But when she saw Harold, a dreadful certainty took possession of her. It was as if a long-expected letter, with a black seal, had come at last.

Harold's face told her what to fear the more decisively, because she had never before seen it express a man's deep agitation. Since the time of its pouting childhood and careless youth she had seen only the confident strength and good-humoured imperiousness of maturity. The last five hours had made a change as great as illness makes. Harold looked as if he had been wrestling, and had had some terrible blow. His eyes had that sunken look which, because it is unusual, seems to intensify expression.

He looked at his mother as he entered, and her eyes followed him as he moved, till he came and stood in front of her, she looking up at him, with white lips.

"Mother," he said, speaking with a distinct slowness, in strange contrast with his habitual manner, "tell me the truth that I may know how to act."

He paused a moment, and then said, "Who is my father?"

She was mute: her lips only trembled. Harold stood silent for a few moments, as if waiting. Then he spoke again.

"*He* has said — said it before others — that *he* is my father."

He looked still at his mother. She seemed as if age were striking her with a sudden wand — as if her trembling face were getting haggard before him. She was mute. But her eyes had not fallen; they looked up in helpless misery at her son.

Her son turned away his eyes from her, and left her. In that moment Harold felt hard: he could show no pity. All the pride of his nature rebelled against his sonship.

CHAPTER XXV.

*Nay, falter not — 'tis an assured good
To seek the noblest — 'tis your only good
Now you have seen it; for that higher vision
Poisons all meaner choice for evermore.*

THAT day Esther dined with old Mr. Transome only. Harold sent word that he was engaged and had already dined, and Mrs. Transome that she was feeling ill. Esther was much disappointed that any tidings Harold might have brought relating to Felix were deferred in this way; and, her anxiety making her fearful, she was haunted by the thought that if there had been anything cheering to tell, he would have found time to tell it without delay. Old Mr. Transome went as usual to his sofa in the library to sleep after dinner, and Esther had to seat herself in the small drawing-room, in a well-lit solitude that was unusually dispiriting to her. Pretty as this room was, she did not like it. Mrs. Transome's full-length portrait, being the only picture there, urged itself too strongly on her attention: the youthful brilliancy it represented saddened Esther by its inevitable association with what she daily saw had come instead of it — a joyless, embittered age. The sense that Mrs. Transome was unhappy, affected Esther more and more deeply as the growing familiarity which relaxed the efforts of the hostess revealed more and more the threadbare tissue of this majestic lady's life. Even the flowers and the pure sunshine and the sweet waters of Paradise would have

been spoiled for a young heart, if the bowered walks
had been haunted by an Eve gone grey with bitter
memories of an Adam who had complained, "The
woman ... she gave me of the tree, and I did eat."
And many of us know how, even in our childhood,
some blank discontented face on the background of
our home has marred our summer mornings. Why
was it, when the birds were singing, when the fields
were a garden, and when we were clasping another
little hand just larger than our own, there was somebody who found it hard to smile? Esther had got far
beyond that childhood to a time and circumstances
when this daily presence of elderly dissatisfaction
amidst such outward things as she had always thought
must greatly help to satisfy, awaked, not merely vague
questioning emotion, but strong determining thought.
And now, in these hours since her return from Loamford, her mind was in that state of highly-wrought
activity, that large discourse, in which we seem to
stand aloof from our own life — weighing impartially
our own temptations and the weak desires that most
habitually solicit us. "I think I am getting that power
Felix wished me to have: I shall soon see strong
visions," she said to herself, with a melancholy smile
flitting across her face, as she put out the wax-lights
that she might get rid of the oppressive urgency of
walls and upholstery and that portrait smiling with
deluded brightness, unwitting of the future.

Just then Dominic came to say that Mr. Harold
sent his compliments, and begged that she would grant
him an interview in his study. He disliked the small
drawing-room: if she would oblige him by going to
the study at once, he would join her very soon. Esther

went, in some wonder and anxiety. What she most feared or hoped in these moments related to Felix Holt, and it did not occur to her that Harold could have anything special to say to her that evening on other subjects.

Certainly the study was pleasanter than the small drawing-room. A quiet light shone on nothing but greenness and dark wood, and Dominic had placed a delightful chair for her opposite to his master's, which was still empty. All the little objects of luxury around indicated Harold's habitual occupancy; and as Esther sat opposite all these things along with the empty chair which suggested the coming presence, the expectation of his beseeching homage brought with it an impatience and repugnance which she had never felt before. While these feelings were strongly upon her, the door opened and Harold appeared.

He had recovered his self-possession since his interview with his mother: he had dressed, and was perfectly calm. He had been occupied with resolute thoughts, determining to do what he knew that perfect honour demanded, let it cost him what it would. It is true he had a tacit hope behind, that it might not cost him what he prized most highly: it is true he had a glimpse even of reward; but it was not less true that he would have acted as he did without that hope or glimpse. It was the most serious moment in Harold Transome's life: for the first time the iron had entered into his soul, and he felt the hard pressure of our common lot, the yoke of that mighty resistless destiny laid upon us by the acts of other men as well as our own.

When Esther looked at him she relented, and felt

ashamed of her gratuitous impatience. She saw that his mind was in some way burdened. But then immediately sprang the dread that he had to say something hopeless about Felix.

They shook hands in silence, Esther looking at him with anxious surprise. He released her hand, but it did not occur to her to sit down, and they both continued standing on the hearth.

"Don't let me alarm you," said Harold, seeing that her face gathered solemnity from his. "I suppose I carry the marks of a past agitation. It relates entirely to troubles of my own — of my own family. No one beyond is involved in them."

Esther wondered still more, and felt still more relenting.

"But," said Harold, after a slight pause, and in a voice that was weighted with new feeling, "it involves a difference in my position with regard to you; and it is on this point that I wished to speak to you at once. When a man sees what ought to be done, he had better do it forthwith. He can't answer for himself tomorrow."

While Esther continued to look at him, with eyes widened by anxious expectation, Harold turned a little, leaned on the mantelpiece, and ceased to look at her as he spoke.

"My feelings drag me another way. I need not tell you that your regard has become very important to me — that if our mutual position had been different — that, in short, you must have seen — if it had not seemed to be a matter of worldly interest, I should have told you plainly already that I loved you, and that my happiness could be complete only if you would consent to marry me."

Esther felt her heart beginning to beat painfully. Harold's voice and words moved her so much that her own task seemed more difficult than she had before imagined. It seemed as if the silence, unbroken by anything but the clicking of the fire, had been long, before Harold turned round towards her again and said,

"But to-day I have heard something that affects my own position. I cannot tell you what it is. There is no need. It is not any culpability of my own. But I have not just the same unsullied name and fame in the eyes of the world around us, as I believed that I had when I allowed myself to entertain that wish about you. You are very young, entering on a fresh life with bright prospects — you are worthy of everything that is best. I may be too vain in thinking it was at all necessary; but I take this precaution against myself. I shut myself out from the chance of trying, after to-day, to induce you to accept anything which others may regard as specked and stained by any obloquy, however slight."

Esther was keenly touched. With a paradoxical longing, such as often happens to us, she wished at that moment that she could have loved this man with her whole heart. The tears came into her eyes; she did not speak, but, with an angel's tenderness in her face, she laid her hand on his sleeve. Harold commanded himself strongly, and said,

"What is to be done now is, that we should proceed at once to the necessary legal measures for putting you in possession of your own, and arranging mutual claims. After that I shall probably leave England."

Esther was oppressed by an overpowering difficulty. Her sympathy with Harold at this moment was so strong, that it spread itself like a mist over all previous thought and resolve. It was impossible now to wound him afresh. With her hand still resting on his arm, she said timidly,

"Should you be urged — obliged to go — in any case?"

"Not in every case, perhaps," Harold said, with an evident movement of the blood towards his face; "at least not for long, not for always."

Esther was conscious of the gleam in his eyes. With terror at herself, she said, in difficult haste, "I can't speak. I can't say anything to-night. A great decision has to be made: I must wait — till to-morrow."

She was moving her hand from his arm, when Harold took it reverentially and raised it to his lips. She turned towards her chair, and as he released her hand she sank down on the seat with a sense that she needed that support. She did not want to go away from Harold yet. All the while there was something she needed to know, and yet she could not bring herself to ask it. She must resign herself to depend entirely on his recollection of anything beyond his own immediate trial. She sat helpless under contending sympathies, while Harold stood at some distance from her, feeling more harassed by weariness and uncertainty, now that he had fulfilled his resolve, and was no longer under the excitement of actually fulfilling it.

Esther's last words had forbidden his revival of the subject that was necessarily supreme with him.

But still she sat there, and his mind, busy as to the probabilities of her feeling, glanced over all she had done and said in the later days of their intercourse. It was this retrospect that led him to say at last,

"You will be glad to hear that we shall get a very powerfully signed memorial to the Home Secretary about young Holt. I think your speaking for him helped a great deal. You made all the men wish what you wished."

This was what Esther had been yearning to hear and dared not ask, as well from respect for Harold's absorption in his own sorrow, as from the shrinking that belongs to our dearest need. The intense relief of hearing what she longed to hear, affected her whole frame: her colour, her expression, changed as if she had been suddenly freed from some torturing constraint. But we interpret signs of emotion as we interpret other signs — often quite erroneously, unless we have the right key to what they signify. Harold did not gather that this was what Esther had waited for, or that the change in her indicated more than he had expected her to feel at this allusion to an unusual act which she had done under a strong impulse.

Besides, the introduction of a new subject after very momentous words have passed, and are still dwelling on the mind, is necessarily a sort of concussion, shaking us into a new adjustment of ourselves.

It seemed natural that soon afterward Esther put out her hand and said, "Good-night."

Harold went to his bedroom on the same level with his study, thinking of the morning with an uncertainty that dipped on the side of hope. This sweet woman, for whom he felt a passion newer than any he had expected to feel, might possibly make some hard things more bearable — if she loved him. If not — well, he had acted so that he could defy any one to say he was not a gentleman.

Esther went up-stairs to her bedroom, thinking that she should not sleep that night. She set her light on a high stand, and did not touch her dress. What she desired to see with undisturbed clearness were things not present: the rest she needed was the rest of a final choice. It was difficult. On each side there was renunciation.

She drew up her blinds, liking to see the grey sky, where there were some veiled glimmerings of moonlight, and the lines of the for-ever running river, and the bending movement of the black trees. She wanted the largeness of the world to help her thought. This young creature, who trod lightly backward and forward, and leaned against the window-frame, and shook back her brown curls as she looked at something not visible, had lived hardly more than six months since she saw Felix Holt for the first time. But life is measured by the rapidity of change, the succession of influences that modify the being; and Esther had undergone something little short of an inward revolution. The revolutionary struggle, however, was not quite at an end.

There was something which she now felt profoundly to be the best thing that life could give her. But — if it was to be had at all — it was not to be had without paying a heavy price for it, such as we must pay for all that is greatly good. A supreme love, a motive that gives a sublime rhythm to a woman's life, and exalts habit into partnership with the soul's highest needs, is not to be had where and how she wills; to know that high initiation, she must often tread where it is hard to tread, and feel the chill air, and watch through darkness. It is not true that love makes all things easy: it makes us choose what is difficult. Esther's previous life had brought her into close acquaintance with many negations, and with many positive ills too, not of the acutely painful, but of the distasteful sort. What if she chose the hardship, and had to bear it alone, with no strength to lean upon — no other better self to make a place for trust and joy? Her past experience saved her from illusions. She knew the dim life of the back street, the contact with sordid vulgarity, the lack of refinement for the senses, the summons to a daily task; and the gain that was to make that life of privation something on which she dreaded to turn her back, as if it were heaven — the presence and the love of Felix Holt — was only a quivering hope, not a certainty. It was not in her woman's nature that the hope should not spring within her and make a strong impulse. She knew that he loved her: had he not said how a woman might help a man if she were worthy? and if she proved herself worthy? But still there was the dread that after all she might find herself on the stony road alone, and faint and be weary. Even with the fulfilment of her hope, she knew that she pledged herself to meet high demands.

And on the other side there was a lot where everything seemed easy — but for the fatal absence of those feelings which, now she had once known them, it seemed nothing less than a fall and a degradation to do without. With a terrible prescience which a multitude of impressions during her stay at Transome

Court had contributed to form, she saw herself in a silken bondage that arrested all motive, and was nothing better than a well-cushioned despair. To be restless amidst ease, to be languid, among all appliances for pleasure, was a possibility that seemed to haunt the rooms of this house, and wander with her under the oaks and elms of the park. And Harold Transome's love, no longer a hovering fancy with which she played, but become a serious fact, seemed to threaten her with a stifling oppression. The homage of a man may be delightful until he asks straight for love, by which a woman renders homage. Since she and Felix had kissed each other in the prison, she felt as if she had vowed herself away, as if memory lay on her lips like a seal of possession. Yet what had happened that very evening had strengthened her liking for Harold, and her care for all that regarded him: it had increased her repugnance to turning him out of anything he had expected to be his, or to snatching anything from him on the ground of an arbitrary claim. It had even made her dread, as a coming pain, the task of saying anything to him that was not a promise of the utmost comfort under this newly-disclosed trouble of his.

It was already near midnight, but with these thoughts succeeding and returning in her mind like scenes through which she was living, Esther had a more intense wakefulness than any she had known by day. All had been stillness hitherto, except the fitful wind outside. But her ears now caught a sound within — slight, but sudden. She moved near her door, and heard the sweep of something on the matting outside. It came closer, and paused. Then it began again, and seemed to sweep away from her. Then it approached, and paused as it had done before. Esther listened, wondering. The same thing happened again and again, till she could bear it no longer. She opened her door, and in the dim light of the corridor, where the glass above seemed to make a glimmering sky, she saw Mrs. Transome's tall figure pacing slowly, with her cheek upon her hand.

CHAPTER XXVI.

The great question in life is the suffering we cause; and the almost ingenuity of metaphysics cannot justify the man who has pierced the heart that loved him. — BENJAMIN CONSTANT.

WHEN Denner had gone up to her mistress's room to dress her for dinner, she had found her seated just as Harold had found her, only with eyelids drooping and trembling over slowly-rolling tears — nay, with a face in which every sensitive feature, every muscle, seemed to be quivering with a silent endurance of some agony.

Denner went and stood by the chair a minute without speaking, only laying her hand gently on Mrs. Transome's. At last she said, beseechingly, "Pray speak, madam. What has happened?"

"The worst, Denner — the worst."

"You are ill. Let me undress you, and put you to bed."

"No, I am not ill. I am not going to die! I shall live — I shall live!"

"What may I do?"

"Go and say I shall not dine. Then you may come back, if you will."

The patient waiting-woman came back and sat by her mistress in motionless silence. Mrs. Transome would not let her dress be touched, and waved away all proffers with a slight movement of her hand. Denner dared not even light a candle without being told. At last, when the evening was far gone, Mrs. Transome said,

"Go down, Denner, and find out where Harold is, and come back and tell me."

"Shall I ask him to come to you, madam?"

"No; don't dare to do it, if you love me. Come back."

Denner brought word that Mr. Harold was in his study, and that Miss Lyon was with him. He had not dined, but had sent later to ask Miss Lyon to go into his study.

"Light the candles and leave me."

"Mayn't I come again?"

"No. It may be that my son will come to me."

"Mayn't I sleep on the little bed in your bed-room?"

"No, good Denner; I am not ill. You can't help me."

"That's the hardest word of all, madam."

"The time will come — but not now. Kiss me. Now go."

The small quiet old woman obeyed, as she had always done. She shrank from seeming to claim an equal's share in her mistress's sorrow.

For two hours Mrs. Transome's mind hung on what was hardly a hope — hardly more than the listening for a bare possibility. She began to create the sounds that her anguish craved to hear — began to imagine a footfall, and a hand upon the door. Then, checked by continual disappointment, she tried to rouse a truer consciousness by rising from her seat and walking to her window, where she saw streaks of light moving and disappearing on the grass, and the sound of bolts and closing doors. She hurried away and threw herself into her seat again, and buried her head in the deafening down of the cushions. There was no sound of comfort for her,

Then her heart cried out within her against the cruelty of this son. When he turned from her in the first moment, he had not had time to feel anything but the blow that had fallen on himself. But afterwards — was it possible that he should not be touched with a son's pity — was it possible that he should not have been visited by some thought of the long years through which she had suffered? The memory of those years came back to her now with a protest against the cruelty that had all fallen on *her*. She started up with a new restlessness from this spirit of resistance. She was not penitent. She had borne too hard a punishment. Always the edge of calamity had fallen on *her*. Who had felt for her? She was desolate. God had no pity, else her son would not have been so hard. What dreary future was there after this dreary past? She, too, looked out into the dim night; but the black boundary of trees and the long line of the river seemed only part of the loneliness and monotony of her life.

Suddenly she saw a light on the stone balustrades of the balcony that projected in front of Esther's window, and the flash of a moving candle falling on a shrub below. Esther was still awake and up. What had Harold told her — what had passed between them? Harold was fond of this young creature, who had been always sweet and reverential to her. There was mercy in her young heart; she might be a daughter who had no impulse to punish and to strike her whom fate had stricken. On the dim loneliness before her she seemed to see Esther's gentle look; it was possible still that the misery of this night might be broken by some comfort. The proud woman yearned for the caressing pity that must dwell in that young bosom. She opened her door gently, but when she had reached Esther's she hesitated. She had never yet in her life asked for compassion — had never thrown herself in faith on an unproffered love. And she might have gone on pacing the corridor like an uneasy spirit without a goal, if Esther's thought, leaping towards her, had not saved her from the need to ask admission.

Mrs. Transome was walking towards the door when it opened. As Esther saw that image of restless misery, it blent itself by a rapid flash with all that Harold had said in the evening. She divined that the son's new trouble must be one with the mother's long sadness. But there was no waiting. In an instant Mrs. Transome felt Esther's arm round her neck, and a voice saying softly,

"O why didn't you call me before?"

They turned hand in hand into the room, and sat down together on a sofa at the foot of the bed. The disordered grey hair — the haggard face — the reddened eyelids under which the tears seemed to be coming again with pain, pierced Esther to the heart. A passionate desire to soothe this suffering woman came over her. She clung round her again, and kissed her poor quivering lips and eyelids, and laid her young cheek against the pale and haggard one. Words could not be quick or strong enough to utter her yearning. As Mrs. Transome felt that soft clinging, she said,

"God has some pity on me."

"Rest on my bed," said Esther. "You are so tired. I will cover you up warmly, and then you will sleep."

"No — tell me, dear — tell me what Harold said."

"That he has had some new trouble."

"He said nothing hard about me?"

"No — nothing. He did not mention you."

"I have been an unhappy woman, dear."

"I feared it," said Esther, pressing her gently.

"Men are selfish. They are selfish and cruel. What they care for is their own pleasure and their own pride."

"Not all," said Esther, on whom these words fell with a painful jar.

"All I have ever loved," said Mrs. Transome. She paused a moment or two, and then said, "For more than twenty years I have not had an hour's happiness. Harold knows it, and yet he is hard to me."

"He will not be. To-morrow he will not be. I am sure he will be good," said Esther, pleadingly. "Remember — he said to me his trouble was new — he has not had time."

"It is too hard to bear, dear," Mrs. Transome said, a new sob rising as she clung fast to Esther in return. "I am old, and expect so little now — a very little thing would seem great. Why should I be punished any more?"

Esther found it difficult to speak. The dimly-suggested tragedy of this woman's life, the dreary waste of years empty of sweet trust and affection, afflicted her even to horror. It seemed to have come as a last vision to urge her towards the life where the draughts of joy sprang from the unchanging fountains, of reverence and devout love.

But all the more she longed to still the pain of this heart that beat against hers.

"Do let me go to your own room with you, and let me undress you, and let me tend upon you," she said, with a woman's gentle instinct. "It will be a very great thing to me. I shall seem to have a mother again. Do let me."

Mrs. Transome yielded at last, and let Esther soothe her with a daughter's tendance. She was undressed and went to bed; and at last dozed fitfully, with frequent starts. But Esther watched by her till the chills of morning came, and then she only wrapped more warmth around her, and slept fast in the chair till Denner's movement in the room roused her. She started out of a dream in which she was telling Felix what had happened to her that night.

Mrs. Transome was now in the sounder morning sleep which sometimes comes after a long night of misery. Esther beckoned Denner into the dressing-room, and said,

"It is late, Mrs. Hickes. Do you think Mr. Harold is out of his room?"

"Yes, a long while; he was out earlier than usual."

"Will you ask him to come up here? Say I begged you."

When Harold entered, Esther was leaning against the back of the empty chair where yesterday he had seen his mother sitting. He was in a state of wonder and suspense, and when Esther approached him and gave him her hand, he said, in a startled way,

"Good God! how ill you look! Have you been sitting up with my mother?"

"Yes. She is asleep now," said Esther. They had merely pressed hands by way of greeting, and now stood apart looking at each other solemnly.

"Has she told you anything?" said Harold.

"No — only that she is wretched. O, I think I

would bear a great deal of unhappiness to save her from having any more."

A painful thrill passed through Harold, and showed itself in his face with that pale rapid flash which can never be painted. Esther pressed her hands together, and said, timidly, though it was from an urgent prompting,

"There is nothing in all this place — nothing since ever I came here — I could care for so much as that you should sit down by her now, and that she should see you when she wakes."

Then with delicate instinct, she added, just laying her hand on his sleeve, "I know you would have come. I know you meant it. But she is asleep now. Go gently before she wakes."

Harold just laid his right hand for an instant on the back of Esther's as it rested on his sleeve, and then stepped softly to his mother's bedside.

An hour afterwards, when Harold had laid his mother's pillow afresh, and sat down again by her, she said,

"If that dear thing will marry you, Harold, it will make up to you for a great deal."

But before the day closed Harold knew that this was not to be. That young presence, which had flitted like a white new-winged dove over all the saddening relics and new finery of Transome Court, could not find its home there. Harold heard from Esther's lips that she loved some one else, and that she resigned all claim to the Transome estates.

She wished to go back to her father.

CHAPTER XXVII.

*The maiden said, I wis the loade
Is very fair to see,
But my true-love that is in bonds
Is fairer still to me.*

ONE April day, when the sun shone on the lingering rain-drops, Lyddy was gone out, and Esther chose to sit in the kitchen, in the wicker chair against the white table, between the fire and the window. The kettle was singing, and the clock was ticking steadily towards four o'clock.

She was not reading, but stitching; and as her fingers moved nimbly, something played about her parted lips like a ray. Suddenly she laid down her work, pressed her hands together on her knees, and bent forward a little. The next moment there came a loud rap at the door. She started up and opened it, but kept herself hidden behind it.

"Mr. Lyon at home?" said Felix, in his firm tones.

"No, sir," said Esther from behind her screen; "but Miss Lyon is, if you'll please to walk in."

"Esther!" exclaimed Felix, amazed.

They held each other by both hands, and looked into each other's faces with delight.

"You are out of prison?"

"Yes, till I do something bad again. But you? — how is it all?"

"Oh, it is," said Esther, smiling brightly as she moved towards the wicker chair, and seated herself again, "that everything is as usual: my father is gone to see the sick; Lyddy is gone in deep despondency to buy the grocery; and I am sitting here, with some vanity in me, needing to be scolded."

Felix had seated himself on a chair that happened to be near her, at the corner of the table. He looked at her still with questioning eyes — he grave, she mischievously smiling.

"Are you come back to live here then?"

"Yes."

"You are not going to be married to Harold Transome, or to be rich?"

"No." Something made Esther take up her work again, and begin to stitch. The smiles were dying into a tremor.

"Why?" said Felix, in rather a low tone, leaning his elbow on the table, and resting his head on his hand while he looked at her.

"I did not wish to marry him, or to be rich."

"You have given it all up?" said Felix, leaning forward a little, and speaking in a still lower tone.

Esther did not speak. They heard the kettle singing and the clock loudly ticking. There was no knowing how it was: Esther's work fell, their eyes met; and the next instant their arms were round each other's necks, and once more they kissed each other.

When their hands fell again, their eyes were bright with tears. Felix laid his hand on her shoulder.

"Could you share the life of a poor man, then, Esther?"

"If I thought well enough of him," she said, the smile coming again, with the pretty saucy movement of her head.

"Have you considered well what it would be? — that it will be a very bare and simple life?"

"Yes — without atta of roses."

Felix suddenly removed his hand from her shoulder, rose from his chair, and walked a step or two; then he turned round and said, with deep gravity,

"And the people I shall live among, Esther? They have not just the same follies and vices as the rich, but they have their own forms of folly and vice; and they have not what are called the refinements of the rich to make their faults more bearable. I don't say more bearable to me — I'm not fond of those refinements; but you are."

Felix paused an instant, and then added,

"It is very serious, Esther."

"I know it is serious," said Esther, looking up at him. "Since I have been at Transome Court I have seen many things very seriously. If I had not, I should not have left what I did leave. I made a deliberate choice."

Felix stood a moment or two, dwelling on her with a face where the gravity gathered tenderness.

"And these curls?" he said, with a sort of relenting, seating himself again, and putting his hand on them.

"They cost nothing — they are natural."

"You are such a delicate creature."

"I am very healthy. Poor women, I think, are healthier than the rich. Besides," Esther went on, with a mischievous meaning, "I think of having some wealth."

"How?" said Felix, with an anxious start. "What do you mean?"

"I think even of two pounds a-week: one needn't live up to the splendour of all that, you know; we might live as simply as you liked: there would be money to spare, and you could do wonders, and be obliged to work too, only not if sickness came. And then I think of a little income for your mother, enough for her to live as she has been used to live; and a little income for my father, to save him from being dependent when he is no longer able to preach."

Esther said all this in a playful tone, but she ended, with a grave look of appealing submission,

"I mean — if you approve. I wish to do what you think it will be right to do."

Felix put his hand on her shoulder again and reflected a little while, looking on the hearth: then he said, lifting up his eyes, with a smile at her,

"Why, I shall be able to set up a great library, and lend the books to be dog's-eared and marked with bread-crumbs."

Esther said, laughing, "You think you are to do everything. You don't know how clever I am. I mean to go on teaching a great many things."

"Teaching me?"

"Oh yes," she said, with a little toss; "I shall improve your French accent."

"You won't want me to wear a stock?" said Felix, with a defiant shake of the head.

"No; and you will not attribute stupid thoughts to me before I've uttered them."

They laughed merrily, each holding the other's arms, like girl and boy. There was the ineffable sense of youth in common.

Then Felix leaned forward, that their lips might meet again, and after that his eyes roved tenderly over her face and curls.

"I'm a rough, severe fellow, Esther. Shall you never repent? — never be inwardly reproaching me that I was not a man who could have shared your wealth? Are you quite sure?"

"Quite sure!" said Esther, shaking her head; "for then I should have honoured you less. I am weak — my husband must be greater and nobler than I am."

"O, I tell you what, though!" said Felix, starting up, thrusting his hands into his pockets, and creasing his brow playfully, "if you take me in that way I shall be forced to be a much better fellow than I ever thought of being."

"I call that retribution," said Esther, with a laugh as sweet as the morning thrush.

EPILOGUE.

*Our finest hope is finest memory;
And those who love in age think youth is happy,
Because it has a life to fill with love.*

The very next May, Felix and Esther were married. Every one in those days was married at the parish church; but Mr. Lyon was not satisfied without an additional private solemnity, "wherein there was no bondage to questionable forms, so that he might have a more enlarged utterance of joy and supplication."

It was a very simple wedding; but no wedding, even the gayest, ever raised so much interest and debate in Treby Magna. Even very great people, like Sir Maximus and his family, went to the church to look at this bride, who had renounced wealth, and chosen to be the wife of a man who said he would always be poor.

Some few shook their heads; could not quite believe it; and thought there was "more behind." But the majority of honest Trebians were affected somewhat in the same way as happy-looking Mr. Wace was, who observed to his wife, as they walked from under the churchyard chestnuts, "It's wonderful how things go through you — you don't know how. I feel somehow as if I believed more in everything that's good."

Mrs. Holt, that day, said she felt herself to be receiving "some reward," implying that justice certainly had much more in reserve. Little Job Tudge had an entirely new suit, of which he fingered every separate brass button in a way that threatened an arithmetical mania; and Mrs. Holt had out her best tea-trays and put down her carpet again, with the satisfaction of thinking that there would no more be boys coming in all weathers with dirty shoes.

For Felix and Esther did not take up their abode in Treby Magna; and after a while Mr. Lyon left the town too, and joined them where they dwelt. On his resignation the church in Malthouse Yard chose a successor to him whose doctrine was rather higher.

There were other departures from Treby. Mr. Jermyn's establishment was broken up, and he was understood to have gone to reside at a great distance: some said "abroad," that large home of ruined reputations. Mr. Johnson continued blond and sufficiently prosperous till he got grey and rather more prosperous. Some persons, who did not think highly of him, held that his prosperity was a fact to be kept in the background, as being dangerous to the morals of the young; judging that it was not altogether creditable to the Divine Providence that anything but virtue should be rewarded by a front and back drawing-room in Bedford Row.

As for Mr. Christian, he had no more profitable secrets at his disposal. But he got his thousand pounds from Harold Transome.

The Transome family were absent for some time from Transome Court. The place was kept up and shown to visitors, but not by Denner, who was away with her mistress. After a while the family came back, and Mrs. Transome died there. Sir Maximus was at her funeral, and throughout that neighbourhood there was silence about the past.

Uncle Lingon continued to watch over the shooting on the Manor and the covers until that event occurred which he had predicted as a part of Church reform sure to come. Little Treby had a new rector, but others were sorry besides the old pointers.

As to all that wide parish of Treby Magna, it has since prospered as the rest of England has prospered. Doubtless there is more enlightenment now. Whether the farmers are all public-spirited, the shopkeepers nobly independent, the Sproxton men entirely sober and judicious, the Dissenters quite without narrowness or asperity in religion and politics, and the publicans all fit, like Gaius, to be the friends of an apostle — these things I have not heard, not having correspondence in those parts. Whether any presumption may be drawn from the fact that North Loamshire does not yet return a Radical candidate, I leave to the all-wise — I mean the newspapers.

As to the town in which Felix Holt now resides, I will keep that a secret, lest he should be troubled by any visitor having the insufferable motive of curiosity.

I will only say that Esther has never repented. Felix, however, grumbles a little that she has made his life too easy, and that, if it were not for much walking, he should be a sleek dog.

There is a young Felix, who has a great deal more science than his father, but not much more money.

THE END.

www.ingramcontent.com/pod-product-compliance
Lightning Source LLC
Chambersburg PA
CBHW030752230426
43667CB00007B/932